RUSSIA—MY HOME

EMMA C. PONAFIDINE

RUSSIA—MY HOME

An Intimate Record of Personal Experiences Before, During and After the Bolshevist Revolution

by

EMMA COCHRAN PONAFIDINE

(Mme. Pierre Ponafidine)

Illustrated

Prefatory Note by
WILLIAM LYON PHELPS

THE BOBBS-MERRILL COMPANY
INDIANAPOLIS · PUBLISHERS

To
my life-long friend, Carolyn J. Clement
and
my nephew, Clement H. Cochran
through whose devoted efforts and unfailing help I was
able to escape from a Russia that was no longer home
and to find security and peace in this friendly land

PREFATORY NOTE

WHEN I was in St. Petersburg in 1911, I spent a pleasant evening at the urban home of Mr. and Mrs. Ponafidine; and I should like to bear witness now not only to the kindness and courtesy of my hosts, but especially to the Old-World grace, wisdom, intelligence, tolerance, benevolence of the character of Mr. Ponafidine. He had lived long in many countries; experience, instead of making him cynical, had given to his face, manners and conversation a mellow charm. I envied those who knew him well. Mrs. Ponafidine had lived with him many years; I saw him only for an evening. But I shall never forget him.

I am very glad that Mrs. Ponafidine has written this book; for it is a straightforward story of things that happened. If we are ever to get at the truth about the Russia that was and the Russia of the transition and the Russia that is, and to form any intelligent conjectures of the Russia that is to be, we need veracious narratives. Advocates and denouncers will not help us very much; we want witnesses.

Mrs. Ponafidine is an American who was happily married to a Russian gentleman; they lived in the cities in Russia, on their estate in the country, and had a wide and varied experience in foreign capitals. Her years of country life brought her into intimate contact with village officials, with the representatives of the varied activities of small-town life and with the muzhiks. This book is not exactly an autobiography, but it sufficiently reveals her own character and temperament. We know that her testimony is true.

Her book begins with the outbreak of the war, and tells the story of what that war and its red afterglow meant to her, to her husband, to her sons, to her environment. There are occasions in an historical narrative when no adjectives and no exclamations are necessary; the facts speak for themselves. Such are the experiences which the author of this book observed and which she almost miraculously survived.

After the first chapter which tells of the sudden outbreak of the World War, Mrs. Ponafidine has fortunately given us nine exceedingly interesting and instructive chapters on Russian life in city and country during the first fourteen years of the twentieth century. This narrative enables us to come close to the daily life of the peasants in winter and in summer—to see their activities, their superstitions, their point of view. She particularly emphasizes the fact that their ignorance and poverty were not treated by the government with indifference and disdain; measures were being taken which would have led to a steady improvement.

Mrs. Ponafidine's insistence on the tremendous advance made during the first fourteen years of the twentieth century in the education of the peasants should not be forgotten; and I candidly admit, that of all the strange things narrated in this book no one thing astonished me more than the last paragraph of Chapter X.

In regard to illiteracy, that of the older peasants showed a decreasing percentage each succeeding generation. In 1918, my son Alec, who was for a time during the World War military instructor in our volost, found that among approximately seven hundred recruits drawn entirely from the peasants, only six or seven were illiterate. Yet nothing is so generally believed in regard to Russia as that the peasants were illiterate, and that the illiteracy was caused by the deliberate policy of the Tsar's Government.

Her story of life in Russia during the war is told with a restraint that makes it more dramatically impressive; and though, in her account of the tragedies that followed the war, one might easily expect much bitterness and denunciation, she seems wisely to feel that the story itself is sufficient. The account of her escape certainly needs no embellishment.

That it is darkest just before the dawn is a familiar saying; but we sometimes forget that the dawn may be worse than the darkness. The deepening shadow of the war in Russia was followed by the flaming dawn of Revolution. I sometimes wonder if all those who regard the "next war" as inevitable realize that what is coming after it is also inevitable.

Faithfully Yours

Wm Lyon Phelps

INTRODUCTION

THIS book has not been easy to write. For years, friends have urged me to put on paper some of the memories of my life passed in so many different countries, and filled with unusual events. My sons, too, have been urgent, as the only family records will be what I can give them, for we brought out from Russia only what could be carried on our backs, and so far as we know, of a large family but six Ponafidines survive, scattered in different lands.

During the Revolution we ourselves burned all documents, diaries and letters that might have injured us or our friends, so that for the most part I have only my memory to fall back on.

Aside from these difficulties, there was a still greater obstacle. My lecture audiences have been kind and indulgent, and their interest has inspired me in speaking, but I found that a piece of blank paper is a very different thing. Many times in recent years I have made a beginning that remained only such. At last, however, a day came when the past took shape and pictures rose to my mind. The old charm of the Orient again captivated me, and the stirring events we had witnessed and at times been a part of again became vivid, as I lived them over in my thought. I began to write; but when my work was done I found that, in view of the deep and wide-spread interest Russia now has for the world, I had devoted too much space to those eastern lands. It seemed better, therefore, to give to my readers the latter part of my narrative first, the chapters which deal with my life in Russia during the tragic period of her history beginning with the collapse of the Empire in the World War, leaving the rest of my story for a later volume.

For the photographs in this volume I am indebted to

many friends, who sent those which they had received from us in former times or which they had taken when visiting us.

That these pages have been written is largely owing to the help and inspiration of friends. My warmest and most appreciative thanks are given to Mr. Arthur Detmers, the friend whose understanding and sympathetic handling of my manuscript helped create order out of the chaos of my memories. I am grateful, too, to Mrs. Hazard Clarke, my friend and neighbor, and to Mr. Daniel Streeter, for generous contributions of their time and for many valuable suggestions. I would also express my thanks to Miss Frances E. Carpenter, to whom fell the lot of deciphering and typing an almost illegible manuscript.

CONTENTS

ILLUSTRATIONS

RUSSIA—MY HOME

Russia—My Home

CHAPTER ONE

Darkness

ONE afternoon in the midsummer of 1914, as I was sitting at my desk, the manager o   tate appeared in the doorway, out of breath. In a   e he vainly tried to control, he said, "Madam, war has been declared! Yakov (one of our men who was killed early in the War) and I are called, and in an hour all our horses must be at the mustering point in Staroye Syelo."

A bomb thrown into our midst would not have caused a greater shock. None of us had grasped the idea that the disquieting articles in the papers during the past month meant actual war. Our horses were scattered, some at work, some in the pastures; similarly the workmen; but in an incredibly short time all were rounded up. The buckboard was harnessed with a troika for us, and, surrounded by men and boys leading horses, we started. The mustering place was in the second village from us, not over two miles. Everywhere we saw the peasants unharnessing plows and leaving them where they were, catching and mounting their horses. The women scrambled upon the shaggy little ponies, joining the procession. Excitement prevailed, but a sober one; there seemed to be no panic, certainly nothing sullen. The peasants, like ourselves, responded to the call of their country. Officers with measuring sticks examined all horses over five years old, except brood mares. Those which passed the requirements were ordered immediately sent to the headquarters of our volost, ten miles away. We went home. Two cartloads of fresh hay were at once loaded as ordered. The wife of our manager was busy cooking and packing, sobbing as she worked. Yakov had gone to his home in a neighboring village. It was now about four o'clock. Peasants began to pass along the highway that ran through our estate; some were riding their horses to the mustering place, others, surrounded by family and friends, were starting for Ostashkov, our county town, twenty miles distant.

Our two eldest sons, George and Alec, with a couple of workmen driving the loads of hay, and others riding and leading horses, started for the rendezvous. We walked sadly by them for some distance. In the presence of the mothers and wives accompanying their dear ones perhaps for the last time, I felt ashamed to show my grief for our horses. Many of them were home-bred; all would come to my call, but of two of our carriage troika, one, Smelie (Daring), particularly appealed to me. We knew he was above the required age, but he did not show it and in absence of documentary evidence he had been drafted. He above all others knew and loved me, and when we came back to Bortniki from Turkey every spring, on hearing my voice he would whinny before seeing me. I walked close to him (Alec was riding him), and he rubbed his soft nose against me as if he knew it was farewell. The ever-swelling procession moved slowly while yet so many were seeing their boys off. The dusk was gathering as we turned back in the beautiful silent woods. The great pines, trees that had looked down on generations of Ponafidines, were destined, like so many of the human beings we were seeing off, to be destroyed in the coming holocaust.

Had we been permitted to lift the veil and look into the future, that day would have broken our hearts and spirits. The boys rode out of our sight into the deep shadows of the forest. My husband, Oka and I returned home, the three who were to be longest together. Though there was

much of sadness, an optimistic belief that the war would
not be long prevailed. "In three months at most they will
be back," was heard on all sides, and no word of complaint
from the peasants at the prospect of losing their horses.
Of our own eighteen, nine were taken. The final culling
took place at Ostashkov, and I had hoped that Smelie would
not pass; but as Alec rode him up to the square where
the officers stood, the fine old horse unfortunately showed
all his mettle, and his prancing and snorting attracted the
attention of the judges. "There is the mount for me,"
Alec heard one of the officers exclaim. Our manager,
Karpovich, who had promised to try to save Smelie, ventured with, "That is a good-looking horse but he is old,
unfit for war service." The officer stepped forward, examined Smelie's teeth and legs and then, turning to Karpovich, rebuked him for letting his love for the horse outrun
his truthfulness and patriotism. It does not always pay
to be only as old as one feels; so the fate of Smelie was
sealed.

From Ostashkov, the same night, our horses were forwarded by train to the front—less than thirty-six hours
from the time we heard of the declaration of war, and living
out in the country, too! The boys came back by steamer
the next day, and the same steamer on returning took many
recruits to Ostashkov.

One scene that day remains in my memory a clear-cut picture. Walking up a little hill after watching the steamer
off, we saw a young woman who had flung herself down by
a big stone in a perfect abandonment of grief. Her arms
with writhing hands were thrown over the rock, and such
sobs shaking her whole frame I have never heard. We
stopped and tried to find some words to comfort the young
wife, but what are words! As George and I silently walked
on, in a broken voice he talked to me. He and Alec could

have avoided going to the war at that time, for seniors
in the University were not taken. The war was considered
likely to be so short that the Government did not think it
wise to break in upon so nearly completed an education and
draft seniors whose age would otherwise warrant it. So
by putting off going up for the final examination, our sons
could both have been free from military service. George
talked to me of this and of the young woman who had given
up her husband, and said that he had thought much while
riding his horses. What troubled him was his father's
health, and he asked how I felt it would affect him physically
if he and Alec went at once for their examinations and at
the same time gave in their names as volunteers. I think my
heart skipped several beats. The war was certainly coming
very close to our fireside. I told George that in any case
he must lay the matter before his father, for what he himself thought to be his duty was the first thing to consider.

Weak and ill as he was, my husband met this situation
as he did every crisis that came. He told the boys that he
would not have urged nor even spoken to them, but that
he would have been deeply disappointed if they had not
seen it as their duty to respond when their Emperor and
Country called.

A few days later both boys went to St. Petersburg and
registered for their October examinations, to be followed
by entrance, George into a military school, Alec into the
aviation service. In the same spirit all Russia met the war.
Party feeling was forgotten. An "All-Russian Union of
Zemstvos" for the aid of the wounded was created, and
the Duma in special session voiced its confidence in, and
hearty cooperation with, the Government.

When our sons were in St. Petersburg, my husband and
I avoided talking of them and their future, but they were
never out of our minds. I know my husband slept little

PIERRE PONAFIDINE

The dusk was gathering in the beautiful silent woods.

at that time, and shortly after they returned he one night suffered the worst heart attack he had yet had. We worked for many hours, doing all that the specialists had taught us to do, but it was long before any sign of life appeared. Repeatedly the boys said, "Mother, stop, he is gone." But we went on, and toward morning we saw that life was returning. Finally he could speak, very weakly. He lay with closed eyes, speaking in slow disconnected gasps. Calling each of us, he said his last words, as he thought, giving us his blessing and a message and his blessing for Oka, who had returned to the Lyceum in St. Petersburg. Then he lay quiet, only breathing, and we all thought the end was near. The sun had arisen and it was broad daylight when he opened his eyes. Looking around, he said, "Emma, where are you?" I was kneeling, as were his sons, on the floor by his bedside, close to him. We thought his mind was wandering. I laid my hand on his and said, "Here I am, Peter."

"George, Alec, where are they?"

"Here, Father," they answered.

And then in a quick imperious tone as if suspecting what we did not, he said, "Why don't you light the lamp?"

We looked at one another and each read the horror in the other's face, but no one spoke. He repeated the question and then, clasping his hands, said, "Am I blind? O God, Thy will be done. Let me not murmur."

And he did not complain during the five years and two weeks that he lived in darkness after that, a darkness that made the terrible years so much worse.

George left early in the morning to go to the city for a doctor. Frost had made the deep ruts in the road hard for horses and people. In Ostashkov all physicians were occupied, as reserve hospitals were already being filled with men brought from the front, and of the local physicians no one could be spared. One of them, the doctor who in the following years stood by us in our darkest days, consented to come, after his evening rounds in the hospital, if George would get him back for his morning duties. So he faced forty miles or more over the roughest ground in the pitch darkness of a Russian October night. It was after midnight when we heard the bells of the troika and George came up-stairs with the doctor. There was nothing to be done. We had everything on hand for the heart attacks. The blindness would be permanent, and the doctor said there would be no use in the future of sending for a physician. He told us we must be prepared; death might come at any moment— or the patient might live for years if prompt help were given him and good nursing; and all excitement must be avoided. An easy regimen to carry out, with increasing difficulty in getting drugs and with years of famine, revolution and anxiety before us!

We engaged a man to read to him and be with him when I was busy. We also had a new farm manager, overseeing whom involved much of my time. One after another, however, these managers were drafted into the army. The readers also changed, and we had no small family to look after, as an English couple and an American friend who were with us when the war broke out remained that winter and the following summer, while nearly all other foreigners left the country.

Life was centered around the invalid. We moved my husband down-stairs, turning a large sunny southern room into a bedroom for him and at the same time a living-room for the family. A table was brought in and we took our meals by him. Nights were so long! I always read to him for a couple of hours before going, at five o'clock in the morning, to see to the milking, and again read him to sleep at night. The reader (for he did no nursing) relieved me by day except for three hours in the afternoon. So we

managed pretty well until the Revolution deprived us not
only of some one to help me in reading but also of cook and
maids.

By spring we realized that we and the world were involved in something more than a short local war. The
gravity of the situation was felt everywhere. Russia was
called on during the first year to make great sacrifices, to
undertake advances and offenses she was not prepared for,
but which, though they could only bring defeat to her, were
demanded for the good of the whole to relieve the tension
on the western front. All military authorities agree that
Russia's advance into eastern Prussia late in 1914 changed
the course of the war.

CHAPTER TWO

Russia Becomes My Home

WE WERE now alone, my husband and I. Two sons had volunteered and were in training before being sent to the front. Oka was in the Lyceum. Dark thoughts would come in spite of all attempts to throw them off. After the long years in foreign lands, was this what awaited us in the old home that for three centuries had sheltered the Ponafidines? The happy past and the menacing present I contrasted with a heavy and troubled heart.

How would I, alien in blood, face the crises that perhaps would call for the sacrifice of my sons? My thoughts went back to the far past—to the story my mother used to tell me of another July day, when I was born in a little Syrian village nestling in the folds of a Persian mountain. She told me of a Kurdish raid and the cruel murder of a young Syrian shepherd on that day, how the mutilated body was brought amid the weeping and wailing of the women and laid in the courtyard under her windows, how in after-years the poor mother would come to her periodically, saying, "How old is your daughter? You know I can not count, but my boy was killed the day your daughter was born."

This scene appeared to me now like a portent of the tragedies that were to pass before my eyes in a life more than usually filled with adventures and dangers, which now seemed to be culminating.

I had grown up among Orientals. My father, the Reverend Joseph G. Cochran, lived for twenty-five years a missionary in Persia, and he and, much later, my mother and other members of the family were laid to rest in the little Christian cemetery on the mountainside.

Long after my father's death I was sent to school in the

United States, where I first made my home with Mrs. Samuel Sikes and later with Mr. and Mrs. S. M. Clement, in Buffalo, New York. My only brother, Dr. Joseph P. Cochran, had in the meantime returned from America to Persia, where in our native Urumia he had established, through the generosity of Mr. Clement and the support of the Westminster Church of Buffalo, the first hospital in Persia. It was my dream to go back to him and help in nursing, for at this time he was quite alone, with no trained assistance of any kind. I was able to obtain eighteen months of intensive training in surgical nursing and giving of anesthetics, which though inadequate gave me something for which I was devoutly thankful in many out-of-the-way places where in after-years Fate threw me.

After three years happily spent in Urumia, in 1885 I married Peter Egorovich Ponafidine, then acting consul general in Tabriz. This was a tremendous step for me. My husband and his friends were the first Russians I had known—the country and people and customs a closed book. What knowledge Americans might have had of Russia was at this time overshadowed by the impression made by a series of articles then running in one of the magazines. They were written by Mr. George Kennan, whose vivid and accurate pictures of the miseries existing in the overcrowded and unsanitary prisons, the long agonizing journeys of the Siberian exiles after leaving the railroad and before reaching their destination, the brutal treatment they there received, focused attention on one particular feature of Russian life and government, while the better aspects were disregarded. Everything Russian was held in horror.

This was the feeling toward Russia when I came to the turning-point in my life and when I was no wiser or more tolerant than any one else in my views regarding the "barbarous country." The day before my wedding, my brother came to my room bringing the latest instalment of Mr. Kennan's articles, which he urged me to read and consider seriously. It would be better even now to break off the marriage if I felt I could not cast in my lot with a people among whom such conditions existed. My brother had already learned to admire and love Mr. Ponafidine, but he regarded him as perhaps an exceptional Russian. In after-years, I am happy to say, my brother became entirely satisfied with my decision and came to realize that there were other sides to the Russian question.

The marriage was a most complicated affair as it was to take place in London. Here were a Russian of the Orthodox faith and an American Protestant non-conformer wishing to celebrate a marriage in England that would be valid in all three countries. The ultimate solution was a civil marriage before a British Justice of the Peace (I think he was called), a religious ceremony in a Baptist chapel, and a final tying of the knot in the chapel of the Russian Embassy. At that time I knew no Russian, and Mr. Ponafidine very little English. We had therefore to coach him for the responses in the Protestant service, and the Russian chaplain was able to use English with me during *that* ceremony.

CHAPTER THREE

The Ride to Bortniki

LEAVING England, after a short stay in France and Germany we found ourselves on the Polish frontier, the gateway to the vast unknown before me that as a country and as a factor in my own private life held so much that was untried, mysterious and a little terrifying. We were met in St. Petersburg by one of my husband's brothers and his wife, and also his brother-in-law, Prince Shakhovskoy. These three, the first of my new relatives, gave me a warm welcome, and their love and understanding sympathy never failed me in all the following years.

We were to spend the summer in my husband's old family estate of Bortniki, in the Government of Tver, half-way between St. Petersburg and Moscow. The Nicholas Railway at that time had no southwestern branch, and in the very heart of European Russia was a large triangle with neither railway communication nor any roads worthy of the name, so that we had to travel by post carriages about a hundred versts. The vehicles used, tarantasses (tear and tosses, as Mr. Clement dubbed them), were veritable instruments of torture. Boat-shaped wooden bodies placed on two poles that provided the only hint of anything like springs, for none of the spring vehicles used in towns could stand the ruts and stumps and other natural obstacles with which the road was liberally provided. A troika was harnessed to our tarantass and changed five times along the route. The seats of our chariot were never upholstered, but a so-called cushion was furnished. This was usually a sack filled with hay, which after several hours of jolting had an appalling habit of separating and taking refuge in the corners of the sack, so that one finally was sitting almost on boards.   In case of rain, there were tops that could be raised, but they had evidently been constructed for a stationary condition, and were so low that when the horses went at full gallop and the passengers began to bounce up and down, frequent knocks on the head were the result.   At the first post station, where we went in to wait while the horses and driver were being changed, I was lame and sore, but by the time the last station was reached I could scarcely move.

There was another side of posting, however.   We traveled a large part of the way by night.   It was June, and the beautiful "white nights" that our northern latitude gave us made it possible to read the signs on the mile-posts as we passed.   The magnificent forests seemed more mysterious and beautiful than by daylight, and the sleeping villages were full of interest for me.   We slept for several hours in one of the stations so as not to arrive in the middle of the night at our aunt's, where we wished to stop.   The one room of the station was furnished with sofas, a row of stiff chairs and one or two tables.   Flower-pots stood in front of all the windows.   A big clock on the wall and icons in the corner completed the furnishings.   One could always get a samovar and sometimes eggs, but we had our own well-stocked lunch basket and after supper we each took possession of one of the sofas.   All through the night the hanging lamp furnished bright welcome light to other passengers, who came and went—some having tea at the table, talking, laughing and smoking in good-natured disregard of those sleeping or trying to sleep.

In the winter this trip was a real delight, for then the kindly snow covered the unevennesses of the road, and if one did sometimes get stuck in deep drifts or was delayed by blizzards, there was none of the awful jolting.   Well wrapped in furs, the bottom of the sleigh filled with hay,

Top—Traveling by stage-coach troika.
Bottom—A typical stage-coach (tarantass).

On Lake Seliguer—passing the beautiful old monastery.

we were warm and could enjoy the winter majesty of those great forests. The broad branches of spruce and hemlock bending low over the road with their burden of snow, and the tall pines towering above, made a marvelous picture.

I never ceased to admire the sturdiness and intelligence of the Russian horses, and to regret the passing of the picturesque troikas. These were not vehicles, as some European writers seem to think, but teams of three horses abreast. The middle horse is always the heaviest in build and must be a fast trotter, never allowed to break into a gallop. He is harnessed in shafts the ends of which are kept up by a high yoke rising above the animal's head and from which a bell is hung. The two side horses are of lighter build and are taught to gallop, each curving his head outward and back so that sometimes a spirited horse had his nose nearly touching his shoulder, leaving one eye only to watch the road ahead. I seem still to see them as they rush along, scrambling over narrow ledges, shutting their eyes to overhanging branches, clinging to the bits of space on the little bridges.

And so at last we came to the cobble-stone pavement that led to the town of Ostashkov, a decidedly one-horse town, with no hotel other than the post station run by an old woman and her husband. The only attractive feature of the town was the flowers that filled every window of every house, even to the decrepit shanty on a side-street.

We found my husband's brother awaiting us, and in the evening a little steamer took us the fifteen miles up Lake Seliguer to our home. That ride in the changing lights of the June "white night" among the small wooded islands, past a monastery whose silver dome shone like a pearl, I have never forgotten. On the summit of a high bluff, a church with low whitewashed walls raised its many domes to the sky. An old family estate moved slowly past. At a narrow place a primitive ferry, pulled by cables, lay motion-

less in the still night. Then, at last, appeared a long irregular shore-line of solid forests—tall, straight white pines,
hemlock and spruce forming a deep green background to
the graceful light foliage of the white birch.

As we drew near, we could see the old homestead standing high above the water, with its garden and "linden walk"
running along the edge of the hill. It had been built by the
grandmother, in 1806, to replace a former house, and it
was she who had set out the lindens. Directly back of the
many buildings, and separated only by a narrow strip of
cultivated ground, began the extensive forests. I like to
bring to my mind the beautiful picture of the dear old home,
and to forget what it looked like when, homeless and out-
cast, we were driven from it in 1920. I like to recall the
outline of the woods as they then were, and try to forget
the gaping openings where the trees were later deliberately
burned or ruthlessly cut.

As I write of this time, forming the background to the
terrible years of 1917-22, both periods as now contrasted
with life in America seem unreal, the one a beautiful dream,
the other a fearful nightmare—both unreal.

We were met at the threshold of the old home by my
husband's sister, Princess Shakhovskoy, who represented the
mother, for both parents had died long before. She bore a
silver tray with "bread and salt," the national welcome
which took the place of official presentations of the "freedom
of the city" or the "key to the city," as given in other countries. The Emperor, the newcomer, the returned trium-
phant warrior, the bride for the first time crossing the
threshold—all were met from time immemorial by this
simple, beautiful ceremony, so significant of the hospitality
of Eastern people. Alas, we lived to see the day when
salt was our most coveted and unfluctuating currency, and
bread was valued above diamonds.

CHAPTER FOUR

The Estate of the Ponafidines

As MY husband was in the Ministry of Foreign Affairs, our stay in Russia was only during his furloughs. A younger brother had, on marrying, continued to live in the old home, managing the estate for my husband. There was a small brick bungalow that in the time of serfdom had been used for weaving linen. The hand looms had been set up there, and the beautiful table and bed linen that formed the rich dowry for the daughters of the house and yet left a good supply for my day were made there. This bungalow my husband had ordered fitted up and furnished for us. We had five rooms and a covered porch that gave us a glorious view of woods and lake, of distant villages and a church set high on a hill, marking the estate of a branch of the Tolstoy family, where the great writer visited his aunt in his youth.

We had brought with us from St. Petersburg, as my husband's valet, an ex-soldier, who had been the orderly of my brother-in-law, Colonel Nicholas Ponafidine. My husband had ordered for him the livery of the Foreign Department, and the gilt buttons and crimson piping brought delight and fame to our simple Nikita. He was a huge good-natured fellow, more remarkable for loyalty and willingness than for wits or intelligence, and this livery proved his undoing. If he went anywhere with our troika, Nikita in all his glory on the box by the coachman was the center of the fascinated gaze of the peasants. When we passed through villages, it was this great "general" to whom the people, caps in hand, bowed low, while we came in for only the tail end of the greetings. To us it was a source of much amusement, and it never occurred to us how deep an impression was being made on the man. When sober, he never allowed us to feel his greatness, though tales of his doings among the servants and peasants began to come to our ears. He was a model servant so long as vodka could be kept from him, but this weakness threw us into a constant state of expectancy and of some apprehension as to what he would do. The Russian is seldom violent and dangerous when "in his cups," nor is he given to fighting, as are so many, but the reticent, cunning peasant is then more apt to speak out what is really in his heart.

Once when we needed a doctor, we sent our carriage to town, for this was before the days of telegraph or regular steamer service between the outlying estates and Ostashkov. Nikita was sent with the coachman, bearing a letter and with orders to return with the physician as speedily as possible, allowing for the feeding of the troika. The orders he carried out faithfully, except that he exceeded them by including a good-sized bottle of vodka for himself. During the twenty-five-mile drive, the vodka and the respectful greetings of the peasants began to work, and finally, convinced of his rank and superiority over all others, he climbed down from the box, forced the doctor (who, aside from being a man of peace, was physically ill-prepared to resist) to get up on the front seat, while he himself took possession of the whole of the back of the carriage. I can now see the picture it made as the carriage dashed up to our front door, our "general" sprawled sound asleep in the back of the carriage and our doctor perched modestly on the front seat!

My personal attendant was dear old "Nyanya Katia"— nurse Katia—who had accompanied her young mistress, my husband's mother, to Bortniki as a bride. She had nursed all the eleven children and was adored by the family. Nyanya could not read or write, but she was a good illustration of the strong character and shrewd horse-sense that one so often and so markedly finds among the peasants. She had a quiet dignity that made her respected and that enforced obedience. She acted as housekeeper now, and kept as strict though kindly a hand over the young maids as in the bygone days she had ruled the under-nurses and the children themselves.

Another one of the old serfs was Taniusha, who had been in charge of the laundry, herself doing the fine ironing. Though very old and now drawing a pension from my husband, she would insist upon doing up with trembling hands his best shirts and my dresses.

When any member of the scattered family returned home to Bortniki, these old women came in for almost the first greetings and were kissed and petted as the dearest members of the family. Presents, too, were brought out for them—a package of the highest priced tea for old Taniusha, whose idea of Paradise was to drink as much as she pleased, and as often as she pleased, of the most expensive tea to be had. A box of snuff would be concealed under other gifts for Nyanya Katia, whose secret vice (as she fondly believed) was indulging on the sly in snuff.

I soon discovered that it was indeed a new life, even to the details of living. The manor house was flanked by separate buildings, housing kitchens, ironing-room and ice-house, so that all the odors and noise of cooking were kept from us. In these outer quarters the house cook reigned supreme, while in a separate kitchen one of the last of the serfs who had elected to remain with the family was still, with assistance, cooking for the farm-hands, though she was very old.

In Russia, eating has always been something more than a mere routine for supplying physical demands, and I doubt if dieting simply to attain the required number of calories

can ever be grafted upon that people. Eating is one of
the Russian's greatest pleasures. A holiday was the occasion not so much for arranging outings, sport, receptions
and parties in our sense, but for careful planning of menus.
A caller meant the samovar (with accessories), whatever
the hour. The sound of carriage bells brought housekeeper
and cooks to the window, eagerly craning their necks to
count the numbers arriving and to take measures accordingly. No one, from peasant hut to palace, came and left
without tasting the equivalent of "bread and salt" in this
Russian-Eastern hospitality.

So, even in every-day life, the table meant much. Most
Russians take a very light breakfast, but in addition to our
coffee we always had eggs and hot cakes. At twelve came
luncheon of two hot courses and a dessert. At three-thirty,
what the English call high tea was served. With the hiss-
ing samovar on the table, the tea hour, whether in the
afternoon or late evening, was always the time of delightful
family gatherings. Not only tea was served, but berries
in season, eaten in soup plates with rich cream, preserves
in winter, candied fruits, cold meats, butter and the great
variety of bread that is peculiar to Russia. At seven or
eight came dinner. There was not the English formality—
no dressing for any but official or formal dinners. The
meal always began with a soup—and in no country in the
world can the Russian soups be surpassed, nor the great
variety of *pirojhki,* which are little stuffed patties that go
with them. Three courses and a dessert did not seem to
interfere with a good supper, mostly cold, with perhaps one
hot dish at eleven o'clock. In later years, however, we substituted a simple tea for the supper.

There was always much visiting among the "county
families." The fact that the old estates had been in the
same family for generations brought about ties and rela-

VIEWS OF BORTNIKI:

Top—Rear of house and corner of bungalow.
Bottom—Lake from the front porch.

Views of Bortniki:

Top, View from the lake

tionships that compared, I imagine, with conditions in the South in this country before the Civil War with the difference that there was far less formality. Serfs, and later cheap labor, made possible such free and open hospitality as can never be repeated in our more complicated age. It meant nothing to us to pick up the babies and nurses, fill another carriage with dogs and guns and forester, and drive off, without warning our hosts, for a visit of several days to a "neighbor," perhaps thirty miles distant. Such an inundation coming unexpectedly upon us was also to be looked for, and caused only pleasure—no consternation to either us or the servants, who enjoyed the bustle and importance it brought to them.

Russia was, and is, a country of contradictions—of luxury and primitiveness, of autocracy and the fullest democracy. None of the big country houses in our part of Russia had, at the time I speak of, plumbing or gas. The water was drawn by horses from the lake in barrels, and receptacles in all the buildings on the place were thus filled. Kerosene lamps and candles were used, and my husband could remember when pine splints furnished the only light in peasants' huts and servants' quarters.

Birthdays were of secondary importance, but the "name-day," the day of the Patron Saint, was never overlooked. So with us the twelfth of July, the fête of Saint Peter and Saint Paul, was the name-day of my husband, and, as it happened, my birthday as well, and later that of our eldest son George, while, last but not least in such a family as ours, it was the opening of duck shooting. Naturally, therefore, it was the greatest day of the year for us.

The peasants celebrated, proportionately to their means, even more lavishly than we did. I remember that once, when driving, my husband and the coachman estimated what name-days and the celebration of the village annual fête (for each village and estate had its own patron saint) and Easter cost the peasants. The result was startling! Even the coachman himself was amazed: in proportion to his income, the amount was several times greater than that spent by those of our class.

Wine, as a table beverage, is not drunk in northern Russia as it is in the southern countries. The peasant drinks his tea and kvass, which might be called the national drink. Made at home from rye rusks, and slightly fermented, it is a non-intoxicating nourishing drink. But on fête day, vodka is what he must have, and on those few days or at weddings he drinks for the sake of drinking, until the whole party is under the table. Women did not take part in drinking when I first went to Russia, but during later years this evil began to include many of them. When the fête and the day or days of headache had passed, the peasants, except the comparatively few habitual drunkards, would again go through a long period of soberness. I am sure that among the peasants there were fewer of the habitual wife-beating drunkards than in most countries.

But to return to our particular celebration. We never sent out invitations for the twelfth of July, but we knew our friends would come. Provision was made for lunch, tea, dinner and supper for from fifty to eighty persons, not including the coachmen and the boatmen from the steamer and rowboats. Guests came from many miles by land and water, and huge birthday *piroga,* or pies, stuffed with fish and eggs or mushrooms or cabbage or meat, were baked in the servants' kitchen; these and large kettles of soup were provided for the coachmen and boatmen. Vodka also was served them sometimes by imprudent hosts whose regard for the safety of their guests was not so strong as their sense of Russian hospitality. At such times, how many were to spend the night troubled us housekeepers not at all.

There was always room in house or bungalow, or on hay and feather-beds spread for young folks on the floor of the big Russian bath.

When I began to keep house in the old mansion that had come into the family with the first of the Romanoff emperors (and went out with the last, three hundred years later!), I realized what it meant to live for generations in one place. I wish I had a list of what came to us—and this was after two daughters and three sons had been married and supplied with linen, china and such things. Russian titles and property were shared among all the children, and yet I found the old home stocked to meet requirements in a way that amazed me. Roughly I remember that there were over fifty feather-beds and more than a hundred down pillows. An old English dinner service known to antiquarians as having been in the family for generations still existed in incredible numbers. The soup tureens, six of them, were so gigantic that if full they must have required muscular waiters to carry them. There were a hundred soup plates and several hundred dinner plates of assorted sizes, and platters, vegetable and other dishes innumerable, including a long narrow platter for fish of a size I had never before seen served whole. All these, after several generations had used and, presumably, broken many pieces!

That first summer I came to know much of the life of the country gentry, who are among the most highly educated and cultured people in the world and who, beyond what education, travel and the knowledge of many languages can give them, possess a natural charm that has won the hearts of all who have known them.

CHAPTER FIVE

The Village School

As WINTER approached, many of the estates were deserted. Our neighbors became few, our relatives among them. My husband, too, was called to St. Petersburg on business. I thought it a favorable opportunity, therefore, to get a good start in the Russian language, for I should be left to myself where it would be "sink or swim," since none of the servants or people around us spoke anything but Russian. This way of learning a language has its complications, but I can recommend it as a sure means of opening up what will afterward be an easy matter. I spent many hours each day in the village school on our place, a school that for years my husband had housed and mostly supported. Children from five neighboring villages came, dressed in sheepskin coats, high felt boots in dry weather, leather ones in wet, and with well bundled heads. They brought their lunches of rye bread or patties, but the teacher took her meals with us.

These children were a great help to me in getting a start in the language. They also enabled me to get closer to the peasant life than would otherwise have been possible. The school continued on our place until the zemstvo, or local government, was able to put up buildings of the required uniform type, and then it was moved to the central one of the five villages strung along the shore. This brought the school nearer to all the pupils—a great boon, for they had been obliged to walk nearly three miles. In the short days it meant starting before full daylight and getting home after dark. The road over open country or on the frozen lake with deep drifting snow was more than some of the children could traverse in bad weather, and this was one of the problems faced in bringing education to the country children.

Preparation for the winter is more noticeable in Russia than in most countries where the winters are milder. Double windows are brought down from the attic, put in and carefully calked with a kind of putty. The space between the two window-sashes at the bottom has several inches of sand laid to keep out all the drafts possible, and it is covered with different colored moss. We had in our woods the loveliest moss—pale silver, russet browns and many shades of green that kept their colors all winter and were a link between us and the snow-bound world. In cities where moss is not at hand, thick layers of cotton batting are placed, sometimes brightened by clippings of tinsel or colored paper or everlasting flowers strewed over the cotton. While the housewives are thus getting the homes protected, the police in towns and the headmen in villages are thinking of travelers. As the snow falls and lakes and rivers freeze, they take measures. Young spruce trees are firmly planted in the ice at convenient distances in two parallel rows marking the road. This is a vital precaution in view of the terrible dark blizzards that are to be expected—blizzards so dense that once they caused my husband and the coachman, in the middle of the day, to flounder for hours in the drifts on the lake in front of our house, unable to find the turn. On land, long wisps of twisted straw tied to trees and fences, or, in the open country, little trees were again planted to mark the roads. So after a heavy fall of snow, the little ones had signs to guide them as they trudged through the deep drifts.

The teacher we happened to have at the time I speak of trained an exceedingly good choir from among her pupils. I loved to sit in the little schoolroom listening to them singing the beautiful folk-songs or rehearsing for the church service. Sundays, dressed in uniforms furnished by my husband, this little choir filled our church, peasants coming from a distance to hear them sing.

Christmas was nearing, and we began to think of the tree we wanted the children to have. After dinner, the table was cleared and my little nephews and nieces brought down from the attic stores of discarded toys and invalided dolls and animals. The entire family gathered, and under the direction of a cousin whose nimble fingers accomplished marvels of toy-surgery, we spent many happy evenings. This also served as a fine language kindergarten for me in learning Russian. So when the great night came, with bags of nuts and a practical gift for each child, a toy was added. None of the children had seen such a tree, and their delight was ours.

During the four-year course the children learned to read and write. They learned, too, the barest rudiments of world geography, with some detail of that of Russia and the Bible lands, arithmetic to fractions, and "God's Law." The course was of necessity short and simple, and the children were all of one faith. The religious teacher was the village priest, a part of whose duties it was to drive on given days to the schools in his parish. The children were taught the Slavic rendering of the New Testament, the life of Christ, the prayers in the Prayer-Book, and stories of the lives of the saints. The study of religion was given far more prominence in a Russian's schooling than we find even among the college courses here. To make the teachings in city schools acceptable to the various denominations represented, the class was divided, the Russian Orthodox priest taking the children of his fold, a Lutheran pastor those of German Protestant parentage, a Catholic priest the Polish element, and a mullah for Mohammedans. Thus, while all followed the required course, each denomination had religious study conducted by its own religious leader.

In May came examinations. Pupils who showed ambition and capacity, and whose parents wished them to continue their education, went to the county town for examinations that would pass them into the "city school," where also their tuition would be free. For from the village school on, the way was as open to the public schools and then the universities as it is to any American farmer's children. There were numerous scholarships in the universities, and these with increasing frequency were being applied for by peasants. In any case, the university tuition and the expenses connected with university life were markedly low in comparison with all Western standards. Not only could the peasants and the "proletariat" acquire an education, but education opened all doors, even that of the nobility. In this respect the Russian nobility was a very democratic and flexible one, being constantly augmented from below. Though coming from the humblest and even illiterate families, students were able through education and state service to obtain for themselves and their posterity the title and all the privileges of nobility. The number of peasant students profiting by education was slowly but steadily increasing as the need of education was realized by them. In view of the prevailing belief that peasants were barred from education, I can not emphasize this fact too strongly.

CHAPTER SIX

Peasant Life

THE long years of serfdom undoubtedly left a barrier, a wall of distrust between the peasants as a whole and the *pomeschiks*, or landowners; that is to say, lack of confidence on the part of the peasants, and consequent failure on the part of the *pomeschiks* to understand the psychology of the peasants. This unfortunate misunderstanding has been an important factor in the events of the past chaotic years in Russia.

The Russian intelligentsia who are closest to the peasants are the first to admit that they are to them a sealed book. During the years of serfdom they learned to adapt themselves to existing conditions and to hide their real sentiments. They are reserved and suspicious, and by nature individualistic. Their emancipation they regard as the direct act of the Tsar, against the wishes of the former owners of both serfs and land. That the plans for emancipation were worked out by Alexander II with the hearty cooperation of many of the landowning statesmen and nobles is entirely overlooked by the peasants, and the loyalty to the person of the Tsar has to this day been something quite apart from loyalty to the Government. The peasants believed that the "Little Father" was on their side in spite of courtiers and *pomeschiks*, and that the landowners would, if opportunity offered, gladly bring about the former conditions. This is the basis of the distrust that we always felt we were not overcoming. It was this sentiment of the peasants that caused a deep misunderstanding of their attitude during the Revolution and much incorrect interpretation of the attitude of the *pomeschiks*. While undoubtedly there were isolated exceptions, I know personally none of our class who did not repudiate serfdom as a thing of the past.

The first years of my life in Russia saw the beginning of the great work the zemstvos did for the peasants. As peasant life can not be understood, nor our own position visualized, without some knowledge of this work of the zemstvos, I feel that I must explain briefly.

The zemstvos were instituted by Alexander II. In those days when local conditions and needs varied, and vast distances were emphasized by lack of good roads and telegraph lines, the zemstvo met the situation. It was a local governing body made up of representatives of the landowners, whether peasants, clergy or *pomeschiks*. All local interests, such as schools, roads, agriculture, medical help (including veterinary) came under its jurisdiction. For many years my husband was an active member of our county zemstvo. In timing his vacation, he always aimed to be at the spring meeting, and no longing to be at home and to enjoy the pleasures or attend to the interests of the estate would keep him from remaining to the last day of the sitting of the zemstvo. The functions of the zemstvos grew; the amount added to their budgets for building schools and for increasing the number of normal schools for the training of teachers, expanded, the funds being derived from a special tax on land. This was only one part of their work, but so much information at least seemed needed to explain the significance of these important governmental bodies.

The condition of the peasants, justly sympathized with, is widely talked of, but that a progressively increasing work for their betterment was steadily being carried on is rarely mentioned. That there were twenty thousand agricultural cooperative societies in Russia before the war, that the land was gradually passing into the ownership of the peasants, and that they actually owned more land in 1914 than did the nobles—all this is either unknown abroad or ignored. In emancipating the serfs, the program of Alexander II is the one exception in history, I think, where any provision was made for the future of the class liberated. That the system of land tenure, the "mir," proved to be a clumsy and ineffectual form of tilling the ground in no way gives us a right to forget what the Government had done. Time and circumstances demanded a change, and it was coming; but it should not be viewed from the commonly accepted Western belief that the peasant was the wilfully abused and oppressed victim of the Tsar and all the *pomeschiks*.

I myself went to Russia very ready to criticize and to believe that all evil came from above—from the ruling classes, but many years of close contact with peasants— closer than with townfolk—and of intimate knowledge of government methods and internal and foreign policy, have given me a more balanced judgment. When we take into account the comparatively few years that separate barbaric Russia from civilized Russia, and keep before our minds the numberless nationalities, tongues and mental make-ups of these peoples, and recall the widely various climate and environment included in that vast realm, we get a more understanding view of the causes and defects and mistakes of the past. Realizing the tremendous obstacles in the way of progress, we get a new light on the good, the hopeful signs that pointed toward rapid betterment during the quarter of a century before the World War. Only those who have informed themselves of the facts, or who knew Russia from within, are aware what strides were being made in that short period of time. I do not shut my eyes to the bad in the past; I see the evils that made the collapse of the old régime inevitable. It can not be too strongly emphasized, however, that there were statesmen and *pomeschiks* who worked for the good of the people, that there were sufficient patriotism, integrity and ability in Russia to bring about an evolution—or a wise, rightly timed revolution.

When I went to Russia, the majority of peasants in our part of the country were tilling the land that was owned in common, and living in closely built villages in log cabins. These cottages were snug and warm but built so near together, with the inevitable pile of wood between them, that a fire once started ran through the village, if a wind favorable to such a catastrophe were blowing. After such a fire, the police would give an official statement of the condition of the families and the amount of loss incurred, adding permission to raise funds for rebuilding. Armed with this document, some member of the family would begin a tour of the country, going from village to village, town to town. Few refused their mite. Local landowners were usually generous in giving timber. And so a new village rise. In making a detailed description of anythi Russia, the vastness of the country and the varied cli conditions which naturally cause differences must not be i gotten. Where we lived in Greater Russia, between St. Petersburg and Moscow, is found the type of peasant life that I am describing. We were surrounded by great forests and therefore log cabins or "izbas" were the homes in which the peasants dwelt, while in southern or Little Russia white-washed "khata" and straw-covered roofs were the usual abodes.

The severe climate made warmth the chief objective in all building operations. The Russian stove is therefore the center and most conspicuous feature of the interior of the house. The huge brick oven in which all cooking, as well as baking, is done is so built as to heat the whole of the large compartment. The many turns—forty or fifty, I believe—that the flue makes before the smoke reaches the outer chimney insures every particle of heat being retained. The hot-air chamber is closed as soon as the fire has burned out the dangerous fumes, and we have a huge brick construction before us with a flat "roof" reached by two or three steps built in the side. The stove is warm—the "roof" most comfortingly so, and this platform, some eight feet by six at least, piled with sheepskin coats, quilts, pillows, etc., is sleeping-place, warming-place and comfort for the whole family. The father, coming in half frozen from his work in the woods or from getting fish from under the ice, climbs on top of the stove and in the warmth found there escapes a chill. The baby is taken there to be bathed; the sick turn to it instinctively. The children, always lightly clad in the house, spend hours rolling about on it, playing or sleeping like kittens in a warm basket. The regular sleeping quarters of the family are on wooden benches around the walls or on mattresses on the floor, though sometimes there may be a properly curtained bed in an alcove.

Partitions of pine boards and the walls of the stove break up the large compartment into kitchen, living-room, and generally a best room, or parlor. Neat home-woven strips of matting cover the painted floor where most walking may be expected. Here is the corner cupboard of icons, chief among them those given at baptism and marriage. A table between the windows—another cupboard with the best bits of china—a stiff row of chairs—flowers in the curtained windows—these are the inevitable furnishings of a prosperous peasant's house. The poor izbas have only one living-room, and the kitchen part is probably not even partitioned off. The peasant's life is one of hard toil and little enjoyment. In the long winter evenings the only recreation is the gathering together of the young folk in one of the largest izbas, where the lighting is furnished by the party and probably something paid as rent. Here

the girls take their spinning, crocheting, cross-stitch embroidery, and the boys their concertinas and balalaikas.
Story-telling, dancing, singing fill the evening. It is in these
besedas, as well as by wedding- and fête-days, that the Russian folk-songs have been passed down from time immemorial.

When a fête-day comes in the summer, the village streets
are the ballrooms. Every one is out. The old women sit
in groups on the benches that are built under the front
windows, the old men smoke and discuss crops in little knots
of their own. The fête lasts for two or three days, the
whole village exchanging calls, and as in every house a
bountiful table is spread and vodka flows, the last callers
sometimes have to be carried home, but as often no one is
sober enough to do so, one can see drunken men scattered
about under the trees, sleeping off the effects of such indis-
criminate hospitality.

CHAPTER SEVEN

Medical Work

MY HUSBAND being in the Foreign Office, we looked upon our Russian home as only a temporary one. We could have returned there for short periods every year, had we so wished, but as my husband's appointments were always in distant parts of the Near East, it scarcely paid, since most of the short leaves would be consumed in travel. When therefore, eight months after our arrival in Russia, my husband was appointed Consul General to Bagdad, he decided to continue doing as he had before his marriage and accept this as a five-year appointment.

The very name of Bagdad carries romance and adventure, and though we both had spent so many years in the Orient, this was to be a new life to us. And so, indeed, we found it. The years passed there brought us experiences and contacts that opened a new outlook on life and international affairs.

The climate we did not anticipate with pleasure, nor did I look forward calmly to setting up my first housekeeping under such unusual conditions—for so many months spending the days in the cellar and the nights on the roof because of the heat. Moreover we had heard weird stories of having to share home and bed with scorpions, lizards, snakes and other such slimy creatures that have never been included in my love for the animal world. But this too, is "another story."

It was in Bagdad that our first son was born. George, our longed-for baby, came in 1892 as a "name-day" gift to his father and a birthday present to me on our common fête-day—that of Saints Peter and Paul, July twelfth.

When we returned from Bagdad it was under different

circumstances, with a four-months-old baby and my husband broken in health. The heat of Bagdad had affected his heart, laying the foundation of the heart trouble that, though temporarily relieved, was never cured and ultimately caused his death. Coming as we did in November— from tropical heat to a Russian winter—was what the physicians relied upon to tone him up, but it was a risk for the baby and one that we were fully conscious of. This fear, however, proved to be one of those mythical "bridges" we so often create and look forward to with dread and that in the end never materialize. Some day perhaps I shall write a book on the number of minutes, piling up into days and years, that one spends on this needless occupation, and the loss of energy expended, for my experience has been that I have seldom crossed the identical bridges I fully expected and feared—it was always an unexpected one, and at an unexpected time. In this instance the baby thrived, never having so much as a cold. To be again in a country where the four seasons really existed and to see snow after living through five years of only three seasons—hot, hotter, hottest—was a tremendous delight and one that we sensed as soon as we passed the Black Sea.

We anchored in Odessa at night and in the morning looked out of the porthole to see the ground covered with snow. That winter landscape, the first we had seen since leaving Odessa in 1889, came as a tonic to my husband, and day by day in his own climate his health returned, so that by the time we reached Volochok, where we left the train to take post-horses, he could care for me, for I was about at the end of my strength. Fortunately, during troubled times we always seemed to have turns in being incapacitated. Seldom both of us gave out at the same time.

Winter had set in with severity, but the snowfall had not been so great as usual; the roads were in some places blocked

with deep drifts and in others swept bare by driving winds.
Large sleighs with ironshod runners were therefore too
heavy, and posting was done in the peasants' long, low, seat-
less sledges with broad wooden runners. Sitting deep in hay
with the baby so bundled that I was in constant fear of his
being smothered, we drove mile after mile for two days
in an almost continuous storm. Every time we stopped to
change horses my husband would scrape off the snow to get
at George and lift him out. The baby was not half-Russian
for nothing, for he responded to the winter rigors in a way
that the doctors had little expected, and we brought him
home without a cold, a picture of rosy health and good
nature.

We remained in Russia nearly two years on account of
my husband's health. During this time he was very active in
local work among the peasants. His election on the zemstvo
council followed term after term even during his absence,
so when returning on leave he took his place again. This
gave him the opportunity of furthering the measures in which
he was so deeply interested for the education and general betterment of the condition of the peasants. He was appointed
inspector of the school that was still on our estate, as well as
of several others near by. He was also honorary judge and
attended the sessions of the Circuit Court held periodically
in our county town. Going with my husband to the zemstvo
meetings and coming closer to the peasants' problems, I was
able to get more understanding sympathy with them and see
more clearly the tremendous obstacles they as a mass presented toward any change. Suspicious of the motives of
any move made in their interests that came from above, they
balked the efforts of their real friends and rendered their
work discouraging and often almost hopeless.

In nearly all the zemstvos of European Russia, for instance, the medical work was well established—less so in

Siberia, although there also it was progressing. In our part
of the country, medical "centers" existed at central points,
where there were a free dispensary, a physician, a trained assistant and often a midwife. The villages under their care
were within a radius of perhaps twelve to fifteen miles.
Zemstvo post-horses provided means of transport, so that
the peasants did not have to take their horses away from
their work.

The Russian peasants, like other people of narrow intelligence the world over, had more faith in home remedies
and in old women, or any one else who seemed wiser than
themselves, than they did in regular doctors. Of hospitals,
too, they had a horror. I was constantly besieged by patients and soon realized that I could do a great deal for them
in cooperation with the doctor and by training them to believe in scientific treatment. As I became acquainted with
the personnel of our center, I found how hampered they were
in being unable to trust the peasants with medicine and in
caring for wounds. So we entered into a sort of partner-
ship that continued, whenever we were in Russia, with the
various doctors we had. In surgical cases or severe illness
I would go with the doctor and get instruction that I could
carry out daily, he coming as needed. Or I would give first
aid if the patient could not be taken to the dispensary. We
had one emergency bed in the medical center and a good
zemstvo hospital in the county town, but the need of a small
emergency hospital such as many zemstvos already had in
most of their centers became more and more imperative, for
at certain seasons of the year the condition of the roads
made taking patients so far both painful and dangerous.
The opposition to the extra expense of each bed and finally of
our little "northern hospital" that came into being much
later, had to be fought step by step by patient explaining
and urging. The expense lay on our zemstvo funds, with

some help from the Government health department. I remember the final struggle in a zemstvo meeting in which the
budget for the hospital was read. The peasant delegates
outnumbered those of the intelligentsia, and they fought
against everything that seemed like luxury. The size of the
windows seemed absurd, as their minds went back to the
small windows in their izbas. Painted floors and a bathroom for each of the two stories they regarded as unwar-
ranted expense. One of the members in a long speech
addressed to my husband, who presented the budget, said:
"We are not city people. We are not used to such things.
Our parents before us went to the Russian bath. They never
had tubs in the house. They did not build such big windows
to let in the cold. And unpainted floors are as good to walk
on as your expensive painted ones. It is all right for you
to talk, but the expense comes out of our pockets."

My husband answered that he was pleading for these innovations not for himself; that we were not eligible to the
zemstvo hospitals; that we paid for every visit the doctor
made us, though our share of the taxes was far greater than
that of the individual peasant, as we owned more acres to
be taxed. "I am not complaining of this," he went on. "It
is as it should be. But I wish you to understand that when
I insist on bathrooms and on floors that by being painted can
be kept cleaner and add to the safety of the patients, I am
pleading for your wives and little children and for what I
know is for their good."

It took years to get the neat little building put up on
ground given by our cousin. This winter that we were home
we had an epidemic of typhoid and many children's infectious
diseases. I was out almost daily with the doctor, or alone,
carrying out orders, and saw how much more readily the
peasants obeyed me. My brother when ordering drugs
in America for the Urumia hospital let me put in an order

for large quantities of the most needed preparations, largely in tablet forms. Once, during the absence of our physician, there were a number of cases in villages near us that I attended to, for the assistant was overworked. As soon as the doctor returned, we went together to the villages, and to my delight the doctor agreed with my diagnoses and treatment, but naturally I withdrew, only going to see that his orders were carried out. The first day of the doctor-given medicine, wives and mothers came to me. In one case the "new medicine" had made the patient "all swell up," in another had given heartburn, and so on with a long string of unexpected symptoms. They one and all brought back bottles and powders, begging for my own that were so good. I drove to the dispensary and had a talk with the doctor. He was an understanding man, heart and soul anxious to win the confidence of the peasants and get at the truth of their statements. So he went with me to the houses and told dissatisfied folk that thereafter I would give them medicine. This I did, but it was medicine prepared by him, the same they had been taking, though disguised. Immediately miraculous results followed. All unnatural symptoms disappeared, improvement took place! Several times we made this test, always with the same results. In a paper he read before the State Zemstvo Convention, the doctor cited our experience as an illustration of the difficulties scientific medical work met with among peasants.

The typhoid epidemic happened to be during Lent, when milk, eggs and meat soups are not eaten. Rye bread, sauerkraut, cereals, dried and pickled mushrooms, cucumbers and vegetable oils form the menu. Nothing would persuade them to give milk or the bouillon I took them. The fact that neither I nor the doctor, a Lutheran from one of the Baltic states, was of the Orthodox faith made our words of little weight. My husband then sent for our priest, who accompanied us on a long round of visits. He talked with the peasants, explaining to them that times of sickness made an exception and that it was not wrong during Lent to take whatever the doctor ordered. Some, however, remained firm and died with their own diet or, in some cases, defied all science by making good recoveries. One case that worried me was that of a mother whom with the utmost difficulty I finally persuaded to give her four-year-old child, sick with typhoid, milk and bouillon instead of sauerkraut soup and rye bread.

The zemstvo was very faithful in sending twice a year into every village and house some one to vaccinate the children. This not only met with no opposition but was welcomed.

Alongside our medical work was a veterinarian center. It consisted of a free dispensary and a small stable in which peasants could leave their horses or cattle if necessary, furnishing only the fodder. When epidemics broke out, the head veterinarian in the county town sent out trained assistants to each *volost,* or township. The peasants having been collected to meet him, he explained the symptoms, and told them of precautionary measures and of treatment or of the headquarters they should notify. Here, too, I had as much trouble as with the human beings. Cows and horses were brought to me or I would be asked to go to the villages—and I never refused if I could possibly go.

These experiences opened my eyes to a new side of Russian autocratic rule. No government surely did as much for the peasants in bringing to them free education and medical treatment. But there was undoubtedly an undesirable side to this system. The peasants, deprived of the necessity of initative, developed not at all. As they were not permitted to have any political interests, this too parental care did much to foster the traits that later made it possible for them to submit for so long to Bolshevik tyranny.

CHAPTER EIGHT

Bright Spots and Dark

IN 1893 our second son, Alexander, was born, the only one of our three sons who, according to present United States immigration laws, could be considered a native Russian. The following summer my husband was appointed representative of the Foreign Office on the boundary commission of England (India), Afghanistan and Russia to decide on an unexplored line across the Pamirs. He left for Tashkent in May. I followed with the children in August.

We looked back to our life in Tashkent as among the pleasantest of all our Eastern experiences. Aside from the great historical interest of Russian Turkestan, which included Samarcand and (as suzerainties) Bokhara and Khiva, the climate and conditions of life were delightful. The Pamir expedition that my husband made was one of unique interest that will be told of in the volume covering my life in the Orient. The months spent on the Pamirs at altitudes never less than fourteen thousand feet and running as high as eighteen thousand where strong men suffered from "mountain sickness" almost proved fatal to my husband, for the change from the heat and low altitude of Bagdad (below sea level) to such extremes brought on heart attacks, and I brought him home in a worse condition even than that in which he returned from Bagdad. The state of his health made a longer stay in his native climate imperative; but only a short time was given to actual rest, for he was soon drawn into an activity for which, owing to his past experiences, he was the only available person to be consulted.

It would seem a far cry from cholera epidemics to Mohammedan pilgrimages in Arabia, but only an intimate knowledge of the Mohammedan religion and pilgrimages, of the Great Kourban Bairam, "Fête of Sacrifice," when tens of thousands of animals were slaughtered in one spot and on one day, and a careful study of all the caravan and sea routes that the Russian Mohammedan pilgrims took in returning could discover the clue to the strange periodical outbreaks of cholera in various parts of Russia. This established, and the dates known in advance, my husband's conclusions as given in an article he had published would, it was believed, enable Russia to take precautionary measures that would forestall and prevent such scourges. A commission having been appointed to study this question, my husband was "loaned" to it by the Foreign Office, and his work in this new line kept us in Russia for two years.

This period, now that I had a good working knowledge of the language, brought me closer to the people of all classes, and it was easy to see that unless a more liberal government were granted, trouble was likely. It was not so much from the peasants that open, to say nothing of intelligent, criticism and discontent were heard. It was from the middle classes, the intelligentsia, that the various parties were formed that furnished material for later activities. The peasants in our part of Russia were not "land hungry." Theirs was a life of toil and the special hardships that come with long cold winters; but, in the sense so generally accepted abroad, they were by no means oppressed by the despotism of Tsars, officialdom or Cossacks. The great error of the past was that they were too parentally treated in that they were not given any encouragement to develop individually and acquire initiative.

In 1897 my husband was appointed Consul General to Meshed, the capital of Khorasan, Persia's most northeastern province. This was a very important post, as the Afghan and Indian frontiers presented many problems that the Bagdad and Pamir experiences had qualified him particularly well to meet. And so again our faces were turned toward Persia. Meshed presented many new points of interest as one of the three remaining "cities of refuge." One of the most sacred of the holy places, it fairly bristled with fascinating studies. But that is another story.

After five years spent in this unique spot, we returned home, bringing with us our last son, who had, as the Persians devoutly believed, the stamp of happiness and good fortune on him because of his having been born in Meshed and thus having the privilege of inheriting the title of "Meshedi." Perhaps the length of that title—"Meshedi Jusuph Khan"—drove our little Joseph into inventing for himself, as he did when almost a baby, the shorter name of "Oka," by which he has always been known in the family circle. And so with three fine healthy boys, and my husband in much better health than for many years, we returned to Russia. How bright life seemed!

CHAPTER NINE

The Eve of the World War

IT WAS full spring as we sailed up the Volga. Winter was giving way in loudly tumbling streams and rosy tinted trees, while snow still lay in northern exposures. The river had overflowed its banks to such depths that in places the flat-bottomed steamer left the swift current of midstream and floated over fields and meadows. Nightingales filled the trees, and as we plunged along in the darkness, the branches sometimes touched our windows, and it seemed that one and the same nightingale sang to his love all the night through.

As we went farther north we found ourselves back in the beginning of spring. The trees were just bursting into bud, and banks of snow lay on northern slopes. Nowhere is spring more vitally evident than in northern countries such as where we lived. A peculiarly delicate pink tinges the sky. Streams of melting water are heard gurgling and rushing as they burrow their way under the snow, and their pungent fragrance in the woods speaks of the moving sap in the trees and the pulsations of a new life.

Coming from the bare mountains and arid plains of Persia and Turkestan, to us the woods and green grass never seemed so beautiful. The children, too, found themselves in a new world. Accustomed to playing within walled premises, and always accompanied by outriders as well as nurses or governess when beyond the walls of the Consulate, they enjoyed to the full the freedom that woods and lake gave them. While the boys were care-free in their enjoyment, we were facing a crisis that is always the most painful to those whose calling obliges them to live abroad. We were now realizing that the happy family life that up to this time had made it a matter of indifference to us where we were stationed was

at an end, and that we must think of the education of the
two older boys. To take them with us where there would be
no Russian schools seemed unwise; to leave them in Russia
and be separated from them for years was something we
could not face. With the boys in Russia, our aim would now
be to get an appointment to a place near enough to have
them spend their summers with us, or ourselves go to them.
Distance, then, not promotion or amount of pay, was to be
the controlling factor. So, while the year and a half that
at this time we spent at home brought us much of pleasure
and change, always there was present a deep heartache in
thinking of the coming decision.

This year also gave us reasons for grave apprehension.
Discontent with the Government among what we have
learned to call the intelligentsia was increasing. Alexander
III had been a strong honest ruler. Kindly by nature, he had
been imbued with a sincere sense of his responsibilities, desiring the real advancement of his people. From conviction
of the divine right of his position, he demanded obedience
and reigned as Emperor. Unfortunately, the horrible fate
of his father had very naturally colored his reign and thrown
him into a policy of reaction that might not otherwise have
so characterized it. Though opposing most of the liberal
reforms, particularly in educational programs, he undoubtedly did so in the honest belief that his action was for the
ultimate good of his country.

In 1902 Russia was governed by a man equally honest,
high-minded, loyal to his country and her best interests as
he understood them. He was not far-sighted enough, however, to realize that a turn in Russia's development had
come; that if a representative form of government more in
keeping with the times were not *given*, it would be *taken*,
and that if the form of absolute monarchism were not voluntarily changed to a government providing a representative

body to stand between the autocrat and the people, it would sooner or later be got by force.

It has always seemed to me one of the most pathetic instances of the irony of fate that Nicholas II should have been born to be ruler, above all in a country like Russia. His mentality, inclinations and will power were utterly inadequate. A private country gentleman, happy in his home and family, the center of a circle of congenial friends; a man always on the side of what was good, cultured, idealistic, and kindly toward all around him and loved by all—this is the picture that springs to my imagination as to what *should* have been.

Undoubtedly prompted by a desire to shape his policy for the advancement of his people, he lacked the force necessary to carry it out in the face of opposition, and was absolutely at the mercy of the last adviser. In connection with this, I remember an incident which, because my husband often referred to it, was stamped on my mind. In one of the frequent discussions between my brother-in-law, Prince Shakhovskoy, and my husband, the former, laying his hand on my husband's arm, said very quietly and solemnly, "Remember my words, Peter. That boy (referring to the newly crowned Nicholas II) will bathe Russia and all the world in blood. God help him and us." In response to the storm raised by us, he explained that it was not a reflection on the character of the Emperor as a just, humane, liberal and peace-loving ruler; it was that he foresaw the weakness that would be taken advantage of by unscrupulous influences, and he knew that Russia needed a strong hand.

I am only trying to express the perhaps vague and superficial feeling that I remember was forced upon me at this period. Inasmuch as we returned to Russia only from time to time and after absences of several years, changes for good or bad stood out more impressively than if we had lived

through them. There was a noticeable change among the
zemstvo employees around us, among the country clergy,
and above all among the student class, that took the form
of a decidedly critical, even when not actively hostile, attitude toward the Government. So far as the clergy is concerned, this fact is a refutation of one of the chief arguments
used by Bolshevism to-day as an excuse for persecuting the
orthodox religion, namely, because, as they claim, it was
a "blind tool" of autocracy. My own experience, particularly
among the village clergy, is quite to the contrary. As to
the peasants, they were less changed, at least in our part
of Russia, where, as I have said, land hunger was little felt.
The peasants were as usual—grumbling over their life of
toil, but always in an indefinite way. It was for the Bolsheviki to start into a reasoning, awakened body that great
impassive mass which was not able to formulate its discontent. But the Soviet Government has met with quite unexpected results, for if the peasants are wide-awake to the
fact that their past was far from being a bed of roses, they
realize that their present condition has brought them even
less of roses and many unexpected real thorns. And so in
1902 we felt a strong undercurrent of something ominous
preparing and a realization that no one among the entourage
of the young Emperor had sufficient vision or courage to
point out and insist on the path that, if taken at the right
time, would have saved the country; for Russia could and
would have worked out her own salvation.

But, in spite of clouds, we saw many bright spots—great
advance in the economic and industrial life of the country,
in transportation, in railroad extension, in education. Much
had been done not only in increasing the number of universities and other institutions of higher education, but also in the
country among the peasants. We found our own zemstvo
active in adding annually to the number of schools. The

school formerly housed on our place was now in the center of five villages; it was larger and had been built according to the required zemstvo model.   Veterinary branches had been added in some instances to the medical centers in villages, as well as improvements made in the city headquarters. Winter courses of instruction by lectures and object lessons were beginning to be given in the villages, and specialists were sent to demonstrate agricultural machinery, methods, dairy work and first-aid veterinary treatment.

As to our private affairs, we left the two boys at the Gymnasium, in the "boarding department," where their fellow students were of all classes, peasants included.   All were given a most thorough mental training, but far too little physical culture.   The boys did exceedingly good work, and we had no complaint to make of their progress.

While the winter, always beautiful, brought us many pleasures in Bortniki, and occasional visits to St. Petersburg opened again an almost forgotten world of opera and theater, we were nevertheless oppressed by the uncertainty of the future.   Many were the projects—and cast aside when we thought of the children.   Finally, however, on the retirement of the Consul General in Constantinople, the post was offered to Mr. Ponafidine.

Here was a solution of our problem!   Every year of the ten we spent in Constantinople, either the boys' tutor brought them to us in the summer or, through leave of absence, my husband was able to be in Bortniki from May, when the schools closed, to September, this being his reward for having hitherto remained at his post for five or six years without furlough.   Christmas vacations the boys spent at Bortniki.   They learned to be good shots, and on skiis to track and round up game, and always looked forward eagerly to the winter sports.   And so we were all happy.

CHAPTER TEN

In War-Time

THE ten years spent in Constantinople were fraught with momentous changes not only to Russia but to many parts of the East. The unfortunate Russo-Japanese War with its disastrous results; the Young Turk Revolution; the war between Turkey and Italy—all not only passed before our eyes but were parts of our lives. In our own family the greatest blows were the death of my brother, Doctor Cochran, and my husband's failing eyesight. During these years we returned to Russia in May for the summers and were back in Constantinople in September. This gave us the opportunity of keeping in close touch with the events that, staged in the East, were to have results of world importance and at the same time presented to us a perhaps clearer picture of the rapid changes going on in Russia than if we had been living there uninterruptedly.

We could see with dismay heavy clouds gathering as a result of the Japanese War: party strife, loss of confidence in the Government, and finally the Revolution of 1905. All the bloodshed and misery of this time resulted in half-measures. To be sure a Duma was granted and beginnings of many radical changes for the better followed, but the actual constitutional government—a Duma with ministers responsible to it, and not to the Emperor—was not realized. Had this been achieved by the Revolution of 1905, those of 1917 would not have followed and the history of Russia would not have been written for so many years in blood. During the succeeding years, while not minimizing the rocks ahead, we watched with gratification the steady and in many respects amazingly rapid progress made by Russia in betterment of the educational condition of the peasants, road construction and the various branches of the State's life. This convinced me that Russia was capable of working out her own problems and soon overcoming the obstacles that had made her in many respects behind the times. Russia had honest leaders to guide the country, through evolution and not revolution, to the position its natural and human elements entitled it to—a position in the world that I fully believe Russia is yet destined to occupy. Though we did foresee troubles ahead—possibly a political revolution, that is, a change in the Constitution—we little dreamed of what was actually before us. The War that shook the entire world to its foundations has been almost forgotten by us in the more terrible events brought by two revolutions and civil war.

This was what faced us when my husband's failing health obliged him to resign from government service and as a private citizen take up his life in Russia.

In 1912, when we were settled down for what promised to be years of happy and useful home life, we found our two older sons in the University and the youngest in the Emperor Alexander's Lyceum, all in St. Petersburg. My husband, who could never bring himself to a life of leisure, was full of projects, both in his private life and as a citizen. Always having the progress of his country close to his heart, he considered running for the Duma, and at home he occupied himself in developing the estate along the most modern lines, as he had been doing for years, as far as was possible from a distance, continuing and increasing his connections with school and zemstvo work in general.

His first dream, that of the Duma, he was obliged to abandon on account of increasing trouble with his heart and eyes, and so he concentrated on Bortniki, at the same time getting together his wealth of material for a book on the Boundary Commission on the Pamirs. In spite of continued party friction and universal discontent with many existing conditions, a strong though small and limited current of reform was steadily pushing forward. Had not the war come, I believe that the best elements in Russia would have succeeded, if necessary through revolution, though a revolution not complicated by the passions of war: a political, not a social revolution. The two years of quiet before the war broke out brought us into particularly close contact with the educational, medical and agrarian conditions among the peasants.

The short winter days gave little time for outside work, but long evenings for reading and writing. As soon as the roads were "settled," our volost, or township, composed of forty-odd villages and a number of estates, received notice from the State Zemstvos' headquarters, offering to send specialists to give a course of instruction, as was planned for all the volosts in turn, and asking where it would be most convenient to have it held. Mr. Ponafidine offered our estate as a good center, and invited the Commission to be our guests.

They arrived in a string of sleighs. There were eight speakers, and their exhibits included many bulky pieces of machinery, dairy implements and the like. Notices had been sent to all the villages in our district, giving the hours of lectures and the days when the various villages would be visited. Peasants living beyond four versts (about two and two-thirds miles) of us were to be given the price of a supper that they could get in the village close to us. This money was given by the zemstvo to remove all excuse for non-attendance!

During the morning hours, the members of the Commission visited the villages to get acquainted with the local problems and to set apart one or more cows in each village for experimental purposes. So suspicious of all innovations were the peasants that no one consented to this until it was understood that the zemstvo would furnish the cows' rations—then all the village vied for the privilege! The usual food of the cows was continued for a week, carefully weighed, as was the milk. At the end of the week an estimate of prices was made. Then for a week the cows were fed according to the Danish method that for some time the zemstvo had been endeavoring to introduce into Russia. At the close of the two weeks, a balance was struck that gave remarkable results. I had selected five of our cows, representing various ages and conditions, and had been present at every feeding and milking. We found that we had in our old patriarchal way been spending forty-nine kopecks a day on each cow. With the new method, substituting beet roots and concentrated feed quite within the reach of every peasant, we actually reduced the expense to forty-two kopecks a day with a varying increase in the quantity of milk, running in some instances as high as twenty-five per cent. in a week.

In the evening lectures, the dairy specialist carefully, in popular language, explained the process, showing how the sale of a part of the hay and straw (used almost exclusively as fodder) could be made to cover the expense of other feed, and how the cultivation of beets and turnips would work, and how the high milk-producing flaxseed oil-cakes should be given. We had seen the results. Our own herdsman, whom at the beginning I had with difficulty kept within the bounds of lofty condescending politeness to these newfangled teachers, became an ardent convert, and it was amusing to see how he turned about, lecturing his fellow peasants on their ignorant, stubborn conservatism.

Lessons in milking were given by these men, though in Russia milking is strictly a woman's business, and no self-respecting cow permits a man to milk her. The restiveness

of the cows made it difficult to show the women that the
simple light pressing was much easier for the cow than the
pulling process that was in vogue. The women resented
these lessons strenuously. Some of the milkers were middle-
aged women. Our instructors were young men, and I would
often hear a shrill voice rising above the sound of milk falling into many pails, "Oh, get out, you can't teach me. I
was milking before you were born. This is a woman's business, and you don't know anything about it." In spite of the
most obvious advantages, we made no headway. Our cow
barn was very long, with cows in separate loose boxes, and I
walked up and down while six to eight women milked. When
I stopped or came in sight of a milker, she worked in the new
way, but as soon as I moved on I could tell by the sound of
the milk falling into the pail that she had gone back to the
way of her ancestors. With two or three exceptions no
permanent converts were made in our villages. Farmers are
proved conservatives, but the three-week course held at
Bortniki opened our eyes to the magnitude of the task before
those who were earnestly working for the betterment of
farming conditions among the peasants. Even for us, with
hired help always under supervision, it was next to impossible
to get results, and we could easily see that it would take
many years of these courses to make much impression on the
peasants around us. We found that the more enterprising,
intelligent peasants who had followed Stolypin's agrarian
reforms and had broken away from the village communistic
farming to land owned by themselves, were the only hopeful
progressive element. These same peasants, now known as
kulaks, are the very ones the Soviets in their zeal for sociali-
zation have decreed to be abolished as a whole class!

Afternoons were devoted to practical demonstrations of
machinery, visits to villages, and veterinary work. The head
of the veterinary department of the State of Tver was him-

self present, and his work, next to the dairy, was what came within my province, for I had to give "first aid" not only to our numerous horses and cattle but to those of the surrounding villages.

Evenings were given up to lectures. I remember one evening a lecture that was broken up by a peasant bringing his horse with an acute trouble, and the entire audience going out into the large snow-covered yard with lanterns for an object lesson and talk by the veterinarian.

Some evenings the walls would be hung with specimens of dried grasses with their common names printed under them, and a specialist would explain the methods of the best meadow culture and the nature of the weeds to be exterminated. Again there would be photographs of fields of what was raised in our district, showing the condition of crops as treated in the various ways and with the help of machinery that had been demonstrated during the day. And so on—simple clear talks, with questions encouraged, continuing until late at night.

We were impressed with the zeal and devotion to their work that these zemstvo employees showed in their efforts to make the courses productive of practical results. We personally, I know, profited immensely. The "butter-maker" laid the foundation of our future work that made the Bortniki butter mentioned in the annual reports as the best in the State.

My department was the dairy and general medical care of the horses and cattle, and I gave myself up to it, rising at dawn and personally supervising the feeding, milking and butter-making. My husband had the broader farming interests. He had object lessons for the peasants in shape of experimental plots in fields through which the State road ran. Placards described the amount sown, with various methods of cultivation and kinds of fertilizer used.

Harvesting at Bortniki.

Top—Our tandem in front of village school.
Bottom—The lake in winter: returning from church.

The medical work among the peasants, too, was being improved and increased. When the war broke out, in the forty-three provinces having zemstvos there was a total of thirty-three hundred medical districts, and the average radius of the "medical points" was ten miles, so that the peasants could be certain of getting free medical treatment and medicines.

It is pertinent to speak at this point of the peasants' devotion to the Russian bath. In the villages clustering around our lake, many small square log cabins could be seen. When no lake was at hand, these buildings were to be found near streams, springs or wells. They were "Russian baths." Well-to-do families had their own. Sometimes a bath would be built by several families, each taking its turn in heating it. On Saturdays, along the sandy banks of the lake, the women, while keeping an eye on the heating baths, scoured their samovars and other copper vessels. The izbas, their simple homes, also came in for their share of Saturday routine, and the wooden floors were well scrubbed.

In the afternoon and evening, people began to go to the baths, each with a small roll of clean linen tucked under his arm and a bundle of birch twigs in his hands. Steaming themselves, rubbing and thrashing themselves and one another with the twigs, stretched out on the various steps or shelves, the peasant not only took a cleansing bath but steamed and soaked the soreness out of his muscles.

Women went with children of all ages, down to nursing babies. The old and feeble were helped to the bath. Anything was an excuse for heating the bath at other times than on Saturday: A strained back, a severe chill called for steaming; fever received first-aid treatment in the bath. The result in many cases was a cure, but in others disaster, for the bath might be a considerable distance from the house and the weather might be cold and stormy.

The bath-houses were always at a safe distance from other buildings, as few came to a natural end. Sooner or later the intense heating resulted in a fire. But to live without this kind of bath was incomprehensible to peasants in central and northern Russia. In some parts of the Empire baths were not to be found. When in the hard year of 1918-19 hundreds of our peasants went south in search of flour, they came back with tales as wild as did any of the old Polar explorers—of a new kind of Russian people who had no baths!

As my husband's eyesight became worse, and there were no children to keep me at home, I accompanied him to the zemstvo assemblies. In every meeting that I attended, the peasants were decidedly in the majority. As village schools were almost entirely under the zemstvos (except parish schools), the notion of the peasants not being allowed education is obviously absurd. At a meeting of our zemstvo in the spring of 1914, I listened to reports that gave full reason for believing that within three years we should have enough schoolhouses and teachers to warrant introducing compulsory education throughout the greater part of European Russia. Illiteracy among the younger generations was rapidly decreasing.

A fact often overlooked is that when the serfs (practically all of them illiterates) were emancipated, they made up eighty-five per cent. of the population in a country in which the severe winters and lack of roads created additional problems in bringing education to the scattered hamlets. School facilities, too, were lacking. Undoubtedly, for the first fifteen or twenty years after the emancipation, there were many persons who opposed pushing the education of the former serfs, on the ground of the danger of having a large half-educated element in the population. But the last years of the nineteenth century and the first fourteen years of the twentieth saw enormous strides made in education all over the Empire.

During those later years one could note men whose origin was in the peasant class appearing more and more in positions of civic, scientific and professional prominence. The ranks of the nobility were constantly being filled from what is called "below." Education threw wide open every door as in no other country known to me. It was only through education that one could rise from the lowest class to the gaining of even title and rights of "nobility." I remember how often, when I asked my husband who so and so was, he replied, "A University man." That was as conclusive as with us would be "a successful business man," "pastor of a big church," "head of a large corporation." So great an authority and accurate a scholar as Professor Sorokin himself of the peasant class, and now occupying the ch   Sociology and Economics in Harvard University   is *Social Mobility* that in Russia the percenta   nent men rising from the lower classes was about the s   s in democratic countries.

In regard to illiteracy, that of the older peasants showed a decreasing percentage each succeeding generation. In 1918, my son Alec, who was for a time during the World War military instructor in our volost, found that among approximately seven hundred recruits drawn entirely from the peasants, only six or seven were illiterate. Yet nothing is so generally believed in regard to Russia as that the peasants were illiterate, and that the illiteracy was caused by the deliberate policy of the Tsar's Government.

CHAPTER ELEVEN

The Fatal Year

SUCH were conditions in Russia on that July day when the news of the declaration of war reached Bortniki. Now, in 1915, the Government was facing more than its share of difficulties in getting supplies to the far-scattered army. The number of unarmed troops increased, and this added to the lowering of the morale of the soldiers, who had to depend on the arms of the killed and wounded. These facts lost nothing in the telling as they came back to the villages, to the homes of the men at the front. Moreover, differences between the Duma and the Government increased. To my husband, lying helpless, for he was most of the time confined to bed, following keenly every phase of the war, the clouds seemed to be growing hopelessly black. He foresaw what was coming long before any of us did. He heard with dismay of the increasing split between the Government and the Duma, of the fatal decision of the Emperor to attempt to bridge it by himself taking command at the front, with the vain hope of thus winning the confidence of the army. The Empress, who together with her daughters had been active in Red Cross work, was by this move brought more intimately in contact with the front. This act of hers presented another opportunity for spreading the stories of betrayals of Russian movements or of her influence in bringing about dismissals or appointments that might be profitable to the enemy. That the Empress and Rasputin were responsible for much is undoubtedly true, but that the Empress never consciously said a word or took a step unfavorable to Russia must be equally true in the mind of any impartial student.

It was not only the Duma that advocated drastic changes

at this time. The various members of the Imperial family, beginning with the Dowager Empress, various organizations, among them that of the "Nobility," the most conservative body, brought pressure upon the Emperor, but in vain.

During the first years of the war, we probably felt less than did other nations its immediate effects on our daily life. Luxuries and imported goods were cut off, prices on many necessities rose, but food was not restricted. This was largely owing to the Russian characteristic inclination to live for the day, not look ahead, and also to the belief in the short duration of the war. Our interests, however, became limited. The war filled all our thoughts and all our reading.

In April, 1915, George was married to Vera Semkovsky. The winter of 1915-16 was brightened by having her in our home. George was at the front, Alec in the aviation head-quarters, and Oka still in the Lyceum. But daily came the terrible strain of reading the long lists of killed, wounded and missing. Each reading seemed to take years from one's life. I would hastily run through the lists, dreading to catch the name of "George Ponafidine," and then go over them carefully. How thankful we were for only the words "alive and well" that sometimes came on a postcard from "somewhere."

Daily the peasants came to us with packages which they asked us to address in German to their boys who had been taken prisoners. One old woman trudged on foot several miles to bring a neatly sewed up package for her son in Germany.

"Now give me his address in Germany," I said.

"You are wiser than I, little mother, you write it."

"I will write it if you give it to me."

"Well, write it—you are wise."

"I may be wise but I can not write an address I do not know," I explained.

"But you know everything. You must know where he is."

"Did your son send you an address?"

"Oh, yes, he wrote what to send."

"Yes, but did he tell you where to send it? Have you his letter with you?"

"Why, I thought you were wise enough to know where to send the package."

The poor old soul was diconsolate when she found she had to go back home and bring the letter to us.

At this time the Government offered farmers the use of r prisoners to fill the place of men absent in the army, id we who were very short of farmhands applied. From that time until after the Revolution, we had both Germans and Austrians. We were obliged to clothe and feed them and give them a little pocket money. We were responsible for them under certain conditions. My husband had them brought before him; he explained to them our own responsibility and asked for their loyal cooperation. In return, we would give them all the liberty possible. They would not be guarded if they gave their word of honor not to go off the estate without asking permission. They were amazed to find that all the war propaganda they had been filled with as to the cruelty of the Russians was false. One of them told us afterward that the first weeks he was with us, if he woke in the night and heard Russians talking, he would break into a cold sweat, thinking of the tortures that were supposed to await German prisoners.

It was interesting to see the attitude of the peasants toward them. There was absolutely no bitterness. Often a woman would come bearing a bit of fish-pie or other village delicacy and put it into the hands of one of the men, saying, "Take—eat—I have a son prisoner in your country and your people are kind to him, perhaps. We are friends. You had to obey your Emperor and we ours, but we don't hate you."

The prisoners on their part we found industrious, faithful to whatever work was given them, bringing their German characteristics to it. One of the bridges crossing a tiny stream needed mending; they came to me for a water-level—the only country bridge of a few planks ever laid by water-level. When I told the man so, he grinned and said, "I'll carve my name and date on one of the planks to commemorate it."

At first we anticipated friction and planned to have the prisoners eat as well as sleep separately from our Russians, but the latter asked us not to. Evenings, returning from the harvest-fields, the two groups would often march close together, singing in turn their patriotic marching songs. We never once had any trouble based on national prejudice until the Revolution came. The contradictions and absurdities of war-time were blessedly often filled with humorous situations that would break the terrible strain we were under. The prisoners were supposed to be sent to us with proper military guard and to be received by us in similar formal manner, but it was the busy harvest-time and men were few. One day we were notified that some additional prisoners we had applied for would be delivered by the military authorities to the local volost and by them to us. From the volost we were instructed to "go and get them." Oka and I, therefore, went in his motor-boat across the lake, together with our neighbor, young Tolstoi. On arriving, we found that the prisoners were stationed in a village several miles inland. All the horses were needed in the fields. There was no one to send, so we left Nika Tolstoi to guard the boat and started through the woods and fields to the village indicated. Here we were told that some one from another village was having them help in the field while waiting for us to send for them. After resting on a door-step for a while, we set out and

after several miles found one of the men, then another, in
a hay-field, who responded to the names we had. Taking
our prisoners, we obeyed at least the letter of the command
by "convoying" them home. Oka marched ahead, I behind,
and the two men between us. They enjoyed the situation as
much as we did, asking who was the convoy and who the
prisoners, and we joked and laughed all the weary walk.
The men were delighted to come to us, for Oka could speak
German, whereas peasants could not.

The winter of 1916-17 brought visibly gathering clouds.
Conditions at the front and their reactions on public opinion,
together with a conviction that the war was to be a long
drawn-out one, increased the gloom. When the lake froze,
many were the parties of soldiers passing for a few days of
leave to spend at home. These gray heroes seemed a link
between us and George, and whenever we met one or more
of them, we invited them to stop and rest. When driving if
one passed a soldier, however full the sleigh or heavy the
load, room was made and a "lift" offered. No stretch of the
imagination then could picture a time when the sight of the
soldier's uniform that now warmed our hearts, bringing
out a desire to do everything one could for the wearer,
would ever change.

Vera and her mother went south to Vera's aunt for
Christmas, and my husband and I were left alone. We read
everything we could get. Military censorship, of course,
limited our war news. George's letters could give even less.
But it was the home news, internal politics, that caused
greatest anxiety. Still, we were not prepared for what happened. In the summer the steamer brought a daily mail to
our little branch post-office, some five miles from us, but in
the winter we had only two mails a week. I often drove over
for the sake of a change. Unexciting as it was, I could hope
to see people or to have some incident, if only the capsizing

of my sleigh in a drift, to make a story to bring back to my blind husband. No reporter anxious to make a "scoop" was ever more eager to find material than I was to make my eyes bring something to break the monotony of his life. I tried to have him see everything I did. Looking out of the window, I would put into words everything I saw, and in that way he was able to keep in close touch with all the small details of our surroundings. But we were soon to have news and more than enough for him, news that became worse with every new day.

One clear cold morning in early March I drove to the post-office. The peculiar pink tint that spring paints on the Russian skies, something almost more felt than seen, showed the first struggle against the long gray winter, and somehow with spring approaching in all its beauty one felt that the ugly things in life, war, hatred, revolution, must lose their horror. Arriving at the door, I went up-stairs to the familiar little room where I had pleasant acquaintance with all connected with the post-office. The postmaster had a pretty hard struggle, with his growing family, to live on his small pay. We always tried in a neighborly way to take over to them vegetables, butter, something of our own raising, that could be offered without offense. When he told me once, almost with tears in his voice, of the death of a pig he had bought, hoping to have a good supply of pork and hams for the winter, I told him of an unusually large litter of pigs we had, really too large for one mother to care for, and the next day a fat squealing little porky was put into a basket and presented to the postmaster. And so for several years our relations had been of the pleasantest sort. What then was my surprise this March day in 1917 when I entered the room with a cheery good morning, to have the postmaster himself and his aides look at me in a challenging, almost menacing way, not one moving to touch his hat—something that not

even a peasant fails to do in meeting a peasant woman—
and in a loud insulting voice answer my greeting with, "Well,
we are rid of your Nikolashka" (diminutive of Nicholas).
This was my first intimation of the abdication of the Emperor. The attitude of this man gave the key-note to what
was to come, the "liberty, fraternity and equality" that
showed itself in boorish insults. The "freedom" that was
only to be used as license, the "equality" that was soon to
level all Russia to an equally low grade—a bringing down of
culture rather than a raising, a "fraternity" that was to set
brother against brother, children against parents, and elim-
inate all brotherly love.

A faint premonition of all this came to me in the attitude
of these men; it struck me so forcibly that I found my mind
dwelling on it as I drove home, in spite of the far greater
importance of the news contained in the papers just received. It was the news of that historic interview in the railroad car where the members of the Duma obtained the
written abdication of Nicholas II.

There was no need this time for me to seek something
that would make an interesting half-hour for my husband.
He was able to sit up that day, bolstered in Grandmother
Ponafidine's huge armchair. I read him the papers and told
him of the immediate reaction on the public as I had experienced it in the post-office. As I read, he exclaimed over and
over in awestruck tones, "Poor Russia! God help us, Russia
is ruined!"

This, the March Revolution of 1917, was hailed by most,
even the extreme conservatives, as something inevitable and
even to be desired as the only hope of saving the situation
at home and at the front. To the peasants it came as a surprise; to many of the intelligentsia, as a long-expected and
hoped-for event; to the conservative aristocratic and, in some
instances, Imperial circles, as a perhaps necessary solution,

if the Emperor refused to grant the political reforms demanded by them. Even the most conservative body, the "Nobles," had implored the Emperor in 1916 to place the Duma on a strictly constitutional basis. This political reform was imperative.

The abdication of the Emperor in the name of his son and brother also brought dismay to those who foresaw the need in a country like Russia of a strong central authority, though with what might be merely a figurehead as its source.

Personally, I feel that had the abdication of the Emperor been followed by a parliament acknowledging the ill-fated boy, a parliament with a central figure in the background, it would have steadied nerves, given a confidence that ultimately might have brought about a real democratic or strictly constitutional monarchy without going through the years of bloodshed that came to Russia and established the most autocratic government ever known.

I realized that Mr. Ponafidine's was almost the only dissenting voice in the general optimism. At first it rather shocked me as well as all the members of his family, who could not get his point of view, though we all lived to acknowledge his wisdom. He felt that a political revolution was too vitally needed to risk staging it at an inopportune moment. He realized what few did at that time, that a revolution was more than a coup d'état: it was the crisis of a disease that would be followed by a long, patience-trying convalescence. Could we hope to depend on the patience of the excited, war-weary, propaganda-filled public? Would they be restrained when they found that the millennium did not follow with the rising sun the next morning? "No," he said, "we need political changes too badly to jeopardize achieving them by a revolution of this kind and staged at the wrong time. No surgeon in his senses will perform a major operation if the state of the patient's health clearly shows that the shock will be fatal. He will first work to prepare the patient for it. As it is, the revolution will be drowned in its own waves. We shall never get the good results that might have followed it, and Russia will be at the mercy of the first strong party of adventurers that may rise up. In time of war there is no hope of a revolution for the better."

In the meantime, rumors were many, newspapers unsatisfactory (two posts a week), and we had three sons in the midst of the upheaval and no word from them. One day Oka arrived, a hard-looking, unshaven, disheveled parody of himself. The Lyceum in which he was studying was founded by Alexander I, primarily to prepare men for state service. It was one of three privileged schools, open only to the aristocracy, and entrance was by very severe competitive examination, as the whole number of students was not over three hundred.* Naturally the "Emperor's Lyceum" would be one of the first institutions to be aimed at. My husband and I had not spoken to each other about it, but it was uppermost in our minds. How would Oka escape? A peasant happening in asked me in a whisper as he left, not wishing to worry my husband, "Has Joseph Petrovich any of his own clothes with him in St. Petersburg?" and when I told him that Oka never had any but the Lyceum uniform with him, the man shook his head, "Bad, bad—they'll kill all the Lyceists they see on the street. God grant he gets home." And he voiced what was in our hearts.

When sleigh-bells called me to the window, therefore, and I saw Oka driving up to the house, the load that fell

---

* The time when such privileged schools were needed in primitive Russia had passed, and the leveling of such would surely have come under a more democratic form of government. It was one of the many changes demanded by time that every country faces and that could have been worked out peacefully without bloodshed.

from my heart, as far as that one son was concerned, can be imagined. No, I think it can not be by any one who has not lived through the agony of such days.

As we had anticipated, the Lyceum drew the attention of the revolutionists. It was claimed that the school was armed, and to avoid the expected raid the students were immediately disbanded. Those who lived in the city had civilian clothing brought them, but others like Oka naturally had none available. To diminish the risk, the boys were offered red rosettes to pin on their breasts, but I imagine Oka was not the only student to refuse to wear one. It took Oka two days to get to the part of the city where Alec was. Street fighting was going on in many quarters. Machine-guns stationed on roofs swept the streets, so that he often was driven to seek another route, only to find himself in a fresh field of battle. Sometimes he was forced to lie flat or crawl, and it was only on the third day that he reached Alec's quarters.

A few days later a laconic telegram, "Am well," came to tell us that George was safe up to date.

During the summer of 1917 the position of all officers in the army became unbearable. With the overthrow of the Emperor it had been believed by the army and the people that the war would automatically cease. The decision of the Provisional Government to remain loyal to the Allies, to continue war to the end and only then turn all attention to settling the new internal problems, was a great disappointment to the army. And this disappointment was fanned by strong propaganda. The officers were the visible exponents of this policy. Their loyal opposition to a separate peace with the enemy, their constant encouragement of the men under them to fulfill their duty, brought upon them personally opposition that the soldier could not exert against the Duma that was out of his reach. Every day the officers

carried their lives in their hands, both during the short
period of the rule of the Provisional Government and in the
culminating massacres under Bolshevism.

Some day, I hope a pen more adequate than mine will do
justice to these heroes, the officers who suffered thousands
of small humiliations, who were murdered, shot down like
dogs, only because they endeavored to keep up the loyalty
of the troops. The officers were under the double strain
of being in constant danger of death by their own people
(a very different thing from facing the enemy's guns) and
of knowing that at home their families were in an equally
precarious position, since poverty and famine were added to
the odium of being an officer's family. And yet the cases
in which the officers failed in loyalty were almost negligible.
Many who found their efforts to inspire the men futile committed suicide rather than accept conditions forced upon
them.

The fatal "Order No. I" of March fourteenth, was the
act that set in motion the machinery that was to bring the
army to complete disorganization. Later efforts to change
it were useless; the harm was done: the army acknowledged
no authority but its own. Though this Order No. I came
under the Provisional Government, it was undoubtedly without their knowledge or at least approval. It became evident
that the Committee or Soviet of soldiers and workmen was
dominating and practically ruling the country under its own
initiative, often in direct opposition to the policy of the Provisional Government.

In a few weeks more it became clear that the Government was doomed. The honesty of the individual members
did not make up for their weakness. Another fatal defect
was that the new rulers were theorists, academicians, with
little practical knowledge of the psychology or needs of their
own people. The socialistic Soviets in the meantime were

growing in strength and working for their own party ends rather than for the honor of Russia. This Order No. I, clearly issued as a weapon turned against the new Government's policy in continuing the war, was an example. While issued as a Government order, it was undoubtedly inspired and released by the Soviets, and the Government was not strong enough to suppress it, and later attempts to annul or modify it were futile.

The gist of the Order was:

(1) Soldiers' Committees were to be chosen in each military detachment.

(2) Each military detachment was to obey its Soviet in its political decisions.

(3) Orders of the Military Commission of the State Duma were to be obeyed only if they did not contradict the Soviet's orders.

(4) All weapons were to be under the control of the Soldiers' Committees and were not to be delivered to the officers.

It seems inconceivable that in time of war, complicated by a revolution, any government desiring the speedy and successful termination of the war could be so blind as to issue such an order. Even to the lay mind, the possibilities of treachery, or at best the confusion that would follow, must be evident. Also the fact that this order laid the officers absolutely at the mercy of an already disgruntled army, eager for peace, betrayed its origin. The worst enemies of Russia and the cause of the Allies could have done nothing more fatal than did those who framed this order. The responsible leaders of the Provisional Government felt this and were appalled by the magnitude of what it involved, but all attempts to undo the harm were abortive.

On every side, even we in the rear had proof of what

was coming, with all central authority ignored and the policy and fate of the army in the hands of Soldiers' Committees, even at the front and in active warfare.

To give an instance of what took place near us, that with variations in detail was one of many: An officer sat down in a railway buffet to a plate of soup. The Revolution having wiped out all class distinctions (there were no longer any first- and second-class buffets in the railroad station), a private without saluting seated himself by the officer. Suddenly, pulling out some hairs from his mustache, the soldier reached over and dropped them into the officer's plate of soup. Without a word, the latter rose and, taking his plate back, asked for another dish, with which he went to a distant table. No sooner was he seated than the soldier followed and, seating himself, again dropped some hairs into the soup. What could the officer do? No redress was to be had anywhere. He did all that remained to do. Drawing his revolver, he shot and killed the soldier, then blew out his own brains. There was much that was humiliating and dangerous to the officers personally, but fatal to the country, when an important order was given at the front which, instead of being instantly obeyed, had to be discussed and voted on as provided in the third Article of Order No. I, when it would possibly be vetoed.

The first time that George returned home after the Revolution, he told us of his own experiences at that time. Ever since going to the front, he had been in the line of battle with occasionally a week in the near "rear." Soon after the issuing of Order No. I, a day came when the Germans centered a heavy artillery fire on the position. He reported to his Colonel that an attack was evidently being prepared and that in all probability he would be obliged to call for reenforcements, knowing that the enemy had a greater force than ours at that point. Toward evening an attack was made. Seven times that night George called for help. He also reported the need of ammunition, the supply in his immediate rear having been blown up during the bombardment, and at the same time he gave strict orders for economy of what was at hand. The Colonel at the first call ordered reenforcements to move, but with Order No. I firmly in their minds the soldiers called a meeting to discuss the question. Were reenforcements needed, and how many? Did he really need ammunition? And so on and so on, as only in Russia, and especially at that time, could discussions be carried on. It was morning before the Colonel, who had begged and argued and stormed, could get the men to move. They found only a handful of our men alive. The hand-to-hand fighting had been terrible, but in spite of inequality of numbers George's men were occupying the advance German trenches.

I remember his telling, as one of the curiosities of warfare, that in the complete destruction of the trenches they had occupied, and plowed up, so to speak, by the shells, the huge iron pot full of buckwheat cereal, that back-bone of peasants' menu, though powdered with dust, remained the sole article uninjured. The soldiers had a "meeting" after this incident. George was found guilty of "pro-German attitude" in making feeble resistance by ordering an economical use of ammunition! Also he was blamed for the loss of a machine-gun. These charges were brought up to prove that he was not worthy to receive the reward for "personal bravery" sent by the Provisional Government.

And so we helplessly watched the disintegration of the army and trembled for George as we never did when he was exposed only to what now seemed to us civilized and humane warfare. It was these months that filled us with the conviction that there is something worse than war. Undisciplined mobs, a sense of absolute license and lack of authority, are more terrible in their results and far more to be feared and avoided than what for want of a better word to explain my meaning is "legitimate" warfare. That this is the universal testimony of those who lived through those terrible years, I think can not be doubted.

It was this attitude of the people toward officers, who were to them a symbol of the continuation of the war and, as a class, absolutely devoted in their loyalty to authority, that made us tremble for our sons. We decided that in all that was to follow, our first thought in steering our very shaky bark must be to keep our sons as much as possible in the background. My husband, therefore, sent for a lawyer and gave me power of attorney to act in everything representing him and the estate. At this period it seemed that any mistakes I made as a woman might lead us into less danger than would be caused by involving officers and bringing on the ever-ready persecution by the blinded people.

Events developed rapidly. Following the formation of the Provisional Government in St. Petersburg, local miniature ones were formed in the provinces. Before the latter appeared, we lived in a state of literal non-authority. All the old institutions having been pronounced annulled, and nothing having yet been done to establish their successors, we lived from day to day wondering to whom we should appeal in case of any lawlessness or crime taking place. That during over a week of this ideally primitive status not an act of violence or disorder occurred, to our knowledge, speaks for the natural law-abiding instincts of the peasant. All that developed during the summer that in any way pertained to the ownership of land brought out the worst of the peasant; and this was due to socialistic propaganda, worked at home and at the front. All that we suffered (though in a far less degree than what many endured) was always directly traceable to propaganda, generally by soldiers from the front who came home filled with the idea that the land was being divided up while they were absent and that they might lose their share. These soldiers were the actual firebrands that started the flame of hatred among the peasants toward us during the first two years. It was the peasants we in Bortniki feared at this time and from whom came countless humiliations. Later, when the greater menace, that of Bolshevism, came to them, the peasants entirely changed front. So far as they dared, they helped us, and there is little doubt that our lives were saved by them more than once.

Our State,* and in a short time our county town of Ostashkov, had their representatives in the Provisional Government, and we also in our volost, the members being appointed from local men. The old police became "militia men," and our volost government was centered in a local committee with new powers. The Provisional Government was a figurehead in Petrograd. In the socialistic parties, "Soldiers' and Workers' Soviets" were becoming the real leaders. The same spread to the provinces. The volost, which formerly had dealt with only local social and agrarian problems, was now headed by a "Committee," virtually the government under whose arbitrary rule we lived. The term "local authority" came to be used in connection with this new form of government. That there have been so many discrepancies as to details in these years (and the same to a degree can be said even now in 1931) is owing to this "local authority" or, literally, "power on the spot." All depended on the personnel of the Committee. One volost

* The "Government of Tver" is equivalent to the State of Tver. Within the State is the county (*uyezd*); the volost, canton or township, consisting of possibly thirty or more peasant villages and landed estates; and finally the village mir or community of one or more villages.

might be under men of violently revolutionary temper who hesitated at nothing, looting and bloodshed included. Next door, in a volost a few miles distant, the Provisional Government might be represented by a more humane, conservative element, and life would be tolerable. Then again, we ourselves came in for a variety, for the Committee changed with kaleidoscopic rapidity. A raid would be made on us, the house searched, laws laid down, protocols drawn up, and in a day or two the same process would be repeated by new men, with new details, fresh protocols perhaps quite dissimilar from yesterday's.

When we expressed bewilderment as to what line we were to follow, and whom to obey, the answer was a very simple one, repeated with a frequency and regularity that became somewhat humorous: "Oh, we discharged the old Committee. They were no good." But sometimes it was, "They were dishonest."

CHAPTER TWELVE

The Beginnings of Bolshevism

THE first act of hostility toward us was in restricting our pasture-lands and hay-fields. Realizing that the next step would be the restriction of live stock, we forestalled this action by selling them off as quickly as we could, keeping only as many horses and cows as we could feed on what land was left us. When later we were accused of selling what was "the people's property," we justified ourselves by pointing out that we had received no orders prohibiting the sale, and that, in any case, we had disposed only of such animals as the Committee, by their own action, had left without food.

Later we were visited by a deputation of peasants, who stated that, although we no longer had any rights to the land, the woods, or anything on the estate, they would not touch or expel us until a "paper" came, saying how the property was to be divided among the people. An inventory of everything on the place and in the house was made by a delegation of peasants who, in spite of the tragedy of the moment, furnished us with considerable amusement. They were armed with paper and pens and, dividing up into different parties, scattered themselves through the various rooms, counting the contents. When they compared notes, it was found that, in counting tables, chairs and pieces of furniture, the names and uses of which were often unknown to them, they had become hopelessly mixed. I remember, one day (for this process was repeated over and over) they failed to note down all the large mirrors. "No one will believe us if we say there were only ten mirrors in such a big house; let's put down fifteen." "No, better say twenty," interposed another; and they wrote down twenty.

We were informed that, as long as we did not sell or hide anything, we should be permitted to remain in our house; but they took care to see that we fulfilled their orders. Without so much as "by your leave," they would often go through the house, rummaging in bureau drawers, and sometimes calling me to account if they happened to find fewer articles of linen than when they last counted; and I had to explain that the missing garments were in the wash or being mended.

From this time we might be said to have been the unpaid managers of the estate. We did the work and paid taxes, but could sell nothing, and were even restricted in the use of milk and flour. Our old employees were turned off— in some cases faithful men who had lived, together with their families, on our estate for years. In their place were put men quite incompetent in some instances and decidedly hostile to us in others. All these questions and changes were discussed and settled in hours spent at the village meetings, or *skhodkas*, and ratified after long talks with the Volost Committee. At this time all Russia attended meetings of some sort; from the soldier at the front and the working man at the mills, down to the men and women in the villages, all gave up to such gatherings what should have been working hours.

Our own village commune included three villages. When a question came up for discussion, raised by an individual or by the Canton Committee or by ourselves, the headmen would be asked to summon a *skhodka*. Generally a boy was sent around with a stick to knock at the windows of each house and shout the hour and place of meeting. If it happened to be winter, the gatherings would be held in different houses, in turn; but in the summer the street is the place for holding meetings; the whole village, including children, can gather and listen.

During the summer of 1917, and up to the spring of 1919, when our estate was turned into a state farm, we were constantly called to attend *skhodkas,* whatever the object might happen to be.

If a cow calved, we had to lay the matter before the village commune, and a long discussion would take place as to what should be done with the calf. If a litter of pigs appeared on the scene, their future would be settled in the same way, after long parleying, sometimes with orders to sell them, half of the proceeds going to the Canton Committee, and the other half to us for our "trouble" in caring for them.

One day, toward evening, one of our cows broke her leg while at pasture in the woods. The herdsman came running in, crying from three streams, as they say in Russia, and declared that she ought to be put out of her misery My son went to the village; but by the time he could get three responsible citizens to come and examine the cow, it was too late to kill her that night, and the poor beast had to lie where she had fallen, suffering, until morning. Then a "paper" was given us, stating that, as the cow had evidently broken her leg by accident, and in no way owing to our carelessness, the meat and skin were ours.

As it was warm weather, I immediately went to work cutting the meat preparatory to salting it. While I was thus occupied, some raftsmen, who were making rafts of our— or what had been our—timber to float down the lake, came to me with a proposition. It seemed that they were negotiating for the purchase of a young bull in the next village, to butcher for meat. They knew we were in need of a bull, and proposed that we give them the meat in exchange for their live animal. Now this would strike any one as a very simple proposition, one that we might decide ourselves; but alas, the process of free revolutionary government is

not so easy. We should have been accused of speculation—
that heinous crime which is linked with the ominous words,
"capitalist," "landowner," "noble," "clergy."

So we called a *skhodka* about ten o'clock in the morning.
We appeared, the raftsmen and I, and stated our cases. I
pointed out our need of a bull, and that of the village, which
had always profited by our having one. I undertook to keep
this animal until one which we had, of better breed, should
grow up; this promise of course holding good as long as
we ourselves were permitted to remain on our estate. It
was for them to fix the price of the bull and of a pound of
meat, and then they could easily decide how much meat I
was to give in exchange for the bull. A simple proposition,
was it not?

We all gathered in the street, women as well as men—
for a woman is permitted to represent a householder and
vote as such. For a long time every one talked at once,
as they always do. Then they proceeded to select a chairman and secretary. At noon we adjourned for lunch, no
decision having been arrived at. Then we took it up again.
After hours of talking, it looked as if the decision were
turning in our favor, and one of the raftsmen went down
the street to buy a keg in which to salt the meat. He soon
returned, rolling a small barrel in front of him, which was
immediately seized upon and set on end to be used as a
table for the secretary. The powwow continued until evening; and when we saw the village herd approaching, the
young bull was rounded off, a rope was thrown about its
neck, and it was brought up to take a passive part in de-
ciding its own case. Finally, when it was almost dark, the
secretary, who had gone through agonizing throes of com-
position, handed me a remarkable document. It was signed
by every householder present; illiterates made their crosses.
It stated the amount of meat I was to give for the bull, and

emphasized the fact that the skin of the cow, as well as the live bull, was my "personal property"; and this, remember, at a time when private property had been abolished!

We went home triumphantly in the gloaming, I leading my bull, the men trundling the keg and helping me to persuade the refractory beast whenever he rebelled, as he often did, against changing his abode and his masters. The next day, Alec and I rowed over to the Volost Committee headquarters. There we found a long table, around one end of which were seated the Military Sub-Committee and, at the other, the Agricultural. The members of both Committees were local peasants with whom we were acquainted. None of them had any education other than the course of four winters in the little village schools.

We showed the document given by the village commune, and asked to have it endorsed by the Committee. The chairman read it over and remarked, "It is very simple. In the inventory of your live stock under your care, one cow must be erased and a bull substituted."

"No," said the secretary; "you see, the village has voted that so long as the cow's meat has been given to them, that is, would have belonged to them, the bull that replaces the meat must be recognized as belonging to them."

After this extremely complicated, but decidedly logical, explanation, the chairman solemnly wrote a resolution on the document, agreeing with the village commune in considering the bull the "personal property of Citizen Ponafidine, who had a right to sell and eat the same at the expiration of the time she had agreed to keep it." This precious document was made legal and imposing by being repeatedly stamped. It may be of interest to note that, after all the energy spent on the wonderful document, in the end this, our only "personal property," was taken from us when our estate was turned into a state farm by the Bolsheviki.

What saved the landowners in our part of the country from many of the horrors experienced in other places, was the fact that, in 1918, owing to bad crops, no one had seed enough to sow his own land and therefore our fields were not coveted at this critical moment, when passions ran high.

I am not speaking now of the Government as seen in large cities, but as we, living in the country and provincial towns, were affected by the Revolution in its various stages. Since the peasants, however, made up three-quarters of the population, this part of Russian life, though unfortunately the least known abroad, is not to be ignored. To have given the peasants a leading part in State matters, and then to blame them for the disastrous results, is like censuring a child for setting fire to gunpowder, rather than calling to account the person who gave the child the explosive and the matches.

But it was not only with the village commune and the Volost Committee that we had to deal during these years. Questions of State interest had to be taken to the County Committee of the Provisional Government, and I had occasion to make the acquaintance of various types here.

One interview of the kind we shall never forget. We received a notice demanding taxes, based as in former years upon the number of acres in our estate. We at once drew up a protest, in which we pointed out just how much land had been left for our use, and while consenting to pay on that number of acres, objected to paying anything on the remainder. This I took with me to the Commissar of Agriculture in Ostashkov.

He was a former sailor, who had taken part in the historic mutiny on the *Potoemkin* of the Imperial Navy in the Revolution of 1905 and 1906 when the crews brutally massacred their officers and for weeks terrorized the Black Sea. So this Commissar had passed through a pretty good school, and was a formidable person for us to meet.

The Commissar had been in the village next to us, addressing a meeting, a short time before. In his speech he reproached the peasants for having allowed such an estate as ours to exist, adding that if they needed live stock or agricultural implements they were to help themselves. If they needed houses and buildings, they were to turn us out. Here a woman rose and said: "We will never drive the Ponafidines out; they have always been good to us. When I had no milk, they gave me milk for my child, and our lady gives us medicine when we are sick."

"And you thank her for it?" the speaker asked.

"Of course," she replied.

"The more fools you. *She* should thank you for so many years letting her and her family live there and profit by the land and woods and all that by right belongs to the people. *She* should thank *you* that you have not turned them out long ago; and here you thank her for a bottle of milk or a box of pills!"

Is it a wonder, with such encouragement from above, that the peasants did not all rise and turn us out?

Well, this was the man whom we had to face. From the first I had tried to take upon myself the responsibility of dealing with the Bolsheviki, as it seemed so much more dangerous to have the men-folk of the family implicated. In this case, however, the man was so notorious that my sons would not hear of it; so we compromised, and one of them went with me, though I made him promise to stand in the background and take no part in the conversation if he could avoid it.*

It was with a beating heart that I went up the dirty stairs and into the disorderly room where the Commissar of Agriculture received. Stating the subject of my visit, I

* Also we feared the Commissar might remember my husband as the Consul General who in Constantinople had been the cause of the arrest of his comrades.

asked to whom to present the written statement, and was motioned toward a secretary, seated behind a handsome desk which we recognized. Indeed, nearly all the furniture in the various rooms we identified as having belonged to families of our acquaintance.

The secretary looked over my paper and, handing it to the Commissar, remarked, "It seems reasonable, doesn't it?"

After reading it, the Commissar said, "Certainly, they are quite right; there is no justice in their paying taxes on land that in no way belongs to them now." Glancing at me, however, and then at the signature, he said, "Who is it? I did not notice the name."

"Ponafidine," I replied calmly, never dreaming, after his peaceful reception of us, what a storm the mention of our name would raise.

"Oh, Ponafidine! I have heard of that mischievous family."

And then a scene took place, so wild, so utterly savage, that could I remember the exact words and repeat them, they would scarcely be credited. He ran back and forth, raving, and from time to time beating his breast with clinched hands, or stopping to strike the table with his fists, as we had heard he was in the habit of doing when greatly excited. He harangued us all, stopping in front of various persons, who were astonished, and in some cases evidently pleased, spectators, telling them of this family of "blood-suckers," "oppressors of the poor, who under the protection of a blind husband and lazy minors were continuing to live as bloated capitalists, keeping their work-people little better than serfs"; and more of the same kind.

Then, stopping in front of me, he would repeat over and over, "I know you, I know you, I have heard all about you! We will call you to account yet. We are very busy, but your turn will come, and when I take you in my mailed fist, my conversation with you will be short, Citizen Pona-fidine. You have been a lady long enough. I'll teach you to work." He continued his tirade, running back and forth, literally foaming at the mouth.

My son could keep out of the fray no longer and, stepping to my side, tried to explain to the madman the conditions under which we were living, adding, "Look at my mother's hands, and see if they look like the hands of a lady."

"That's nothing," he answered sneeringly. "You think she works, but she'll know what it is yet. I'll teach her. I'll get her tamed by 1920, and then she'll know what it means to work."

We always remembered that date, and strange to say it was in October, 1920, that we were finally expelled from our last place of refuge on our estate.

When we went out, I felt as if I had received a stunning blow on my head. We were both so dazed that we went on and on down the street without saying a word, until we realized that we were far from the place for which we were bound. Never in my life had I been so treated or heard such language; but that was not what stayed with me and haunted me,—it was the consciousness of the fierce, horrible hatred toward me—that is, toward our class—which the Commissar had shown in his voice and look. It was appalling to be so hated! It took me days to get over the shock; and so long as that man was in power, I took care to avoid the very street on which the Agricultural Department was situated. But it was not for long, for the personnel of our government changed as often as did their decrees.

The reader may wonder why we did not appeal to headquarters. Some did, and while in some cases they received justice, it brought down the persecution of the local powers worse than ever when the revising Commission had left. We, therefore, always endeavored to avoid conflicts, and with this one exception I was never treated with anything but comparative politeness. But we were not in a position to demand much. The Commissar who searched our persons more or less politely, or who was good-humored as he loaded boats or sleighs with our personal effects and household goods, was regarded by us as quite a "decent fellow," and the next time we met him on the street it was with a pleasant bow on both sides.

Throughout the summer of 1917, "instructors" were always coming to the villages, no matter how busy the season, haying-time or reaping. Everything was dropped to hear what they had to say. These men were sometimes soldiers, and always men of little education, both at this time and later, when the same methods were carried on by the Bolsheviki.

When the time approached for voting for the ill-fated Constituent Assembly, an instructor, a young Esthonian soldier, was sent from Tver, the capital of our state, to teach us how to vote. I was obliged to attend, as neither of my sons was at home. The meeting was held in the one street of the village, and I drove my cart up near the speaker and remained sitting in it. He began by explaining what the Assembly was, and what the candidates stood for. He first read off the numbers of the cards bearing names of candidates. "Nobles, landowners—you don't want them!"

Cries of "No! No!"

"Priests—you have had enough of the long-haired clergy lording it over you."

Cries of "No! No! We have had enough of them."

"Landowners, who have taken the land that belonged

to you, and the forests where for generations they have cut down trees that did not belong to them."

"No, no, we don't want landowners."

Then he explained what list would bring them the representatives of the people. Candidates who, if elected, would work for the peoples' rights, secure the land and the woods for them.

"Now," he concluded, "you go to the schoolhouse to-morrow, every one of you, men and women, no matter how busy you are. Drop everything and go. Cast the vote that will secure the land for you and for your children. If you can not write, no matter: make marks, and it will be just as good as if you could write the numbers."

The next day we assembled and, for the first time in my life, I voted—though, I am afraid, not according to the desires of our instructor.

Where the effects of Bolshevism were first felt by us was in the suppression of all private trade, and the disappearance, as if by magic, of everything buyable. This was the period when, in the cities, one might die of starvation while possessing millions. Peasants ran every risk to take bread and other food supplies to Moscow and Petrograd, where they were sold at exorbitant prices.

Of course, we in the provinces did not suffer as much by hunger, having our own bread, butter and vegetables. But all groceries, dry-goods, soap, kerosene and the thousand and one little things without which the civilized woman is supposed not to be able to exist, were not to be had. How often has the want of a button, a needle, or a spool of thread faced us! Imagine never shopping for four and a half years!

This was the time for real ingenuity. Joseph, in his coat of many colors, was not more brilliantly arrayed than were the sons and husbands whose women made them suits of bright blue or green, often sewed with cotton of a different color from the garment.

In the winter of 1917 and 1918, owing to partial failure of the crops, armies of men and women went back and forth to the "bread states," the same Volga Basin which later in its turn starved. So many were these northern pilgrims, going south and returning with bags of flour on their backs, that a new word was coined to describe them—"baggers." And soon these baggers were recognized as the greatest menace to the country.

Having succeeded in getting the flour, our people brought back with them the epidemics of typhus and Spanish "flu" that were raging in the south. The railway stations were horrible beyond description—packed with ragged, unwashed humanity, many already ill. The floors were so covered with people lying on them as to make it almost impossible to find a spot to place one's foot. As the trains left, those who could, boarded them; but every day many were left on the floor, dead or dying.

In this way the epidemic was brought to us, and at a time when we were beginning to feel the lack of drugs. The little state hospital and free dispensary for the peasants near us, which in olden times had always been supplied with necessary drugs, was now poorly stocked. I had always kept myself provided with medicines. First-aid cases were always brought to me, both for men and beasts. This outburst of typhus and Spanish flu kept me busy. In all those months I do not remember a single case among those I attended that could not be traced to some member of the family who had been south and had brought the germs—generally vermin being the direct means.

Attempts were made to stop the baggers from traveling; but this was not easy to do. They were of two kinds: speculators, and those going for their personal needs. This was when the Bolsheviki were making their experiments in the first steps of Communism; an experiment that carried off many and shattered the health of more.

Private trading was abolished, and all buying and selling set down as illegal. Each citizen was supposed to receive all he needed of food and clothing, either as payment for work done, or as rations for those too old to work and for children under age. This was a lovely thing on paper, and still more so as heard from the lips of an eloquent Communist. But Bolshevik doctrines in practise and in theory are, as we all found to our cost, as different as daylight and darkness. Food products were duly nationalized and vanished, together with markets and shops, as projected; but somehow the second part of their program fell through, and the rations were never given out at the time and in the quantities promised.

The result was that, had it not been for these same questionable baggers, who constantly succeeded in smuggling bread, meat, vegetables and butter into Petrograd, Moscow and other cities, the mortality would have been even greater than it was.

It was interesting to note how quickly the peasant women adapted themselves to the new order of things. Women who had never seen a train, and had scarcely ever left their homes, went fearlessly to the far-off Lower Volga states under circumstances that would appal experienced travelers. Others would carry on a regular traffic with Petrograd. Going to Moscow, they would lay in a supply of articles most needed in the villages, such as warm head-kerchiefs, calico, thread, sugar, soap, matches. These they would take to a county adjoining ours, where the people lived mostly on small farms and were more prosperous than those about us. In these villages the speculator exchanged her goods for flour, baked bread, butter, cereals, eggs, to take back to Petrograd and Moscow, returning home to repeat the operation. Women gave up all former occupations, young mothers left the children to the care of grandmothers and aunts, and for years practically lived on the trains. Some who came under our own observation kept this up until their careers were ended by disease, which sooner or later one must contract if constantly traveling in vermin-stocked cars, or by accidents. One woman whom we knew well was pushed from the car platform and had both legs cut off. Thus outwitting the Bolsheviki, these baggers, while doing harm as vehicles for contagion, and causing infinite discomfort by overcrowding the cars, yet did a service that can not be overestimated in feeding the large cities and in furnishing the villages with much-needed goods.

The good crops that we in the north had in 1919 and 1920 naturally led to the falling-off of baggers; but the number of speculators was sufficient to overcrowd the limited transport.

CHAPTER THIRTEEN

Lootings

THE autumn of 1917 began with signs of gathering storms in the political world and with fresh causes of anxiety to us. When the Bolshevist Revolution broke out, George was at the front, and Alec, an officer in the Imperial Army, was stationed in Petrograd. Oka had gone to Moscow to take our silver and jewelry there, for, with the disorganization of the army and the threatened advance of the Germans on our railroad lines, we felt that at any time we might get into the sphere of action, or at least be raided by the disorderly elements that were showing themselves.

For two weeks we suffered great anxiety for the fate of our sons. There were no newspapers, no telegrams could be sent, and rumors that were flying about represented the streets of Moscow and Petrograd as flowing with blood, and it was said that all old officers had been massacred. Though we knew there must be much exaggeration, there was still much cause for worry.

To our great relief, Alec arrived one day, but changed by what he had seen and experienced. He had escaped with his life, thanks to the men in his company. Up to the time we left Russia, he had to remain in the Red Army, as did all others of his class whose lives were spared. The Bolsheviki, all through, have shown a profound knowledge of human nature. They have known how to deal with each class, to arouse enthusiasm, or terror, as their policy in each case might dictate. For the officers of the old régime whom they wished to keep in their service, they invented a measure diabolical in its cleverness. Each officer was made to sign a paper stating that, in case of his joining the Whites, or disappearing, his parents or family would be held responsible; and, knowing full well the significance of these words, however fearless they might be personally, none of the officers had the courage to desert those dear to them.

Oka had sent us a telegram from Moscow the day before the Revolution, saying that he was leaving for home that night; and for two long weeks we heard nothing of him, until one day he too walked in, haggard and worn.

The same winter an event took place—it was one of many—that made us realize how much we personally had to be thankful for. At the end of the lake, some three miles from us, was the estate of my husband's sister, the Princess Shakhovskoy, who lived in Petrograd during this time, suffering great privation. It was never considered safe for her to return and try to save anything on the estate or in the house; but her husband's brother had a place adjoining her land, and kept an eye on her property. From the beginning of the Revolution he had suffered much indignity on account of his title, but his property had not as yet been even controlled. On Christmas Day, my husband asked me to go to see the Prince, as he was rather infirm, and also to take him a secret letter from his sister, sent in our care

I drove the few miles across the lake on the ice, and found the Prince sitting down to a tea-table. As we sat chatting, a maid announced that three soldiers wished to see the Prince. Excusing himself, he went out, but soon returned, half-angry and half-amused, and told me that a soldier of the adjoining village and two bluejackets from a village farther on, came to ask why I was there. They were not satisfied with his telling them that it was not the first time I had been there, that my husband was his cousin as well as connected by marriage, and that I had come knowing he had been sick, and to wish him a Merry Christmas. They insisted that I had come at his request, to take off and hide his valuables, and they threatened him and me with dire punishment if it was found that I had carried anything back with me. Neither of us regarded the matter very seriously, and I left without forebodings. The next morning, very early, we were surprised to see our cousin drive up to the door. He asked me if we would take him in, as he had lost everything. I took him to my husband's room and brought him something to eat, while he told us his story.

It seems that, as I drove through the village on my way back the day before, the soldiers had shouted to me to stop; but I had not heard the voices as it was a very stormy, windy day and my horse was a fast trotter. They claimed that "the more they called, the faster I went, evidently wishing to escape something." Taking this as a starting-point, they succeeded in arousing the whole village. Now every person in that village, if taken separately, was friendly to the Prince, who had always been good to the peasants. Indeed, he had been a sort of father and counselor, to whom they went in trouble. But here were a few hot-headed youths, with revolutionary arguments on the tips of their tongues, who had succeeded in getting the whole village and soon a second one to join in an attack on the Prince. They gave him only a short time to gather a few belongings and changes of clothing, such as he could carry in his hands, and turned him out. He, as had every one else, had hidden money and valuables in various places in the house; but in the excitement of the moment he could not remember where, and so saved next to nothing. After much talking, he persuaded them to let him have one of his own horses with which to drive to a neighbor's, where he had spent the night.

The peasants had immediately looted his house and that of my sister-in-law. Later they burned the house down, and when we left Russia, of the Shakhovskoys' house and estate nothing was left but ruins. Rare plants and trees were torn up; the books dumped into the street. Large mirrors, too high to get into the houses in the village, were sawed in two. One such was placed in an open shed pending the operation; and the herd coming home in the evening, a ram caught sight of a handsome rival, and immediately running back a few steps, with lowered horns charged the intruder— and shattered the mirror.

Our cousin did not feel that he was safe with us, so went on to Tver the same day, where he remained some months, finally returning to the country in the summer, but to an adjoining county. Here he was one day falsely accused of setting the peasants against the Bolshevik military service, and was arrested on a Thursday, with the assurance that he would be tried Monday morning. Early Sunday morning he and seven others, one of whom was a priest who had publicly prayed for the Tsar, were led out, half-dressed, to be executed without trial.

But I have anticipated, in following out this case to the end, and we must go back.

Shortly after the looting of my cousin's home, the village adjoining our estate held a secret meeting, at which it was decided to "loot the estate and house and turn the Ponafidine family out of Bortniki for ever." The document bearing this declaration was signed by every householder but four, and was taken to the other villages for their endorsement. I think that this movement was largely due to the speeches made in that village by the Commissar of Agriculture, as already described.

We were saved in this instance by a neighbor, R, a peasant who was always loyal to us, at the cost of much persecution standing by us in every crisis throughout the years that followed. Whatever success we had in hiding and saving anything was due to his help. We always knew that, day or night, we had a faithful friend who would come at our call.

Learning of this plot against us, he went to our parish committee and told them that, if this resolution was carried out, it would be an everlasting disgrace to our parish; that all the Ponafidine property, when divided among so many villages, would mean so little for each individual that it would not pay for the stigma that would be left upon them. The Volost Committee immediately sent R to us with seven armed men, among them the president of the Committee himself. Sitting by the bedside of my husband, I saw, with a thrill of horror, Alec passing the window, surrounded by a group of armed men. My heart sank; his life was always hanging by a thread, as he was an ex-officer of the Tsarist régime, and I thought that this time the thread had snapped. A moment later, I saw him laugh, and realized, with a gasp of relief, that these men could not be enemies.

Assuring my blind husband that the steps he would soon hear in the house were those of friends, I went to the door to meet them. They told me the story, and said that they would spend the night with us to protect us, and that they had already sent to summon a *skhodka* of all the five villages nearest us.

I put the omnipresent samovar on to boil, and after tea they went to the village to attend the *skhodka*, while I set to preparing dinner for them all, as best I could with our meager supplies.

About two o'clock in the morning they returned, very much excited and heated from the long and violent meeting—where lungs counted for more than logic—and between bites of supper they told us the result of the meeting, often jumping up and walking about in their excitement. They said that the *skhodka* had been so violent that the president of the Committee had been obliged to dismiss it and to give directions for having a general parish council held at the volost headquarters in two days, with delegates from each village. Until the result of that meeting could be known, they promised to have a well-armed company of our friends stay with us.

The volost council was duly held, and passed a resolution to the effect that we were not to be molested in any way until the time came when the fate of our estate and property, along with that of all others around, should be officially decided by the Central Committee. The resolution ended by saying that, if these orders were disobeyed, the offenders were to be "drowned in the iceholes of the lake."

After the delegates had returned to the house, a deputation came to us from the village where the whole trouble had originated. I wish I could portray that scene. About a dozen peasants stood in our large living-room, looking as sheepish as boys caught stealing their neighbor's apples. My sons and I faced them, and our guard, including the Commissar, stood in the background. The spokesman began by dwelling on the good relations that had always existed between us, and regretting that certain young people, carried away by revolutionary propaganda, had got out of hand. But he denied that they, as a village, were against us, and claimed that the matter had been greatly exaggerated by R, and that we might be assured of their friendship, and so on and on.

The president of the Volost Committee listened to it all, and before we could answer, stepped up to the spokesman and said:

"So you as a village took no official action in regard to turning out the Ponafidines, after looting them?"

"No, no, we never wished it," they all answered.

"Then what is this? Listen." And he drew out a copy of the minutes of the first meeting and read off the signatures, pointing to each one of those present whose name was mentioned. "Is this true?"

They all stood twirling their caps, and finally one stammered out:

"Everything in life is possible; perhaps we did do foolish things."

It was such a flat childish explanation that we all smiled. After a few friendly words, they filed out, and we had no more trouble with them.

Control visits, but usually good-natured ones, still took place, and they, more than anything else, showed us what children these were playing at governing the country. I remember one such visitation, to search our house for "alcohol, arms and counter-revolutionary literature." The men went all through the place and house, and finally settled down by my husband's bedside, to write the protocol. The chairman of the Committee spent many perspiring minutes over it, but could produce nothing satisfactory, and one after another of the party attempted it with much sucking of their pencils. Finally, united efforts resulted in a remarkable document. It was to the effect that "the undersigned, after carefully searching the estate and house of Citizen Ponafidine for alcohol, arms and counter-revolutionary literature, found nothing suspicious except agricultural implements!"

After signing this formal document, they all examined it carefully, to see if it could be improved on; and at last some one suggested that they add the words, "Legally testified to that this copy is a correct one."

"That's the way all official documents end," he explained. And the rest, awed by his superior knowledge, laboriously made that amendment to their protocol.

All that winter of 1917-18 we continued directly under the peasants' rule, seldom coming into contact with the city Bolsheviki. We had, however, to go to town occasionally on business; and during such a trip, Oka was witness of

one of the many terrible sights of those years, which must
always remain impressed on his brain.

As he was passing through the streets of our little
country town, his attention was arrested by an unusual
scene. The president of the Executive Committee, on a
bicycle, whip in hand, was chasing a Red Army man, who
was running down the street as if for a championship. They
were soon out of sight, and my son went on, rather amused,
wondering what it all meant. On his way back, passing
the square that is the busiest part of the city, he again saw
these two, surrounded by a crowd of people. Some one was
reading a document. Curious to know what was going on,
Oka went up and heard enough to realize that the paper
being read was a statement declaring that the fleeing Red
Army man was accused of stealing a suit of clothes from the
Commissar of Agriculture, and that he was condemned to
death. Oka and every one else in the square supposed that
this was merely a preliminary trial, or, at worst, that the
man would be taken back to prison and then to the place of
execution; so they all waited to see what would happen
next.

The young man was made to sign his own warrant, and
then curtly told to turn around. He did so, and a man in
the dress of a bluejacket stepped up and, placing a revolver
at the base of the accused man's skull, fired, killing him
on the spot. The effect on all present—men, women, even
little children—was terrific. Not a word broke the still-
ness. The crowd simply melted away, while a cab drove up
and the body was tumbled into it. My son came back to the
inn where I was awaiting him white with horror at the sight
he had witnessed.

CHAPTER FOURTEEN

Arrest of Alec and Oka

NOT long after this, our two sons, who happened to be in the city on necessary business, were arrested by the chief of the militia himself, accompanied by a number of Red Army men. No explanation was given. They were carefully searched, all valuables were taken from them and a receipt given. They were confined separately, in rooms so full as to make it impossible to find space on the bare floor to lie at length. Nor were there seats enough, so that most of the prisoners had either to stand or to sit on the floor during the day.

Late at night, a member of the Secret Service of the Cheka went his rounds; and, to their astonishment, my sons found him to be an old acquaintance. He had practically grown up on our place; his mother had been our laundry woman, and his father, of whom we were fond, had been our waiter, when he was sober. Both his parents had been devoted to us. He at once gave orders to have the brothers placed in a room together, and promised to do all he could the next day for their liberation.

The hostess in the primitive little inn, where we always put up when in town, as did my husband's parents before us, took the arrest of the boys greatly to heart, and ran all over the city to our friends for advice; and she gave them what was still more practical—bread and potatoes. She also wished to telegraph me, but our sons asked her not to do so, hoping that they might be released before the news reached us.

On the second day there came to me a man who had seen the arrest, and he told me all he knew, which was not much. I was in despair. I had never left my husband overnight since the stroke that had caused his blindness in 1914. The state of his heart also was such that I feared the shock. On the other hand, I knew with what calmness and heroism he always met a crisis, and I felt that there was nothing to do but to tell him. He took the blow as I expected, and told me I must go at once to the town and that he could get on quite well alone.

A school-teacher near us was an old friend, and I at once wrote, begging him to come and spend the night with my husband. I also sent to our friend R, asking him if he would come and take me to the city, as the daily steamer had already left, and I had no one on the estate whom I could trust. He had just killed a steer for his winter supply of beef; and when my message reached him, he was beginning to skin the carcass. Laying down his knife, he said to his wife, "Go and find some one to help you. I can not leave our lady in her trouble." And only washing his hands, without even waiting to change his clothes, he came to us on a run.

While he harnessed a horse, I got together some food-supplies, not knowing how long the prisoners might be kept, and prepared everything to leave my husband as comfortable as possible. His was by far the harder fate—to lie there in darkness, imagining the worst; for he knew that some of the hostages taken in connection with the lately discovered plot had already been executed.

Soon after I left, a cousin came to visit us; and as my husband heard her carriage drive up, he was convinced that it was some one from the city, come to arrest us. When our cousin entered, she found him almost in a collapse, and had she not possessed considerable medical knowledge, I doubt if she could have pulled him through the severe heart-attack. She stayed with him until I returned; had I known it, I should have had one worry the less.

In the meantime, we were driving swiftly to a village from which we hoped to get a row-boat to take us across the lake. The village, unfortunately, was celebrating its annual fête, and no one would go on a fête-day for mere money. But when we arrived, not only the relatives on whom we had counted, but a number of peasants whom I knew, on hearing of my trouble, said they would take me if no one else would.

I shall never forget that night's row. The evening was so beautiful that it seemed to mock my sorrow, and never did five miles seem so long. R and the rowers, all of whom were simple peasant-folk, showed their sympathy with exquisite tact, trying to keep up my courage without seeming to do so.

It was dark when we reached the town. At the little inn, we learned that my sons were still awaiting trial, and that food had been sent them each day. That night I could do nothing but walk around their prison, wondering behind which of the barred windows they were lying.

Early in the morning, R, under pretense of carrying them food, managed to get word to the boys that I was there. A little later I went to the prison, and as I came up to where a number of guards and Red Army men were standing, one of them, a huge burly fellow, stepped forward and with profane words almost pushed me off the sidewalk, laughing loudly, but at the same time he managed to whisper, "Meet me in the garden." I gave a second look and recognized him as a man who used to work for us. I walked away rapidly, followed by the laughter of the company.

Going to the little lakeside garden, I strolled about until I saw my friend sauntering around at the opposite side. He passed me several times before he managed to slip a note into my hand, and whispered to me to come at nine o'clock to see the chief of the militia. "Ask him to hasten the trial, and forgive me if I am very rough with you again," he said as he left me.

In a safe spot I opened the note, which proved to be from Alec, asking me to demand a trial. He said that there were many confined with them who had been there for months, and might remain much longer unless some one pushed their cases; that if I made a sufficient demonstration, I might succeed in hastening the trial.

Our steamer was about to leave the pier, and I wanted to send a note by the captain to my husband. I had nothing much to tell, but I felt sure I should succeed; so I wrote him cheerfully and said that no later than the next day I hoped to be home with both boys. But my heart was heavy. As I went to the boat, a lot of peasants were there buying their tickets, and they surrounded me, expressing their sympathy and denouncing the Bolsheviki in such terms that I was frightened. I begged them to stop, for fear we all should be arrested, and then who would remain to fight? The attitude they took touched me very much, as well as their indignation that our sons, "who had never done anything but attend to their own business and never went to meetings or political gatherings," should be arrested. They offered to go home and gather a *skhodka*—panacea for all things—and draw up petitions. I thanked them, and told them that they had better wait and keep still as yet; perhaps, later, I should have to ask their help.

At nine o'clock I appeared at the prison door, and brought on myself again a volley of abuse from my friend. "There she comes again, to bother my life out about her precious sons. To get rid of her, I'll take her in and turn her over to the chief." Continuing to mutter, he led me into the prison. Before opening the chief's door, he whispered, "Stick to it that they be tried to-day"; and I went in.

It is awful to stand before a man who holds the destinies

ALEXANDER PONAFIDINE

Joseph Ponafidine (Oka)

of those you love in his hand, and to feel that you personally may be able to win, or may antagonize him. In those days the passage from the faintest suspicion or accusation to the "wall" (where executions took place) was often very short, and we had little hope of a fair trial when one of our class was accused.

I was greeted very roughly at first; but when I gave my name, the chief of the militia softened and asked me to be seated. I told him I had come in regard to my two sons. I did not know what the charge was, but could say in advance that I was sure there was some misunderstanding, as they kept strictly to farm work, and had not been connected with any political movements; and I asked the chief, as a great favor, that he have them called that day to be questioned, since I feared to leave my husband so long. I also asked permission to see my sons.

He promised me that he would send them immediately to the Cheka (none of my readers can know the thrill of horror that name gave us in Russia). He added that I could see my sons now, or after the trial; but, if at once, I must understand that I would go with them under convoy to the Cheka, and share what came to them. I thought fast, and just then, seeing our doctor pass the low open window, I asked the chief if I might speak to him before answering.

"Yes, if you speak to him in my presence."

So, leaning out, I called the doctor back and asked him if, in case of my detention, he could send a trained nurse, or doctor's assistant, at once to stay with my husband. The doctor took the situation in at a glance, and said I could be assured that he would see to it that my husband would be cared for. So, thanking him, I turned to the chief of the militia, who had been standing close to me, and said, "I am ready. Take me to my sons."

He took leave of me very politely, and ordered a guard

to escort me and then to have us all sent to the Cheka.

We passed through long corridors, and then to a small courtyard, upon which opened one window of the room where the boys were confined, and I saw, among the thick mass of heads crowding at the barred window, my sons. The door was unlocked, and they came out.

We were marched like convicts through the well-known streets, where every one knew us, but no one dared show signs of recognition, much less of sympathy. Brought to the Cheka, we had long to wait in the anteroom; but the door leading to the room occupied by the chief of the Cheka and his secretary was often opened. The president of our local Cheka was one of the most sinister men in the Government at that time—a former railroad engineer, known for his brutality. He invariably questioned people with a revolver and a Cossack *nagaika* (a Cossack whip) on the table before him; and in moments of excitement flourished one or both around the head of the unfortunate being he was questioning. And it is said that he sometimes did more than flourish the *nagaika*.

Among the guards who had accompanied us was our friend, who considerately drew off all the guards but one, and told him he need not keep his rifle in evidence—this, to spare our feelings. The anteroom in which we sat served also as an approach to the room occupied by the *Ispolkom*, or Executive Committee; so that many were constantly passing back and forth. One of our friends, seeing us sitting there, managed to say to me, "Tell the boys not to mind the revolver when they are questioned: he may strike them but he won't shoot." I passed this word of encouragement along.

At last our names were called and my sons went in separately. Our loyal R had hung round us all day, and was now seated by us in the anteroom. How brave that act was

can be understood only by those who know how dangerous
it was at that time to be classed as the friend of an aristocrat,
or in any way to attract the attention of the dreaded Cheka.
Our young Chekist also passed through repeatedly, and
always stopped to offer my sons a cigarette.

When the boys went in, the secretary, whom we happened
to know, made no sign of recognition, and was very curt;
but when his chief left the room for a moment, he offered
the boys cigarettes in silence—which were refused in silence;
but my sons knew that they had a friend at court.

After each of us was questioned, we were told that we
must write separately all we knew on a certain subject, and
a list of questions concerning our movements and those of
George was given us. The secretary, bustling around the
place, contrived to leave us alone for a few seconds, and this
was long enough for us to plan in English what we were to
write, so that our information, set down separately, tallied
at every point. After many questions and much talk, to our
infinite surprise we were told that we were free; and all that
was demanded of us was that we sign a paper declaring that
we would not leave the county without the permission of the
Cheka. And so, without making the acquaintance of the revolver or the *nagaika*, we were escorted back to the prison,
where, on presenting the receipt, my sons were given back
their money, watches and pocketbooks.

I think that, after all, it paid to be arrested, to experience
the full sweetness of liberty. I thought then that nothing
would ever make me complain again. All the supplies I
had brought for my sons we left for their less fortunate comrades; and with our good R, who was as happy as we were,
we returned home, even before the time I had promised my
husband to do so.

We afterward discovered that the arrest had been caused
by information being given that our sons had gone to the

city to meet members of the counter-revolutionary party.

Immediately after the release of my sons, Alec was made military instructor in our volost, where he superintended the military training of young men in the various villages; and so we had the comfort and help of his being with us.

During this winter of 1918-19 we first came in direct contact with the Bolshevik authorities in the city; and the peasants came to us, advising us to join their commune, arguing that they might be able to protect us if we belonged to it. They passed a resolution in a *skhodka* held without our presence, stating that as the "Ponafidines had always been friendly and good to the peasants, and whereas, since the Revolution they had never shown any political activity but had always been ready to submit to all the revolutionary laws of the parish committee and commune," they asked to have Citizens Ponafidine and their sons registered as members of their community.

This was, of course, not a political confession of faith, but a purely agrarian step. That it never had any practical result for us was not the fault of the peasants. In all that followed, when they repeatedly asked us if they might interfere in the action of the Bolsheviki against us, we advised them to keep still, for we doubted if their resistance would have any weight, while it surely would bring down on them the wrath of the Bolsheviki.

Our first visitor from the Bolsheviki was the County Commissar of Agriculture, an Esthonian, a butter-maker by profession, who arrived with secretaries, assistants and professional farm managers. He was exceedingly polite, and altogether won our confidence. We heard later from one of those present, that he said, "That is the way I always treat them, until they lose their fright and show me everything. Then, when I have got what I want out of them, I begin to squeeze." And he certainly did squeeze us later on.

He went all over the estate, and then came in and discussed matters with us in a friendly and apparently open manner. He said that the chief object of the Commissariat was to see that no ground remained uncultivated, and that the greatest number of cattle and horses were raised. He assured us that we might remain in possession if we would guarantee to cultivate all our land as it had been done by us formerly, in order to give as much to the market as we did in former times. Under such circumstances, we could be permitted to have hired help, as was the rule on state farms.

We explained that it was out of the question. We had no horses to plow with, nor cattle to furnish manure, as in other years, nor means with which to hire help. Also, we should cause bad feelings among the peasants, who now had the greater part of our grass-lands. The strongest argument of all, that we did not trust him and his fine words, or any other Bolshevik, could not, of course, be expressed.

His next suggestion was that they make a state farm in Bortniki, and I remain to manage the dairy for them. This last I evaded, claiming the right to do so because I was over age for such work, and could not leave my sick husband. The question of a state farm was left open, but everything they said pointed to such a fate for our estate. Before he left, I said to the Commissar, "What is to become of us in case the estate and all our property is taken from us? My husband and I are, unfortunately, still alive; how are we to be supported?"

In reply, he threw up his hands in a comprehensive gesture about the room, and said:

"Oh, all this, your house and personal belongings are yours. They can not be touched. We only take the farming implements and live stock. You and your husband can receive rations as issued to old people; your sons, of course, will be in the military service."

He left us feeling, on the whole, reassured; we had not sufficiently learned the lesson that the Bolsheviki were teaching us, and therefore took the word of the Commissar as worth something.

A short time after this incident, going out into the hall one day, when I was alone in the house with my invalid husband, I found three big strapping Red Army men standing in the doorway, who, on seeing me, raised their rifles as for "Attention," and with one voice shouted out:

"In the name of the Russian Socialistic, Federative, Soviet Republic, we arrest—your property." And at the last words they brought down their rifles to "At ease."

I went up to them and asked them not to make so much noise, as my husband was sick, and added, "Now just put down your rifles—you won't frighten me—and I'll get the samovar ready. We'll drink tea, and afterward you may tell me what you want."*

At the sound of the word "samovar," instantly all their bellicose instincts were subordinated, and they asked eagerly, "Where shall we put them?" And standing their rifles in the corner I indicated, they followed me into my husband's room.

I hastily explained to him in English that I thought the boys were all right if handled carefully, and to them I said, "You sit down and talk to my husband, who is blind and lonely, while I prepare the samovar for tea."

I left them cozily chatting and smoking cigarettes (such cigarettes!) that my husband offered them. With tea and black bread, all we had to offer, they became still milder; and finally, when they handed me a small piece of paper (we were having a paper famine and even official documents were written on scraps, sometimes even on packing paper), it

---

* "Tea" had long been made of dried fruits or plants, even carrots.

proved to be from the Commissariat of Agriculture, and began: "Take from the Ponafidines thirty table-cloths, ten pairs of curtains, ten pairs portières, ten window-shades, twelve upholstered chairs"—and I forget how many tables, books, bookcases, mirrors and wardrobes, all to be taken for the "Communistic Club of Ostashkov," our county town. The paper was signed by the County Commissar of Agriculture.

As no business is ever done in Russia without bargaining, I did not see why this should be an exception; I began, therefore, to use all my powers of persuasion—so successfully that they came down from thirty table-cloths to eighteen; and when I took them around the house, to choose curtains and tables, they were kind enough to say, "Oh, give us what you care least about"; and on leaving, they gave me a receipt for all they took. This, by the way, was the only raid made on our house where the Commission went through the form of giving us a receipt.

We parted touchingly. They invited us to come and see their club, and all went up to the bed to shake my husband's hand very politely and to apologize for disturbing him. Later on, one of our acquaintances told us of a big military dinner given to all the Commissars and other Communists of importance—a very fine dinner for those hard times. Our friend said, however, that all his appetite left him when he saw the table spread with a handsome cloth for twenty-five persons, with my monogram and crest in the center.

This shows how uncertain our life was, and how our fate always depended on the kind of persons, or the mood of the persons, who visited us. It was one of the most wearing of our experiences during those long years, this uncertainty. Many a bridge we dreaded to cross, we found, on approaching, did not exist; but again, when we least expected it, a flood would burst upon us. What has driven the refugees in tens of thousands from Russia has not been altogether the fear of starvation, but in some measure the impossibility of leading the life that made us each evening thank God for one more day of peace, and in the morning to ask Him for help to bear whatever the new day might have in store for us.

CHAPTER FIFTEEN

Letters to America

THE story of our lives from the middle of 1917 to the middle of 1918 can best be told, perhaps, through letters which I succeeded in getting to my friend Mrs. Clement. Some of these letters were given by Mrs. Clement to the *Atlantic Monthly*, and later I added a few articles. With the permission of the *Atlantic* I reproduce some of these letters. My readers will be interested, I trust, in this contemporary record of events as they affected us.

Bortniki, July 9, 1917

My dear Carrie,—

I often want to write, but there is so much one wishes to say and can not, that I have little heart for writing. If this state of things keeps on, most of us will be candidates for mild types of insane asylums. How Peter stands it! For several nights we have had the most exciting powwows until eleven o'clock, in Peter's room, with peasants.

Finally, seeing matters were getting too complicated for our local Committee to handle, I went to town and had an interview, where I felt myself as in the coils of a boa-constrictor. Still, I was advised to send for them in case matters became worse.

A few days ago I telegraphed, and yesterday, as I was sitting by the window reading to Peter at seven o'clock in the morning, I saw two men coming up from the landing, one of whom I recognized as a member of the Central Committee. I hurriedly dressed Peter and led him out into the big room. The city man had come in answer to my telegram, and had arranged that members of the two committees interested in our harvest-fields meet him here; also about fifty peasants.

If you could have seen and heard what we went through from then until two-thirty P.M., when they left!

Our neighbors were violent, menacing and brutal; the city man, quiet, polite, tried to prevent excesses; but the result is the same—all our fields, except as much hay as will carry us through the winter, by *their* estimate, taken—the price fixed but the money confiscated; "as all the burden of the war falls on, the peasants, the gentry can not be permitted to get any profit."

The fields left for our own use were valued, and *we* must pay the same rent for the land. Then they claimed we had more horses than we needed and they have the right to confiscate the extra ones, *gratis*. When we told the use to which each horse was put, and proved that in the winter and plowing season we found we had not enough, every peasant present, though all knew the facts and most had worked for us, when fifteen to eighteen horses a day were used, swore that never were more than six horses harnessed in Bortniki.

I turned to one and another by name, and said, "Have you a conscience and a God? Answer me truly if, the year around, fifteen to eighteen horses are not too few." And they all in chorus replied, "She lies, she lies; they never use more than six; take them from her!" And not a man was there whose wounds, or those of his household, or horse, or cow, I had not treated, and whom we had not helped, sick or poor, and given boards for coffins, or timber to build, if a fire came!

The whole day was a nightmare. Such a noise, one could hardly hear, and one never knew when the noise might not change to worse. I gave Peter brandy, etc., repeatedly, and he talked quietly, when from time to time the chief came to him. But Oka and I kept the mob in the other side of the house. We are forbidden to sell more cattle, and they haven't left us enough to feed them. Horses I think we can sell, but *we* shan't get the money. Altogether, we and our kind are being hunted like rats. Schools like Oka's, and of fine arts, are being turned into syphilitic hospitals; and the worst of all is the army.

I don't know if you will ever get this. I have had nothing from you for a long time. Last night Peter slept very little, but is better to-day than I feared. We have a new intendant, and that complicates matters.

Bortniki, August 11, 1917

I keep writing, though I get nothing and do not know if you have received the letters and cards I have sent you. The post is suffering now like every other department of our poor country. Alec in Petrograd is two or three weeks without word from us, and I write two or three times a week. His letters are often twenty days on the way. George's come very quickly and regularly of late, thank God! But he, poor fellow, in addition to miseries untold, gets nothing from us. He has had but one letter in one and a half months! We are very anxious about him, for officers are being mown down by friend and foe alike—"thousands and thousands," as is officially admitted. He just wrote under fire after two hundred versts marching, footsore and dirty; for since his leave (he was here in the middle of June for seventeen days) he has not once slept under a shelter of any kind, and rains are almost constant.

Last week I had a telegram to go to town to the local Civil Commissariat Department. As I could not get away that day, we sent Oka. They demanded that we gather in and thresh our rye as soon as possible, and give all we can for seed, offering a price far less than it cost us to raise it. When a protest was made, the reply, very politely couched, was, "If you give it voluntarily we pay four roubles [the price peasants are selling for is eight to ten roubles]; if not, we shall requisition it at 2.60 roubles."

We asked for more prisoners to push the work, and they told Oka they had just sent a supply for our parish and there were three we could have. . . .

Everything is given by cards: two pounds of cereal and fifty of wheat flour are given per month, to children under five, and to invalids. This month, when I went with a physician's certificate to get the above for Peter, I was re- fused, as "half the country come with certificates," though they knew me personally and were aware of Peter's state. In every way the present "freedom and equality" is far more one-sided than ever. The only classes that have no protec- tion, and that no one raises a voice to justify, are landowners and officers. Mill-hands and day laborers are demanding from twenty to thirty roubles, even more, a day, and eight hours' work, and Sunday and one other day off. Officers who have to dress well and are in hourly danger and peril get, in George's position, two hundred roubles a month. We are all in rags, for not a yard of material can we get. I had put off needed replenishing till cheaper times, and now can get nothing.

We heard that shoes had come to Ostashkov, but by the time we went, every pair was sold. Those costing in times of peace ten or twelve roubles sell for one hundred and sixty roubles! Eggs that at this season should be seventeen ko- pecks for ten are now two and a half and three roubles. Everything in proportion, except when we wish to sell. In many places the peasants won't let the squires sell an egg or a pound of butter. All our class would leave if they could, but they can not. They are not allowed to take money with them nor transfer abroad their capital.

Peter keeps up the greatest interest in everything, but is broken-hearted. He *will* have the papers read to him, though often sobs when we read.

Day after to-morrow I am going to town to try to get

some help from our Committee in the way of giving us legal prices, etc., but do not hope for much. I shall keep on my feet as long as I can. It must be much easier to fall fighting than eating out one's heart.

Sometimes I feel as if I *must* go myself and join the brave women regiments; but even if I were free, they would say I am too old, but I am *not!* Was there ever a time when the world was so full of heartache? Millions of hearts bursting! Truly the last days must be at hand.

October 5, 1917

I have not had a word from you for many months. Anyway I write again, to try to get a word through while I can; for later, when "Tommy comes marching home,"* our real personal troubles will begin. . . .

The anarchy and lawlessness are awful. One of Oka's classmates was here this summer. His father, an admiral, a very genial, kindly chief, loved by all, was brutally murdered in his bed, simply because he was an officer. His ears and nose were cut off, and his eyes gouged out, while alive. I could tell you many such instances, the victims of which we knew personally. This is my great dread for our boys; if it is God's will that they be killed in battle, doing their duty, it is one thing; but to be butchered would be worse to bear.

My brother-in-law Neil has just had his house cleared of silver and all other valuables, in a way reminding one of the times of Robin Hood. He was alone in the house, reading his paper, late one afternoon, and did not hear when seven horsemen rode up to the door and entered the room. As he looked up, the leader came forward, saying, "Are you Mr.

---

* This first example of camouflage later used in our letters. I remember how I puzzled over expressing in a safe way our dread of the soldiers.

Ponafidine? Charmed to make your acquaintance. Don't get excited, I beg of you; we can pass a pleasant half-hour together while my lads relieve your house of all valuables. I see you have a piano; that's good, we won't be dull."

And drawing up an armchair, he seated himself beside poor Neil, who, I fancy, was hardly in a state to enjoy the music, though he says it was brilliant. About the time, which Neil estimates as "hours," the other men came back, saying that it was all done. The leader arose to go, and then re-seating himself, said, "I'll play you a farewell march." And this done, he shook hands very cordially and left. The same thing was done in three adjoining estates.

Yesterday I heard there was lentil flour in our coopera-tive shop, and at once went there. They give us five pounds on each member's book. I know how to cook lentils, but we never saw the flour and I am experimenting. We had a kind of gruel of it last night which, though not very palat-able, must be nourishing, and that is all we look for these days. Fish and rye bread are all we have in abundance. Po-tatoes failed all about us. Few got back the seed. Cabbage the same. I have about two bushels each of beets and car-rots, and a keg of sour cabbage—my whole vegetable supply for the winter. Potatoes I give out by weight. If we are not molested, we shall not starve, but I have no hope of being able to keep what we have, or our few cows. So far we have butter and milk for ourselves, but none to sell. Nothing cuts me so much as the destruction of the dairy. I worked so hard to get it as near perfect as possible, and could support the family now had I back my cows.

I am not hiding anything, as we can not move Peter. I think the best hope of saving his life is to give up everything, asking them to spare him. I have been putting up curtains, etc., and getting the house ready for winter as usual. I had no heart in it, but decided it was best, for though Peter can't see, I like to have him feel that all is neat and pretty around him, and he asks to know just how each room looks. Also, I don't want the servants to think we anticipate anything. It is hard now with the people. I am losing things steadily, linen, etc.; my overshoes taken and, I know, by my maid, who has lived with us for years; and overshoes are not to be had for money now. One can not keep everything locked. I think I must have fighting blood in my veins, for I feel like fighting for our rights; and when the time comes, I feel I *must* go down, revolver in hand; but I keep trying to prepare myself to be patient and tactful for Peter's sake, to try to save him. One comfort is that, if the worst comes, his heart won't endure protracted suffering, and it will soon be over.

The boys have your address, and I have told them that if they survive us, to let you know if anything happens to me. . . . Peter is very brave. We both send you and all your family our best love, and may God bless you for all you have been to us! Perhaps better days will come. I wonder will you receive this!

November 2, 1917.

I have written you a number of cards and letters, but though I thanked you in words, you do not know how we thank you for the help you sent, for it is what we are living on, and Peter's pension; but that, as prices go now, is a very tiny drop in the bucket. I wrote you we had (in June) sold a part of the woods, receiving ten thousand roubles as guaranty money; but a clause in the contract makes us obliged in one month's time to return the money if the timber operations are stopped; so we have placed the money in the bank and, however great our need, dare not touch it.

We have sent Oka off on a delicate and dangerous mission. Feeling that there is little hope of escaping looting,

we must try to get our silver in a place of comparative
safety. You remember our beautiful Persian service; then
your Father and Mother Clement's wedding-gifts to us; a
service for twelve given us on our silver wedding anniversary
by Peter's brothers and sisters—these and all that I have in
the way of jewelry we have sent to Moscow to be stored in
the Government bank.

Then, too, we are trying to hide as we can some flour
and cereals, oatmeal and buckwheat, our main support now,
for bread-riots must soon begin, and if we can save a little,
it is something. I never could have imagined such a state
as our great country is in. Sending Oka to Moscow, we
supplied him with rye bread, oat-cakes and butter. He has
just returned from Petrograd, where he had to go; and he
and his classmates lived in the latter's house, empty, the
family being on their estate. The boys lived for five days
on bread and cold meat I gave them, for they could get
nothing in Petrograd except at impossible prices.

In Ostashkov most of the shops are closed, and the remainder have a big display of empty shelves, and to save
strength and time, hang out notices on the doors and windows: "We have no buttons, no yeast, no wool, no manufactured goods," etc. Of course, all groceries, flour, etc.,
you get by cards; five pounds of flour a month, one of sugar,
and sometimes tea and matches. Cereals, rice, macaroni,
candles, we have not seen for over a year; and we, who have
our own rye flour so far, get no white flour, of course. Prices
are fabulous. Shoes (if one is lucky enough to find any)
that used to cost twelve to twenty roubles, are one hundred
and fifty to two hundred. Not a yard of any stuff can we get,
and it takes the greatest ingenuity to dress ourselves and the
seven prisoners. For instance, I am footing winter socks
for them with some light felt Caucasian hats I had, and we
patch instead of darn stockings.

If we could look upon the war as the limit of our troubles! But it will be the beginning of the end, when they come home to take the land and divide the spoil. If you only knew what the boys are enduring! I write to George four times a week, and he has been six weeks at a time without word from us, and when he knows our danger. I never write the boys any but cheerful letters, and keep back all I can. But they read the newspapers and understand what is going on.

All the peasants are well supplied with money. The war has so raised the price of labor that the peasants and working class get far more than the brain-workers. The artificially cultivated (on German money) class hatred is our greatest menace. The most constantly repeated phrase is, "If we kill off all the bourgeoisie, we shall have peace, and then we can ourselves govern the country." I have talked calmly and quietly with the soldiers, who say it must be done. Even the "bourgeoisie"—landowners, capitalists, even priests, who are for some reason included—who have been kind can not be permitted to live. "We must root them all out, even children knee-high."

I wish I could write to you more freely. I think of you so often and so tenderly. Friends are the greatest comfort these days, and the knowledge that there are those who love us and think of us even at a distance is an immense help.

How Peter keeps up is a wonder. We who are well are quite unstrung. It has been said, and with considerable truth, I think, that there is not a perfectly normal person in the country. Nerves are strained, and no one, even the richest, gets the accustomed nourishment. Personally I feel the absence of sugar most. We always, in the East, had so much in the form of fruit, that one's organism evidently demands it, for I have such a craving for something sweet—

anything. Our apples were stolen while green, or we should have had a supply for the winter; but that is a minor trouble.

Bortniki, November 6, 1917

I want to write you of the last two days. It will give you some idea of the volcano upon which we live. Last evening two soldiers were here until late. They came to inform us that our woods are no longer ours: that, if we need to cut a tree, we must get permission and prove that we need it. In the meantime they brought us a paper authorizing peasants of one village to cut eighty trees for timber and eighty-five cubes for wood. A cube now costs three hundred roubles, so you can see how much we could get if allowed to sell; and this is only for one village!

This morning early I had to go on important business to the post. I hated leaving Peter without Oka, but had to do so. When I came back, I found poor Peter trembling in every limb, and almost unable to speak. The yard was full of women with bags: it seems a report had been spread that we have been selling flour and sending it in boats by night. The peasants about are greatly excited, and went over to our local Committee and warned them that they would loot us and burn us out.

The Committee sent three members, three soldiers, and two soldiers from our neighboring village to examine the charges. As soon as Peter was calm I went out to the barns where they were weighing our grain. I told them that I was deeply cut that such a false charge should be laid to us; that since the orders given us, we had faithfully kept from selling a pound; and that they were at liberty to search the place, as the people said we had hidden grain.

I myself went everywhere with them, showing them every place from attics to cellars, insisting on opening trunks, etc. When they went through our empty cellar and store-room and saw the lack of everything, they were amazed. After weighing all our provisions and calculating how much we would need (at least three pounds of cereals a day for twenty-two persons, and one pound of bread a day), they declared we could spare nothing; but the women raised such a menacing row that the whole delegation came in to consult with us.

They had begun by being very reserved, if not hostile, in their bearing toward us. The leader said to me when he had gone through a part of the buildings, "I almost believe you speak the truth!" At the last he stood up for me bravely, and privately advised me to try to send away what valuables we have, as he doubted if we could escape looting at the least. It was finally decided to take twelve poods to the next village, and there have it decided who was in need; for many who came to-day have bread.

When the women were told that twelve poods would be given them now, their spokeswoman said, "I tell you now, in the presence of the lady, when this flour is gone we will come to her again and ask her to give her supply willingly. If she does, we won't touch her; but if she does not do it willingly, we will take it and burn down the whole place." In vain the men argued, explaining that, even if hunger drove them to take food, it would not justify them in murdering and burning, nor would it give them bread. Nothing would move them.

The delegation came back to me and said, "What will you do?"

I replied: "As you represent our authority and government, it is my place to put the question to you, and ask you what we can do?"

They all laughed and shrugged their shoulders. When the Committee left us, in a very friendly spirit, it was with little comfort and with no encouragement.

It is now seven o'clock in the evening; all is quiet. Peter is undressed, and his old man is reading to him the papers, which are full of accounts of horrors; yet he will read every word. We shall have supper in a few moments, and I am ready for it, as I have had nothing since my morning coffee, as I could not eat my dinner when they were all here. Would you like to know our war menu? For dinner we had a gruel of oat flour and a souffle of squash. To-night we have tea, and potatoes boiled in milk.

We are being overrun with wolves, and a seventeen-year-old girl was eaten near Pakrovsky. I had a letter from George yesterday, dated ten days ago, saying he was "alive and well." In his last seven days in the reserve, he had shot a wild boar and a wild goat in addition to small game. It is not only an immense help in their very meagerness, but the sport is the one thing he has to take him out of himself and his surroundings. . . .

Bread-riots one can pardon, for to see one's children without bread can easily upset all one's morals as to rights of personal property, etc. We have now, according to this month's report, seven hundred and seventy thousand in the government of Tver who have no bread and are dependent on the miserable pittance of five pounds a month. About us are many such; and what aggravates the case is the almost complete failure of our potato and vegetable crops. If we were just ourselves, I would risk sharing our last pound; but we are twenty-two souls in Bortniki, among them refugees and prisoners who must be fed; and we are on such short rations, as it is, that it goes to my heart. They often go out to work lazily, and say they are so "empty." It seems cruel when a woman comes and begs me for only "three pounds for the children." I would gladly give it but dare not. Even the soldiers to-day warned me not to, for if we give to one we shall immediately have so many that our whole supply won't go around, and we shall be accused of partiality, with bad results; so one does not know what to do.

November 8

I go about as usual, quite alone, driving or walking, and so far have had no trouble. To-day one of the women who screamed the loudest at me yesterday brought her sick child to me, with many low bows and sweet words, as they know so well how to use them when they ask for a favor. I did what I could for the baby, and neither of us alluded to the past.

For some time I have been in the habit of going out at dusk and making the rounds of all our hay barns in the fields; but now I am a little afraid of the wolves, going alone. When Oka is back we can go together. It is a comfort in one way when the boys are here, and yet I am relieved when they are not, for I am afraid of their resenting bad treatment of us and only perishing themselves without helping us, especially George. He would never stand calmly by and hear what they say to us, though he bears worse for himself.

Bortniki, November 18, 1917

Since my last to you, great events have taken place. How great and of what shadings we know not, for our last newspaper was of October 26 (O.S.) and to-day is November 4. The telegraph is not working, and we only get conflicting rumors of great bloodshed in Petrograd and Moscow; and Alec and Oka are there. The same day Oka was to have left Moscow, civil war broke out. Eight days in succession I drove to the steamer to meet him and then gave it up. The first day I did not go, George came unexpectedly, *via* Kiev. You can imagine what it was to see him; and now, when I lie awake, it is such a comfort to feel he is sleeping over my head, and not somewhere in cold wet trenches and perhaps lying stark and still "somewhere in Austria."

He came to Kiev the evening of the day his little girl was born. The baby, though small, is well and strong. He divides his time between us, poor fellow; but so much of his meager leave is swallowed up by the long journey, that it only gives him nine days with each of us. With events rushing as they are, we feel that we must profit by every moment together. If I leave the room, George asks me as he used to when small, "Mama, are you coming back soon?" It seems as if I *can not* let him go again!

November 20

We are still in great uncertainty. Great fighting is going on in Moscow, and no trains leave. How it fares with Oka we do not know.

Alec got a few lines to us. He was alive nine days ago, but under fire. In the meantime, famine is approaching, for no food-supplies are coming in. In many of our villages there is flour only for two weeks. If you could see how we spend our evenings! In the *fluegel* we have cut a trap-door to the shallow cellar under the floor, and in pitch darkness George and I carry things down there. We have put there clothing, copper utensils, albums (at Peter's special request), extra samovars, etc. The *fluegel*, being brick, won't burn so easily, and perhaps we can save something.

One of the most cynical episodes of these dark days is the placard just over the bridge in Finland, where thirty officers were drowned, prodded under water with bayonets when they rose to the surface of the river. The placard reads, "Swimming school for officers." Do you wonder that wives and mothers of officers find the nights long?

It is a moment that tries one's faith. Why does God allow such horrors as the world has lived through the past four years? I feel so frozen, I can not get any comfort. Strange to say, I feel no personal fear. It is not bravery, but callousness. The days pass with less strain. It is the nights, and I am getting worn out for want of sleep.

Snow has fallen, and we soon shall be cut off for a time from the city. George insists on my having everything at hand to leave; but where can one go? No one is allowed to leave the country with money, and Peter can not be taken far, anyway. The whole country lives in a nervous, waiting, expectant frame of mind that makes all minor interests and troubles forgotten. The one impulse that grows and deepens is the class hatred, fostered and fed by the clever Germans.

Bortniki, November 24, 1917

I imagine that you have known through the Associated Press more of what has been going on in our poor tortured country than we have. . . .

The day before George left, Alec, as unexpectedly, came in, looking like Lazarus raised from the dead! He had lived through the horrors of arrest, nearly been lynched, as so many of our poor officers have been. His soldiers and chauffeurs stood up for him, and he had to order them to keep from violence. It is a long and complicated story, and that he was liberated is a marvel. He said the prospect of execution lost all its horror in the face of lynching. His colonel told him, when he was released, that he had better go home for a time.

We saw dear George off yesterday, and to-day Oka came, having been through real war. Trench cannonade in Moscow turned the whole city into a war camp. . . . He placed our silver in the Government treasury, on the eve of the day when all deposits stopped for want of room. We feel very thankful to God that all our boys are safe in spite of the risks they have been in.

The political outlook is very dark but still worse is the specter of famine. Some of our neighbors in a near-by state have smuggled a little flour over the border, for selling grain from one state to another is forbidden. If help does not come soon from the United States or elsewhere, I see nothing but death before us all. Even if they don't rob us, we can not hold out longer than the last of April. In Petrograd, Alec, for a long time, has lived on three-quarters of a pound of bread for two days! At noon, soup of such old salt beef that they put mustard and pepper into it to hide the smell! Aside from soup they have a mush of cereal, and the cereal again for supper; of course, without milk, butter or sugar. And this is officers' mess.

The memory of the two famines we lived through in Urumia haunts me still, and when I think of seeing the same things here, it makes me shudder. What the next days will bring forth, none can tell. The coup d'état has been the final push, plunging us into anarchy.

Our new commander-in-chief, an ensign (!), says in an order of the day, that he will "bring the country to peace over the dead bodies of the officers," as they are trying to persuade the soldiers to be true to the Provisional Government.

We pray for a strong united government, of whatever party it may be, before the demobilization of our millions, who will come back like locusts. George saw something of an army in retreat, and says he shall never forget it. The excesses were horrible, and we must expect the same thing when they come back if there is not a stronger hand at home than we now have. The whole country is tired of this reign of terror and lawlessness.

December 1

Since writing, the curtain has fallen on what I think is next to the last act in our agrarian drama. Early one morning, our Local Committee and two witnesses from the village nearest us came, announcing that they had heard I had sold a bull, a cow and three horses, and asked on what grounds I had done so. I told them we had not enough fodder for the winter; also, the cow was Tolstoi's.

They declared that we had no right to sell anything, and showed us a paper, fruit of the last coup d'état, saying that the estate passes into the hands of the Committee. The peasants are ordered to watch us, to see that nothing is taken out of the estate; and they proceeded to write down all our property.

We had for two days been negotiating the sale of a young blood-mare that I had brought up and broken myself. She followed me like a dog, even into the woods and fields, never going beyond my voice. She is a very fast trotter, and we hoped to sell her well before we were officially forbidden to do so.

While I went out with these people with the books to verify everything—live stock, farm implements, etc.,—the buyer came in the back door to Oka, and said that he would get the mare off if we wished. It was our last chance of raising a cent on the place, and Peter and Oka sold her for seven hundred and fifty roubles, the man taking advantage of our position.

When we went to the stables and saw Mushka's stall empty, I at once suspected what had happened, but did not know what to say. The first thing they asked was to see her, for she is famous around here. I told them I did not know where she was; that yesterday my husband had almost made a bargain, and perhaps she had been sold. They made a great deal of trouble, but we talked them down.

All day the boys and I worked with them and had to sit at dinner and entertain them! They wrote down even our personal effects, to the last table, chair and bed, which by the laws of Russia are not liable to be seized, even for debt. Then we were made to sign a paper that we would not sell, or take out of the place, a thing. If we leave to-morrow, we can not take a pillow or a quilt! We can not kill a chicken or calf for our own use, without going to the Committee for leave. When we told them that we may have to diminish still more for want of fodder, they said they would not permit it, but would force us to buy hay. When I said we could not afford it, they smiled and said they would make us find the means.

When they left us in the evening, we were all quite crushed. We are in the position of unpaid intendants who bear expenses, and of debtors whose property has been seized, and of criminals who are deprived of all rights. We are surrounded by spies, for the woods are teeming with peasants, cutting trees as they wish, and each one has the right to stop and control our work and ask what I have in the sleigh, etc. One can not stay in the house and get no air, and yet to go out is pain. The woods we sold are being rapidly cut, but the money each two weeks, as we verify the material hauled, goes to the Committee! The ten thousand roubles guaranty money we received we are hoping to hold on to for worse days. One never hears talk of the war or politics, only bread, bread, bread! To-day a pood of flour is sixty roubles.

As the lake freezes, I fear we shall be eaten out of house and home. Yesterday eleven soldiers passed and demanded dinner. To-day I fed three, and yet few can pass, as the ice is not strong. Yesterday was Peter's sixty-ninth birthday.

Bortniki, January 28, 1918

Your good letter of October 28 came yesterday. It is so long since I had a word from you or any one outside of Russia. Every estate around us is wiped out. Horses, cattle, farm implements, fodder, provisions, furniture, food-supplies, all divided up among the surrounding villages, which recognize no higher central power and refuse to return anything in spite of the orders from County, State and even P. Committees. Every day we expect to be turned out, but so far the villages are divided, the majority voting to let us live on but to take the farm. If they will only let us have the house and vegetable garden and a horse and cow, to have something to eat!

Last week I had a terrible ordeal, which I think took several years off my life. I was summoned very bruskly to a council of our five villages, with all our documents regarding the sale of our woods. Fortunately Oka was home, and the two of us went. They charged me with effecting the sale after the land had been recognized as the people's. They talked about "forgery," "deceit," "bribes," etc., threatening me with dire punishment, a score of hoarse voices yelling at once, shaking their fists. A number of my ex-patients surrounded me in a close ring, and though they dared not say much, they opposed violence. They kept us nearly two hours in that awful mob, but finally we left under more friendly feelings. Only a very small portion of the material is cut and lying on the shore, but they say they will confiscate it. If so, the contractors lose what they have spent in the work—about sixty thousand roubles—and we the money we hoped to get, that would have insured our future during these hard times. The ten thousand we received as guaranty money, and the Committee voted last month we could have, they now demand. I don't know how it will end. We have not dared touch that and have it intact in the bank, but probably will lose it. Also what O—— took to Moscow.

I went to the city two days ago, and came back so depressed by all I saw and heard there of the hunger. We have let a soldier's family (six little half-naked children) live here in one of our now too many empty houses. We

can give them lodging and fire-wood, but in my own house
I have to make up by night little packages of flour to smuggle to them. We are obliged to keep more people than we
can afford to, for the Committee won't let us discharge them,
as they have no bread at home; and we have to pay and feed
them, and they watch me as cats do a mouse to see that I
don't give a piece of bread to any one, and they steal everything they can lay hands to. You can not imagine the strain.
I go to bed dressed, except on very stormy nights, when I
don't fear their coming. The favorite hour for ejecting is
at night.

Oka has received a telegram that was nine days coming
from P——, calling him immediately for his examinations.
They will take six weeks, then he graduates with his degree
as lawyer, and he is not over twenty. Of course he won't
be able to do anything in his profession, but will try to get
some job. I think of writing to the U. S. Consulate, to know
if they could give him employment, as he could work in
several languages. . . .

We are now having a very serious kerosene famine, and
and have to plan everything to do all the work by daylight.
My last kerosene bottle I keep for the one reading-lamp for
Peter, and to have a light if he is ill. When it is gone, one
of my patients promised me a gourd if I can send by night.

We have had several Austrian prisoners ever since the
first year of the war, and more conscientious, devoted workmen we could not have. Now they are taken from us and
replaced by good-for-nothing people who were always pau-
pers from laziness and drink.

Bortniki, February 14, 1918

If you have read of the fall of Kiev, you can imagine
how we feared for Vera and the baby. For over a month
no news from her or from George, who is somewhere there.

Peter was nearly sick with suspense when a telegram came this week, signed "George." "All alive and well." From the papers we know that the part of the city where Vera was is nearly destroyed.

In O—— I found a reign of terror. All shops, gates and windows of first floors closed and barricaded. At one minute the streets would be deserted and then, as from the ground, would rise bands of twenty to twenty-five soldiers armed with rifles with bayonets fixed; many with cartridges slung in several rows; some with two rifles, and many flourishing revolvers.

While I was at the Tolstois' word was brought that the next house was being searched, and they were in a great panic, as they had several thousands of roubles in their keeping for others. They had thought of a safe hiding-place, but one that needed a ladder, and the old folks could not get to it without the help of servants whom they could not trust; so I offered to do it. By putting a chair on a table and climbing on top of a high bookcase, I could reach the place; and they brought me all the small valuables. While they were gone for other things they remembered, and I was perched on that undignified place, we heard a loud ring, but we managed to finish everything before the door was opened—to a friend, as it turned out!

The servants watched till the street was clear, for me to get out and go to a place I was very anxious to reach, to try to take away Vera's furs that I had given somebody to hide. I passed safely, seeing people stopped all along with the order of "Hands up!" The search was for revolvers. Suddenly I heard funny little humming noises, that I never realized were balls. Then, just ahead of me, a terrific explosion, followed by shouts of "Come on! Forward!" and the screams of the wounded. In front of me was a battle, and looking back I saw the street full of fresh companies running up with bayonets held at charge, and many firing wildly in the air, I think.

All the doors and gates being locked, a young boy and I pressed ourselves into a doorway and waited for some minutes till the noise quieted down. A bomb had been thrown or dropped, wounding many, but I did not see any one who was dead. A peasant, who was just ahead of me, evidently got a good share of the fragments of the bomb in his head and neck, and his ear was hanging down on his shoulder. I could not do anything to stop the bleeding, my handkerchief being too short. He was put into a sleigh, but the cabby in a panic ran off and the poor fellow lay screaming horridly alone. I begged a soldier who stood there to take him to the hospital and he did so. I saw five taken to the hospital of those who were near me, and don't know how many more there were. When we came home, two sleighs of peasants ahead of us had wounded in them, one a girl of eight or so.

I had to skirt more than half the town to get back to my horse. Street after street I would try, and find firing. What worries me most is being deaf in one ear; I can never tell from which direction sounds come; so, often I would turn to the right to avoid firing that I thought was at the left, only to run into trouble.

After many adventures, I got safely back and told my man, whom I found in great anxiety, to harness and we would leave, though my horse had not had his full rest. We were both glad when we finally reached the lake. It was easier to go *toward* danger than turn and run! I hated the chilly, creeping feeling in the back when I thought they were behind me.

Alec is here on three months' sick leave, a private now. He has had no pay since December. He works all day with the people on the farm, for he can not get anything to do.

Oka is in P——, having his final examinations. If he can not get anything to do and the war stops, he will come home and we will try to get a peasant's share. That is as much as we can plow ourselves (no hired help will be allowed in the spring) and we may be able to get enough to eat that way. The trouble is seeds. There won't be any potatoes left to set out, nor oats, nor rye. We are eating them all up. We are just at the end of our potatoes and sour cabbage. We eat bread, half oats and half rye, and serve it out by weight, giving each one rations for two days. Every one we see is changed. Insufficient food is telling, even where there is not actual starvation. Bread is fifty times the normal price, and it is only by great good luck, going by night, that people can buy any. Soldiers can get flour somehow, but on no account could we get any, and unless a miracle happens, I do not see how we are to avoid death by starvation.

Bortniki, May 8, 1918

We are cut off from all communication with the outside world. We have had no letters since last fall, and I doubt if mine gets through, though I keep on writing. There is so little time to write that I am going to send this to England and then to America, to Mrs. Roper.

We are still with a roof over our heads, though it is no longer *ours*, and bread to eat—three-quarters of a pound a day—milk, and still some salt meat. So we are better off than any of our family and friends, many of whom have been turned out with only what they could carry, and some killed. Last winter was one long nightmare, when for months I never dared to undress nights.

The village next us, after breaking in and robbing us of grain and oil for two thousand roubles, voted by a large majority to turn us out and loot the place. The next village sent word to the Committee, and a party of armed men came to protect us, and seven of them slept here one night. They searched the whole estate (I think the ninth time), weighed out provisions for a week for us, sealed up the barns, etc. Then they called a meeting of our commune, which was so violent that the Central Committee closed it and ordered two representatives from each of the villages in the whole parish (thirty-four villages, fourteen communes) to go there. The council sat all day and late at night and was very stormy, but our friends outnumbered the opposition, and they voted to let us live there if we would work with our own hands, and to give us three-quarters of a pound of bread a day.

A few days later I was summoned to headquarters. Alec and I went. They were exceedingly polite and even sympathetic. It was decided that we can have three horses, four cows and as much land as we can till without hired help. We asked for a man to help us until George comes, for we ask for his share of land. We have had no news from him since February 11, and have no idea where he is. This help they refused.

Two soldiers have been quartered on us for months, one with a family of six and the other of five. We are obliged to pay and feed them! One is permitted to be our herdsman. His wife milks the cows, feeds the pigs, etc. The second family helped cutting wood, etc., in the winter, but were not to help plow.

Finally one commune of three villages sent for us to their council. There we were told we had better come entirely into their commune, and not carry out any of the Committee's orders without consulting them, adding, "The Committee can not protect you from us but we can protect you against the Committee." So now we are between two stools, but at present are friendly with both.

My cook and dairymaid are taken from me, so I have to cook and myself do the churning and separator work. The boys went to work plowing, carrying out the manure to get the hot-beds started, and their work is going on fast. The peasants were so impressed by seeing that we were ready and able to do manual work, that they called us again to a council, where they were very friendly and told us one of the soldiers might help us until George comes. One of them seized Alec's hand, and holding it out that they might see the blisters, said, "Look, comrades, they work like us and I have seen how they work. Their plowing is as good as ours, but can we do their scholar-work?"

We have five cows and two horses that are requisitioned, but so far not taken, and they keep putting it off. I think the crisis for us is passed, so far as peasant violence goes, and there is less danger now they see we are reduced to their level and eat as they do. The famine is getting worse, and though no actual starvation exists about us, *no one* has enough nourishment either in quantity or quality, even the richest. People go hundreds of miles to bring back on their backs a pood of flour, and in many cases are robbed on the way. Of course, all groceries we have forgotten have ever existed. We roast rye for coffee, and drink it without sugar. . . .

Our worst anxiety is about George and Vera, concerning whom we know nothing. In December, Oka was called to P—— to graduate and get his legal degree. He was robbed on the way of his books, clothes and part of his money. He lived with a classmate and they half starved. In April he graduated with honors, and came home as gaunt as from a siege.

Now our life is a very regular one. Up at four-thirty, the boys work without horses to eight, when they come in for rye-coffee and bread and butter. From eight to twelve they work with horses. Then two hours for dinner and sleep. From two to five, work with horses; then tea, and from five-thirty to seven in the garden. At seven-thirty supper—and to bed. I do not get to bed till about ten, as Peter needs a great deal of care in the evenings. It is wonderful how he bears what he does, but he keeps up our courage. His pension is taken from us and all our silver—that beautiful Persian set! My jewelry and all our valuables that were placed for safety in Moscow are lost. There were moments when it seemed our last day here, if not in the world, had come. A friendly peasant said to me the other day, "I doubt whether you realize how near death you were. There was a time when we thought we could not save you, though we swore we would avenge your murder."

Since writing the above, a new decree has gone forth. Our Tver Central Committee has decided that all landowners who wish to plow are to be sent to Siberia and not given land here unless by *special vote* of the commune nearest them. So far the majority are for letting us live on. Their chief argument is that "there will be no one to care for the sick." Never have I had so large and successful a practise as this winter. Medicines are very dear and rare, and our zemstvo doctors and hospitals have none. Now that they are "nationalized," the peasants won't spend money for them. I have managed to keep on hand some of the most needed drugs and, with the faith they have in me, I have made cures that amaze and frighten me, and that are not to be explained on any scientific medical ground. I think God has helped me, and it has more than once turned the tide in our favor. I have gone out nights when the boys were not at home, alone with whoever came for me, though sometimes I was not sure that there was not to be foul play.

In our cooperative shop the other day, as I stood for

SCENES FROM PEASANT LIFE:

Left—Returning from fields.
Right—Corner of village street.
Center—Village fathers.

Top—A village street.
Bottom—Peasant children.

hours in the "tail," waiting my turn, the talk was very animated and mostly about us. The best element is understanding, too late, the immense harm done to Russia by demolishing the big estates and dairy-farms, the chief supply of grain, cattle, butter, pigs. They have ruined us, deprived themselves of between four thousand and five thousand roubles that we spent each year in hiring help, all from our commune, to say nothing of the grain, hay, potatoes, etc., we sold. Some of the people said, "We understand now how wrong we were. You have been ill-treated, but we won't let you be turned out. If we must starve, we will all starve together." And starve I fear many of us must. Rye flour is two hundred and thirty roubles a pood, if you are lucky enough to get it.

This spring very little will be sown, as all the seeds are being eaten up, and next winter must be far worse than now. It seems as if God had forsaken Russia and there is no hope for us but to face a hungering death as bravely as we can. So far Peter has not suffered for anything. I exchanged butter and rye flour for a little sugar and rice for him, and we have eggs. We fed the pigs and chickens all winter on horseflesh, but now the warm weather has begun we can not keep it, so they have to forage for themselves, and we are shooting all the dogs except George's and my Daisy. I will share with them.

Mrs. Roper, please read and send this to Mrs. Clement. I long to hear from you all and have written many times but doubt whether you have received my letters.

(Copy of card sent to Madame Ponafidine's sisters)

Bortniki, June 1, 1918

Still no letters from the outside. Here a great change has taken place in the attitude of the peasants since the approach of the Germans, and they are constantly fawning upon us, and assuring us that they never meant to touch us—"It was owing to outside influence, etc." I do not know which of their fronts shows the worst side of their character. We can get no information in regard to George's fate. A company is formed in Moscow for getting letters through to the occupied states, and we are trying to get into communication with Vera, who is probably in Kiev. A letter costs forty roubles! Everything one needs is not to be had, or too expensive. Not a pen can we get in Ostash-kov, nor any buttons. My sister Jeanne (Princess S.) and family are almost starving. They live by selling in the streets newspapers and various things. No employment is given to aristocrats. Their estates are in ruins. We are better off than any of our family. Peter is as usual. We get him out on the balcony.

Love from
Emma

These letters were the last that were received by our friends from us, and we, too, had no word from the outside world. All communications by letter or newspapers ceased, and we knew nothing of what was happening beyond the frontier of blood-stained Russia. The Soviet papers, printed in too small editions for private circulation, gave us little news and that not of an encouraging character. We were led to believe that all Europe and America were following in the footsteps of Russia, and that communism was being adopted the world over. Surprise has often been expressed by friends here that we should have believed this possible. But we had seen the impossible happen in the huge Russian Empire. Why could not the same thing be repeated in other countries?

We felt as if we were living on an island cut off from all

the world, and our only hope was that if the condition of the rest of the world was not as pictured, there would be intervention. Oh, the hopes that would rise when news passed secretly, carefully worded, that the Allies were moving on Petrograd! We could not imagine that we were forsaken. After the Bolsheviki had made a separate peace with Germany, it seemed impossible that our old friends— the French, for whom Russia had made such sacrifices in 1914-15, the English, who had never called in vain on Russia in those first years of the war to divert German forces from the Western Front—would leave us to our fate. We felt that the world must understand that Bolshevism was not Russia, that the Russian army was the victim and not the cause, that the Russia that was their ally existed, though bound and helpless. And so, month after month, we who had no real knowledge of events "outside," clung to the rosy, very indefinite but deep-rooted faith that means were being taken for our salvation. Even to-day, the Russians have a very hazy idea of the history of the world beyond the Russian frontiers from 1917 on. It is perhaps more correct to say that they have little definite knowledge as to Russia at large beyond the state or village in which they live. There are still trusting souls who look for "them to send us help."

CHAPTER SIXTEEN

Evicted

IN SPITE of the reassuring words of the Commissar we felt that there was a sword hanging over us, and in April, 1919, it fell, when an order came to vacate the house. A Commission arrived, including men from Moscow, who took over the estate. All the people who had been with us before the Revolution were turned off as being tainted with "bourgeois" ideas. Our herdsman, who had a family and had been with us a long time, was told to go. He had no land, and it was condemning him and his family to misery. Though he was a simple peasant, no more mercy was shown to him than to us. Until summer, when he could get a job as village herdsman, he lived on what he could beg. He came to us nights, and I would give him little packages of flour—very little for we had little.

The Commission explained that Bortniki had long enough been in our hands, that it rightly belonged to the people, and that everything raised on it should go to the people instead of to our living in luxury. It was decided to make it a *sovkhoz*, a Soviet farm. An experienced agriculturist was introduced as the representative of the Agricultural Department, and in no way as boss. He was permitted to do nothing without the unanimous vote of the workmen and their wives. The workmen were told that they would be furnished with all they needed, not only quarters and food but also clothing, as payment, and all the balance of what was raised on the place was to be taken by the Government for the "people."

I went around with the Commission and our inventory, and many were the curious incidents that occurred. The new farm manager was a clever, unscrupulous man. He knew his business well, was a successful farmer, a Communist in order to be on the "right side of the fence," determined to adapt himself to the new conditions and profit by every breeze. To us he was as friendly outwardly as he dared be; he was on the side of the Soviet in fleecing us, and on our side in fleecing them. He outwitted us both. He made out the inventory in pencil, and when he had copied it we found he had in many cases halved the number of articles or mentioned them vaguely. In this way he was able to annex much for himself and slip over a great deal to us. At first we were rather staggered. Wasn't this condoning robbery? And yet was it not our own property we were helping him to save for us? This was the beginning of situations so complicated, so bizarre, that we soon lost all sense of "mine and thine," truth and falsehood, honesty and dishonesty.

The new manager V settled in the little cottage where our superintendents had always lived, with a buxom young woman, his mistress, leaving his family in the native village. This woman was also an apt pupil of the prevailing morality. V could count on her loyal help in outwitting the Soviet and us. At the same time she was loyal to us, smuggling us some provisions and clothing if we remained silent when she "stole" from V some of the things he had stolen from us without the knowledge of the Commission. If the above is a complicated explanation, the deeds were not less so!

We were permitted to live in the little bungalow that had been my first home in Russia. We were told that we could "use until needed by the Government" any furniture we wished, and we decided to take the fullest advantage of this gracious permission, hoping to be able to "steal" some of it with what we could foresee would be the tacit consent of V. I made a plan of the rooms to scale and measured furniture when no one was looking. The result was that every room was packed with furniture. We took the piano and many of the best pieces and hangings, though the latter did not fit the windows. With refinement of cruelty that class hatred has made the outstanding method of the Bolshevik leveling process, we were ordered to leave the house on Easter Sunday. Easter is the most loved of all the Church holy-days in Russia, and the peasants broke their stolid apathy in such indignation ("No one would turn a dog out on Easter!" they said) that they obtained a reprieve for us, and we were given that last Sunday in the old home.

A Jewish friend had brought me from Petrograd about three pounds of white flour, half a pound of sugar and a small handful of raisins, and some peasants gave me a few eggs, so that we had a small quantity of the Easter cakes and eggs, without which no one in Russia celebrates Easter. I cooked the last dinner, and (the dining table being the last bit of furniture to be moved) the boys and I sat down with our peasant friends to the last meal. Again a natural delicacy that surprised us was shown by these rough simple men, who tried to keep the conversation going to divert my husband and me.

The next day several peasants came and spent the day helping us move. They lifted my husband's mattress and laid it on a Persian rug spread on the floor, then holding the corners, carried him. As he felt himself being taken through the front door, he gropingly put out his hand and, touching it, said, "For the last time." One of the men hearing him said in such a hearty cheery voice that the words seemed almost possible of fulfillment, "No, no, your Excellency, it is not the last time, and when you are brought back and given your rights, remember, we must be the ones to carry you again."

Five months later, these men did carry him, but it was to take him beyond the reach of any Bolsheviki.

The bungalow had always been used as a guest house, and had neither cooking stove nor pantry. A cousin of ours had a tiny stove with place for two small pots. This was set up in one of the rooms, and all our provisions were placed in boxes in the attic. We were given flour enough to last till the new crops came in, and just enough potatoes to plant, so that we never dared to eat one. A little sauerkraut and a small amount of salt completed our supplies. We had a horse, a cow that was not then giving milk, and two hens. The latter seemed to understand our needs, for they laid as no two hens ever did, insuring one or two eggs every day for Mr. Ponafidine. When he died, one chicken was killed and the leg of the other was broken by the Communist work people on the estate, but we managed to get hold of the wounded hen, and when Alec came home we broke our long fast and had real chicken meat.

We started our new life. Oka left early every morning to row across the lake to his place of work in the Forestry Department. He was supposed to receive as pay all that he would need: thirty pounds of flour a month, boots, ma-terial for clothing, kerosene, soap, a certain amount of fats, cereals, meat, tea and sugar. In fact, however, during two years he had only something like sixty pounds of flour, that is, sometimes a little flour but more often three or four pounds of grain of some kind. We would put this through a coffee-mill. Meats and fats we never had, nor any gro-ceries; soap, only enough for sparing toilet use, none for laundry purposes; matches in a very small quantity, salt the same, and very little kerosene.

The baking problem was my great difficulty. Though there were plenty of ovens in the various buildings on the estate occupied by the Soviet work people, it was a favor

I had to ask, a favor often grudgingly, even insolently granted, though out of our meager allowance I always made a "loaf for the children." When Oka returned in the evening, I had his dinner ready—sauerkraut thickened with flour, rye bread, tea of dried apple leaves or berries. As the spring came on, our soup was made more palatable with the young nettles or wild sorrel, but we did not yet have our own vegetables. One and another of the peasants or acquaintances would smuggle in something for my husband. Sometimes, answering a tap at the window late at night, I would find a little milk, a bit of cottage cheese, a small fish— something that enabled us to give our invalid more suitable food.

His blindness made it possible for us to deceive him, and our sense of truth being by this time blunted, it was easy to get him to eat any little dainty that had come to us, for he would never consent to eat anything unless assured that we had the same. He would ask the boys to tell him what I was eating, and they always insisted that there was enough for us all. One day, when he had something that had been brought him, we happened to have a friend who was sharing with us our usual soup. Mr. Ponafidine called him to the bedside and said, "Please tell me what my wife is eating." I made frantic signs to our friend, and he, seizing the situation, fell in with it but overacted his part by calmly announcing that I was eating chicken: Hopelessly, my poor husband exclaimed, "I knew they were deceiving me, and you are with them." After that it was more difficult to manage him. One of our Jewish acquaintances, a lumber merchant, had been arrested and sent into temporary exile to the south, where he had considerable personal liberty and plenty of food during the summer. From time to time he sent us small packages of rusks, sometimes even adding a few ounces of hard candy, a great luxury, to be used as sugar.

I spent hours reading aloud. Though our Russian library had been taken away from us, we found in the attic a pile of Dumas' works in paper covers. These books with so much action in them were a tremendous source of comfort to us in taking our minds off the present and particularly from the constant fear for George and Alec. Evenings, when Oka came home, after his dinner of soup and bread he had a little rest while I made his father comfortable for the night and read him to sleep. Fortunately, we had been permitted to choose for our vegetable garden a plot near our windows, so that when working out there we could constantly keep watch over the invalid, for we were in constant dread of the heart attacks that were increasing in frequency and violence.

In our part of Russia, the "white nights" from May to July made it possible to be in the garden until very late. So we did our work at this time, and on Sundays, when Oka was home, peasants would help him when they dared.

The summer wore on, broken by occasional domiciliary visits, with various threats and unpleasantness but nothing serious for us. It was heart-breaking, however, to see the work of years in building up our estate to be, as it was considered, one of the most scientifically run farms in the State of Tver, go to ruins. The superintendent V tried to maintain the scheme of nine years' rotation of crops and the proper care of the cattle and horses, but he was hampered by the universal curse of the times, absence of authority. At the meeting held every morning, instead of the preceding evening, to plan for the coming day, he could only suggest, not order or even guide. No one person was in charge of horses, or harness, of feeding of cattle or care of machinery. Each day in the meeting it was decided, or attempts were made to decide, what particular work each man and woman were to do that day. The result was much talking and arguing, sometimes lasting till breakfast time, when it happened more than once that they began the day's plowing with horses that had not been fed, as the workmen had not been able to decide unanimously who was to do it. At noon, the men who had been plowing turned the horses into the stalls for some one else to feed—just who had not been decided—and went to their lunch. In the afternoon, still another group continued plowing, for one of the principles was that to obtain the best results, a man must change his occupation. As in so much of the Bolshevik program, practise and theory are two different things. Unfortunately, change of occupation did not extend to animals, and the same horses, hungry and thirsty, were led out by a fresh, well-fed group of men.

Some days after the estate was taken over, we heard the unmistakable sounds of lashing a horse. I was reading aloud and it was hard to control my voice, but I went on, hoping my husband would not notice what was happening. Suddenly he burst out, "I have thanked God sometimes that blindness prevents my seeing what these brigands are doing, and now I must pray for deafness." The treatment of our horses, each of them my friend, was one of the hardest things to bear. I went out to find one of the strongest, best work-horses, harnessed to a rake, lying passively, enduring the whip rather than attempt to rise. I hunted up V, for I had learned that my own remonstrances made things worse. Indeed, my mere presence would sometimes bring needless cruelty. V went, stopped the man and made an inquiry based on the only argument then in use, "injury to the property of the people." He was unable to find out when the poor beast had last been fed and watered. Certainly, neither he nor any of the others had been attended to during the previous twenty-four hours. By the end of the summer several horses were dead and others wrecks, afflicted with a terrible skin disease covering them like a stiff coat that made free action of the muscles impossible. The veterinarian was sent for several times, but he had almost no medicines nor the needed oil to lubricate the skin.

Our horse had to pasture with those of the Soviet and was under the same conditions, but though he had not had a ration of grain for years, he was glossy and healthy, for Oka and I took good care of him and the cow. Whenever he caught the disease from the other horses, I took him into the lake and scrubbed him well with green soap, and then with my fingers worked into the skin the precious ointment which, together with the soap, the veterinarian had given me. He shared his small stock with me, especially iodine, for he said it was no use giving it to the workmen—they wouldn't bother with the horses anyway. So among the thin, collar-galled horses, our sleek old animal (the poorest of the lot had been given to us) looked better than any of the younger horses. In the herd, too, our cow stood out as almost a different creature from her less fortunate communistic sisters. Our vegetable garden was watered and weeded, in contrast to the adjoining wilderness of weeds where onions and carrots were fighting a losing battle. One of the things that led to our final expulsion, I think, was the demoralizing effect these contrasts had. Commissions from Moscow came several times to inspect the state farms. As the leather-coated, high-booted "comrades" went about, conducted by V and a delegation of workmen and their wives, one would hear the same questions: "What horse is that—so different from the others?"

"Our Lady's horse," some one would say.

"What, have you a 'Lady' still? Remember, ladies do not exist."

In the herd our cow drew attention. "That cow has an owner. She belongs to the Ponafidines," V would say with secret malice, for he had learned the fatal blight of communism on defenseless cattle and children, and was never in sympathy with it in his heart. In the vegetable garden, the question arose as to why only a part was weeded and cultivated. "Because this part is cared for by an owner," again V had the courage to answer. Even in the fields, where the rye and oats had stakes driven to show what we had sown, ours was thicker. Evidently under Communism some of the seeds had been "socialized."

Before the Revolution, horses and cattle had been very differently treated. The peasants' way of handling them was not ours any more than was their way of caring for their own and their family's comfort and health, nor was it marked by any great degree of wisdom or kindness, so that the cattle and horses often came in for rather rough treatment. But on the whole, deliberate cruelty to animals, except when the driver was drunk, was not so great as among the peasants of many other countries. There was far more of the personal touch in the handling of these our helpless servants. Before the war, the Society for the Prevention of Cruelty to Animals was becoming more and more active in the cities, where there was naturally more call for protecting cab and dray horses, but I doubt if even *there* the Society's reports record any more lurid cruelties than do those of other countries, ours not excepted.

That first summer, when our meadowland was curtailed by the peasants, the pasture given us was maliciously chosen at a distance and separated from us by fields assigned to peasants, making it a problem how our animals were to get there. I asked the peasant committee, who were in their most brutal mood, if we could drive our cattle through their fields, and the answer came as quick as a flash, "If you dare do it, we will rip open the belly of your herdsman." As our cows had no wings, it was a serious problem for us.

My sons, however, ingeniously fenced off all the lawn and hillsides within the radius assigned to us into minute enclosures, on one of which they kept the horses until all the grass was eaten clean, then moved them to the next, where the grass had had time to grow. One night a very intelligent little mongrel cow-dog of ours barked and scratched on the wall under our windows so persistently that we were wakened. The boys slept at the other side of the house and, tired out by the work in the fields that was then new to them, did not wake. Tsigan (Gypsy) was so insistent and so human in his calls for help that my husband said I had better go out and see what was up. It was a very warm night, and dark, and I went out barefooted with only a kimono thrown over me. The horses had been penned for the night directly under our windows, but peering as I might in the darkness, I could not see a form. I went to the improvised gate and found the bars down, evidently the work of "Freena," a magnificent heavy-weight Belgian mare that was noted for her cleverness in opening doors and untying knots. Tsigan ran ahead of me, jumping and barking. I followed him into the fields, going farther than I realized, anxious to round up the horses before they damaged the "people's" property by getting into our former fields of grain. At last at the outskirts of the woods I distinguished in the darkness the outlines of Pushka, a light, cream-colored horse, and knew they were together. I called one and another by name, and soon in the darkness big forms loomed up and soft muzzles touched me. Taking one of the horses by the forelock and talking to the others, I started home. Tsigan, true to his calling, barked and rounded up the laggards. When nearly home, I saw, silhouetted against the sky, two figures coming toward me. I dreaded that they might be hostile peasants, but they turned out to be my sons; their father, worried by my long absence, had managed to wake them. Of course I had a lecture from my sons, but it was better than facing angry peasants, as we should have done had our horses been found by them.

The attitude of the kindliest peasants when Communism came to them would be an interesting study to a "behaviorist." Care for property and live stock seems to be primarily associated solely with ownership. Remove all ownership, all individual responsibility and property rights, and wanton or careless destruction and neglect follow, which for animals entail cruelty and suffering. From this distance, that and many other to us novel psychological problems seem of interest, but at the time they were grim tragedy.

Little by little throughout the summer of 1919 the intendant V managed by night to get things away from the estate. His house, already well stocked from the "liquidation" of other estates in which he had taken part, became so filled that it excited the cupidity of his fellow villagers, and they reported to the Communistic Party in Ostashkov that Comrade V was stealing "people's property." A delegation with a Chairman was sent, and property that was easily recognized as belonging to estates was found in V's house and confiscated. At the same time, to make this work more thorough, the house was pretty well looted! V was ordered to the city, arrested, and for some time we knew nothing of him. One day he reappeared, as irrepressible and debonair as ever, and told us the whole story. We, who were forgetting how to laugh, did so that evening. He told us how he was called before his judge, the Chairman of the Committee detached to make the domiciliary visits. When he described this man's perfidy, V's indignation was comical. Turning to my husband, he said, "Do you remember that brown suit of yours that you missed and I had stolen? Well, the rascal was calmly wearing it! Do you remember Alexander Petrovich hunting for your knife? I had annexed it and—there it was brazenly lying on this man's desk! Then I saw the Tolstois' clock I had taken hanging on the wall. Can you imagine it! And this man accusing me of stealing!"

He joined merrily in our shouts of laughter, though I imagine not quite realizing the angle of the picture that most touched our sense of humor. The end of it was what we later learned to expect whenever a great noise was raised about bringing to justice a Communist accused of dishonesty. V was returned to his job. His personal property, together with what he had annexed, disappeared. What became of the stolen people's property, neither we, the former owners, nor V, ever knew. The incident was closed, and V returned with renewed energy to fill his house again.

CHAPTER SEVENTEEN

The Children's Colony

OUR estate was taken over in April, 1919, in as prosperous a condition as possible after four years of war and revolution. The few horses and cows left were in good condition, the barns stocked with sufficient hay and grain. V was an experienced farmer and, with authority over the farm-hands, could have made a success. As it was, he was tied by the comrades, without whose vote he was powerless. We soon saw striking instances of the results of Bolshevik theory.

In the scheme of rotation of crops, clover is sown with oats; the latter is harvested the first year, and then the field yields three years of clover. The first clover year is of course the best, the last two falling off in quality. I had gone through the fields with V when he took charge of the estate, carefully comparing all the boundaries with the plans and explaining the crops that were to go into each field that summer. He was constantly being sent for to the city to attend various meetings, which had no regard for seasons; the farmers would be called to them in the midst of harvest or when a long day's work perhaps would have saved the grain from a coming storm.

And so one day V was ordered to go to Ostashkov at a very busy time in the summer to attend an agricultural meeting of several days' duration. Before leaving, he called all the comrades to discuss what was to be done during his absence. Among the pressing work was the plowing up of the third clover field. From the window where I sat most of the day, reading aloud, I could see what was going on about the place. Several teams harnessed to plows started for the field. After an hour or so, I saw the men returning, the horses unharnessed, and a meeting called. Later the horses were again harnessed, and the men started, but in another direction. It seems that when they found how hard it was to plow the field after its four years (one of oats, three of clover), they had voted to try the first year's field as probably softer and more easily worked! And so the better crop was "by unanimous vote" ruthlessly sacrificed, not only causing an actual loss in clover but upsetting the nine-year order of rotation of crops, a still more vital mistake.

In one way and another we saw the work and plans of years on the estate go to pieces. The workmen had no interest, did the farming in a slovenly way, and cared for the live stock so poorly that there was scarcely milk enough for the families on the place. Butter-making and the furnishing of milk to families of Red Army men were given up.

Soon after we moved out, the house was cleared of furniture. I do not know where it was taken but the house was later prepared to accommodate children. Long tables, cots, etc., began to come, and we heard it was to be used as a "summer colony" for poor city children. Again we saw an excellent program worked out on paper. The children, aged from seven to twelve, boys and girls, were to have a well-planned routine, light house duties, nature study, some gardening, reading, swimming, etc. The menu, too, was well planned and a good supply of provisions that, so far as the general public was concerned, had long since disappeared from sight, such as white flour, chocolate, cereals and even jam, was brought. Butter, eggs, vegetables were supposed to be found in abundance on the estate. The head of the colony was a young man whom we knew well, a teacher in the village schools. The staff of girl teachers included one who was well known as a public immoral character and another who had lost her position in a school for the same reason.

The colony arrived, and for the first week the régime

seemed to promise success. The children were painfully antagonistic to us. I think their attitude the first weeks hurt me more than any of the class hatred directed toward us ever had. I avoided going out of the bungalow on the side toward the manor house. Children's faces at the window were always watching for us, and tongues run out, little fists clinched. Daily they were taught of the selfish *pomeschiks* (squires, landowners) who had lived here in luxury, condemning the laboring mass to poverty and crowded cities.

Gradually the picture changed. The same old story of theory and practise again. The daily routine was replaced by no supervision of games or work. Evenings, the staff had parties that consumed much of the supplies intended for the children, to which young men from the post and telegraph stations near by, as well as others, came. After supper, boating or rambling in the woods attracted every one of those in charge until a late hour. The physician who was to make weekly visits as well as to answer emergency calls came but once during the summer. The weekly Russian bath was given only a few times. The summer had many raw rainy days, and as no toilet arrangements had been supplied in the house, the shivering children would rush down to the lake, dash a little water on their faces, and run back to the shelter of the house. Owing to lack of care, the plumbing got out of order, and the fifty children and a number of adults soon put our lovely old garden with its hundred-year-old linden walk in such condition that, as one of the peasants expressed it in disgust, "One could only walk there with high boots."

Gradually, as the children felt the neglect and the lack of food they began to change toward us. They would stop by our porch, where my husband, often lying in a *chaise longue*, would talk to them. At first their talk was half insolent, then they became interested, and finally they showed a friendly spirit. They began to ask embarrassing questions, to which a truthful reply, if reported, would get us into trouble. "Was this your house before?"

"Yes."

"What right had they to take it from you if it belonged to you?"

"Oh, because in a Communistic country all must be in common."

"Then, if all is in common, why don't you have sugar and such things? Why don't we get a cup of milk with every meal as they promised us?"

Then came other questions that showed the inner workings of the colony. "Why do the teachers have parties and eat up all the jam and sugar and give us none? Why did A. L., when she went home for the week-end, take all the supply of milk, leaving us none?"

It was often difficult to find evasive answers, and though we were very careful, before many weeks the children were ranged on our side—offering to work in our garden rather than grumblingly weed in the Communistic garden.

When an accident occurred, the children would come to me, and when I suggested that they had better go to the teacher, the reply was, "Oh, they won't do anything." The older children would sit and talk with my husband, offering to read to him and relieve me, and even to run down to the lake and get a pail of water. Coming so intimately in contact with them, I saw how ill-cared-for they were—grimy necks and marks on their wrists where washing of their faces and hands ended. They began to complain of not getting enough bread, and we often shared with them. Once one of the children ate a poisonous mushroom, and they came for me. I had never been inside the house since we left it. Even our cats, contrary to the accepted theory of cats caring only for places, stayed by us. To see the child, I had to go to my old room. I saw pinned on the walls many photographs torn from our albums, rooms dismantled, walls scribbled on, a desolation that made my heart ache.

One day a woman from a neighboring village came to me and asked me to come and see her little niece, who had been in the colony and was sick at her house. She said the child had come to her three days before and climbed on her bed, "burning and was now unconscious." I told her I could not interfere, that the colony being responsible and having a doctor, they must attend her. "But they won't. They paid no attention when she was coming down with the sickness and it is useless."

The woman begged so hard that I compromised, saying I would go and see the little girl and then secure the doctor. I went. The child was indeed "burning" and unconscious, and I felt it was typhoid, an epidemic that was raging. Returning, I went to the house and hunted up Ivan, the head of the institution, and asked him if he knew anything of Natasha. "Why, she was around here a while ago. Why do you ask?"

"Please send for her and I will tell you," I replied.

Ivan asked some one to call the teacher "on duty." After some delay she appeared. He asked her where Natasha was. "Somewhere around here," she answered.

"Have you seen her to-day?" I ventured.

"Of course, she was here a minute ago," came the decidedly resentful reply.

"If that is so, she can not be far. Please, Ivan, have her found. I have a very special reason for asking it."

By this time a number of children had gathered around, and one of them piped up, "We haven't seen her for a long time."

"Who sleeps in the bed next to her?" I asked.

As no one seemed to know, the children were called, and

one child said, "Natasha sleeps next to me, but she hasn't been in the bed for several nights."

Then I fear I forgot prudence and told Ivan (who proved later to be a loyal friend of the family) what I thought of him and his care of the children. He sent for the doctor and the aunt, who would not hear of the child's being returned to the "home" but kept her in the village through the long illness that followed.

Another time we were wakened by noises, and found that all had turned out to hunt for the tiniest boy in the colony. Boys in the dormitory, waking, had noticed his empty bed and gone to rouse his teachers. After a long search, the child, almost wild with fear, was found in the woods.

Some parents took their children home before the summer's end, preferring their own poverty and city life to what the children were getting. The parents were indignant, too, at the stories told them of what went on nights among the teachers and their guests. These stories, perhaps exaggerated, certainly had some ground. Several times, children showed us candy which, with sly old looks on their little faces, they said had been given them by such and such a teacher to keep quiet about what they had happened to see.

When I asked one of the teachers how many children they had in the colony, the casual reply was, "I suppose there are fifty at least; that is what we were told, but they never keep still, and when we count them, one time there are more and at others less."

The first of September, the colony broke up. I never heard a parent express willingness to have the experiment repeated, nor was the colony sent to Bortniki again. Nearly all the children came to us to say good-by. Many repeated, "I think it is real mean the way they treat you." "I don't think we have any right to live in your house." "No one had a right to turn you out."

Ivan told us how the children could scarcely be kept off the subject at table; he had to shut up their comments and questions for fear they would do harm. Already we were being accused of putting bourgeois ideas into their heads.

When my husband died in September, I was very much touched by a letter from one of the boys, in which he spoke for himself and others of the children. A year later when, having been turned out of the bungalow, Oka and I took refuge in the city, the welcome children gave us when they happened to meet us in the street or see us from the window often frightened me. I feared it would bring fresh persecutions upon us, for a shrill voice would cry out, "Mama, mama, look—there is our lady the Bolsheviki have driven from her own home." Often a child would rush across the street, on seeing me, and ask breathlessly, "Is it true they have driven you out?" Then I would fairly have to stop his mouth, fearing the torrent of indignation might be heard.

The wonderful official report of the summer colony was a revelation—the foundation for a profound distrust of all Soviet official statistics and reports. The years that followed brought repetitions of this instance. Whenever facts were known to us personally (as in the Forestry and Fishery Departments), we found Soviet reports and statistics distorted.

That the Bortniki Colony was not an exception in the way it was carried on was proved to us by an incident that occurred in the only other colony near enough for us to have personal knowledge. It was situated on a small river, in which the peasants living in a village some distance downstream found the body of a small girl. Inquiry showed that several days had passed from the time she was last seen to the day the peasants went to the colony to know if the child belonged to it. It transpired that the little one was a member of the colony and that she had not been missed.

CHAPTER EIGHTEEN

The Death of My Husband

THE summer of 1919 passed without serious conflict with the higher powers; but we had no news from George, and very seldom heard from Alec. My husband failed rapidly after we left the old home. Though brave and philosophical about it, the blow had sunk deep. It was pitiful to see how troubled he was in not being able to locate himself. In the big house he knew where every picture hung and every chair stood; now, in the bungalow, packed full with furniture, he never succeeded in getting his bearings. When he was well enough to be up, I repeatedly led him slowly around the room, letting him touch things, telling him which way each door and window faced; but back in bed he was again confused and lost.

We were having our own vegetables as the summer went on, but our cow gave no milk, and we were not permitted to have any from the farm. Occasionally the women in milking would manage to steal a little, and after dark bring it to our window. The first time I indignantly refused. It was stolen. "But isn't it the milk from your own cows?" the woman insisted in a tense whisper; "Take it, you must not let the Barin go without milk." What was one to do? The milk I had an undoubted right to—but it came to me through the broken trust of an employee. Yes, but she too was a slave—put as a pawn in this estate, with no individual rights. Though something in me rebelled (I suppose it was what little was left of my Puritan conscience), I took it, but have never to this day been able to answer the question that rises in my mind as to whether I was really condoning a theft! As my husband became weaker and our fare more and more unsuitable, I decided, much against Oka's advice, to go to the city and try to get permission to receive daily a quart of milk from our former cows. Oka was sure I should fail, and lay myself open to unpleasantness, if not insult, but the need was imperative. The question was how to leave my husband for so long, as the attacks of angina were becoming more severe and more frequent. The children's colony was still with us at that time, and some of the children eagerly offered to read to him and sit by him and go for the dairy woman for help if he should be worse. This woman had for years been housekeeper for one of our relatives and secretly did all she could for us, so I decided to leave all remedies where she could get at them and to take the risk.

The official reason for nationalizing the milk was to have it for the children and the sick and aged and poor. Taking with me a copy of this decree, I went to Ostashkov to the Sanitary Department and stated my case. Naturally every doctor there knew well my husband's physical condition. I was very politely received and great surprise was expressed that the *sovkhoz* (Soviet farm) refused to sell even a glass of milk for a sick man. They said they would "give instructions" to the Agricultural Department, but knowing the magic power of "a paper," I refused to leave without one such and well sealed. Armed with this and the decree, I went to the Agricultural Department under which we lived and on whom our very existence depended. Here, too, they were as polite as in the other Department. "But why did you go to the Sanitary Department? We will gladly give you permission to have milk. We supposed you did," etc.

"I went to the Sanitary Department first to get the medical certificate stating my husband's need of milk, without which I knew I could not get any," I replied.

"Well, you certainly are entitled to milk for your sick husband. I am going to Bortniki some time this week and will see that the manager gives it to you," said the Commissar.

Again I was determined not to go without a paper. I told him that each day without proper nourishment meant a great deal, and so asked him to give me a written instruction to V so that we could get the milk at once. It took a great deal of arguing and, finally, seeing there was little hope of getting rid of me, he wrote an order to "give Comrade Ponafidine one quart of milk a day for her sick husband." This was duly signed, but I insisted on seals being added, and went home in triumph. We had milk for two or three days; then came a most characteristic order to V, saying that "all instructions concerning the *sovkhoz* under your care are annulled up to yesterday's date. P. S. Including milk for the Ponafidines."

V brought it in to read to us. He was full of the humor of the situation, though realizing that it carried more of tragedy to us. So great was the suspicion, jealousy and spying on one another that V did not dare to give us milk, as I am sure he would have done all along. Even the woman who smuggled us milk might, under other circumstances, have been the first to denounce him to the Commissar.

So I had to go to the city again, and again I was politely received by the same Commissar who had signed both these contradictory orders. When I told him that V had ceased giving me milk, he expressed great surprise and asked me the reason. It was an awkward moment, but I took the bull by the horns, and said, "He received orders from the Commissariat not to give us any more."

"I never gave any such orders. You can always have the milk. I am coming soon to Bortniki and will tell the manager so," was the cool reply.

"But you did give orders. I myself read them over your signature," I insisted.

"There must be some mistake. Perhaps I signed the wrong paper."

"Then that is simple. Please now sign the right one." And I stayed till he did. This was not the last time that the comedy was repeated—with perfect politeness.

In July my sister-in-law Princess Shakhovskoy had died, really from lack of nourishment, and we had dreaded telling my husband of it, fearing the shock. We broke it to him just after he had been given a dose of heart medicine and Oka and I had everything in readiness for an attack. But after a few seconds of silence he said, "Thank God, she is at rest. Life is too hard."

That was beginning to be the universal attitude toward death. Joy that a loved one was spared the horrors of our life was greater than grief for our loss.

The heart attacks were becoming more frequent and more painful. At last the end came suddenly the evening of September 23, 1919. Oka and I were by him, listening to V, who was pouring out his woes and philosophizing, keeping us in bursts of laughter. I think my husband laughed too much, for he only had time to call my name and lost consciousness. V jumped up and left the room. Oka and I alone worked over him a very long time, using the remedies and means that so far had always brought him back; but this time they failed.

It was about nine o'clock in the evening, I think. We were surrounded by hostile people, or at best by those who dared not show friendship. Only the dairy woman could be counted on, and she came and helped Oka perform the last offices and in the Russian way lay the body on a table, cover the mirror, fold up the bed. Before midnight, when she left, all was in order.

Alec was only about four hours by train from us but was as inaccessible as if he had been thousands of miles away.

Top—Where for three hundred years the Ponafidines had been buried.
Bottom—Sunday—waiting for the church-bells.

Our peasant neighbors.

Letters took days and weeks to come. We, as private citizens, could not send a telegram nor could any one go to take an oral message, as he was stationed in the "military zone" on the Polish front. The military Commissariat of Ostashkov promised to wire at once to the regiment and procure leave for Alec. Whether from carelessness or from intention, the telegram did not reach him till after the funeral.

Oka sent notices as he could to friends and relatives, but it was not a time for thinking of individual sorrow. The only response came from one cousin, who with her son immediately arrived from their estate in the same county. Had it not been for the presence of these two, we should have been absolutely alone, surrounded by hostile faces. None of the occupants of the estate came into the bungalow; even V was afraid to show his sympathy by doing so, though the strange illogical man did a bigger thing by getting us a coffin. At this time when the mills were silent, nails not to be found, coffins were so rare that they were rented only to carry bodies as far as the cemeteries, and then brought back to be used again.

We were determined, however, to have a coffin. There were boards in plenty on the estate, but we were not permitted to have any, though the peasants remonstrated, saying that in past days we had always given boards whenever they had asked for materials for coffins. It might have been possible for us to obtain one in the city if we had had flour or salt to pay for it, but we did not have enough. V, however, as a Communist, might succeed; and he went to the city and did so. Before starting, as we were talking to him about it, the post came, and he silently handed us a letter from headquarters again informing him that "all documents and instructions concerning the estate were annulled." Even he felt the bitterness of this attempt again to withhold milk from him who had gone beyond the reach of further trouble.

In those sad days the peasants rallied around us. The bungalow was filled during each of the several services held, though of course no Communist came. We put off the funeral day after day, hoping Alec would come. In Russia the Psalms are read continuously beside the silent body, generally by some clerical or monastic person. We four took our turn day and night, and from Wednesday to Sunday one of our two cousins or Oka or I knelt there, never for a moment leaving our dear one. It seemed to me that I could not have any one but those who loved him near him, even the unconscious body, and we never forgot the two who shared with us the vigils of those days and long nights.*

At last we were obliged to give up waiting for Alec. The cemetery was on the opposite side of the lake, and the peasants prepared one of the great boats, capable of carrying fifty or sixty persons. We had to go over a mile to the landing place, and the peasants would not hear of our driving but insisted on themselves carrying the casket. There is a beautiful old custom in Russia of halting on the threshold for a short prayer as the owner of the house leaves it for the last time. We were no longer the owners; early in 1917 every one of these same peasants had brutally told us so—that we could not have a stick of wood to heat our rooms without their permission. To-day, the peasants turned to us in friendship and sympathy. Early on the day of the funeral they brought cartloads of juniper boughs from the woods; these, finely chopped up, were strewn the entire length of the road from the house to the lakeshore. When

---

*And yet in her day of trouble we can not even send her a word of sympathy without danger of injuring her. While writing the above, word has come to us in a roundabout guarded way, that this cousin has lost both her sons. The one who was with us at the time of my husband's death has been banished, and the other executed.

the casket was carried out in the face of the assembled Communistic farm-hands who stood at a distance, sullenly, with hats on their heads, these peasants with bared heads stopped in front of the door for the rector to offer the customary prayer. The road wound for some distance through our estate to the place where a gate marked the end of our property and the beginning of that of our village neighbors. Here again, to our amazement, the peasants without a word from us or from their priest, stopped in silent acceptance of what they had so loudly denounced—private ownership. At that time we did not realize as we can in looking back, how deep-rooted and ineradicable in the human consciousness are certain impulses—ownership, family ties, belief in God—impulses which despite arguments to the contrary will, in moments of stress, find expression.

It took real physical courage at this period for the peasants so openly to show their sympathy. The people from the village we passed through joined our procession, and the boat was packed. The occupants of a motor-boat, recognizing us, stopped their engine and stood with bared heads until we had passed. Arriving at the village where in the churchyard the Ponafidines had for three hundred years been buried, again a quiet and apparently sympathetic throng awaited us. We went to the church for the service and then waited for the daily steamer to pass, vainly hoping that Alec might be on it. There were no hostile demonstrations at the church, for the anti-religious propaganda had as yet scarcely touched the villages.

It was not till five days after the funeral that Alec came, having been granted a two-week leave. George never knew of his father's death, for we had lost all communication with him. He himself, as we learned years later, fell in October, 1920.

CHAPTER NINETEEN

Outwitting the Usurpers

WE WHO were left had to go on living, and Alec thought of the long cold winter, when the big Russian stove devoured so much wood and when Oka would be free only on Sundays to replenish the supply. So he went to work quietly, assisted by one or another of the peasants, who would unobtrusively join him in the woods to help with the double saw. The sections thus cut he hauled to the house with the aid of our one horse, and piled close to the door. In the evenings he and Oka sawed the big pieces into shorter lengths which Oka could gradually split for our use. Too soon Alec had to leave us. The days shortened. Oka had to start for work before light, and came back after dark. My occupation gone, the day and night nursing and the responsibility of years ended, I was left stranded. The housework was slight; there was no material to do even the necessary mending; and there were many hours to think.

What added to our loneliness was the darkness. Oka calculated that the kerosene he had a right to hope for as part pay would last us only if we allowed ourselves two hours of light, and this not with lamps, for they consumed too much kerosene. All of northern Russia used bottles. A hole in the cork permitted the passage of a tiny wick, and the light was not only feeble but very unstable, seldom surviving any movement—a calamity, as matches began to be scarce.

As the autumn went on, reading after two-thirty became difficult, and soon after four it was quite dark. I could not hope for Oka's return before six o'clock—on stormy nights he would be later—and I sat in darkness, thinking of his battling his way on foot across the frozen lake, with nothing but a stick for protection if attacked by wolves, for we

were all disarmed. The table was set by daylight, and our
soup and potatoes made ready. Oka would go to his room,
where everything was laid out in his accustomed way, so
that he could wash in the dark; then our precious bottle was
lighted when we sat down to supper, and afterward placed
on the piano, where Oka's music made us both forget for a
time. When the two hours were up, we extinguished our
light and sat in darkness. We could see the windows of the
house lighted up, for some of the workmen and their families
lived there and had kerosene. Looking over at the lighted
windows of the rooms where we and generations before us
had passed happy days made our loneliness greater. We did
little talking, for there was so little we could bear to speak
of—the past?—the present, with the constant heartache
for George? for Vera and the baby? for Alec? And the
future—that would not bear talking of. We simply lived
from hour to hour, day by day, trying to have strength only
for each step as it came—and the strength never failed.

I think the darkness of that winter, added to the long
blindness of my husband that I had to witness, is the cause
of my present love of light. The dim candle-lit dining-
rooms, now so popular, chill me, however bright the company, and I am impelled wherever possible to turn on more
and more light. The kerosene famine I have no doubt was
the cause of more nervous breakdowns, more suicides, than
was any other of the deprivations suffered by Russians during those first years after the Revolution.

Before Alec left, we had a family council, trying to look
the future in the face. We realized that my husband's long
sickness and loss of sight had been a strong protection to
us, and that now we might anticipate worse treatment. Oka,
who had so far escaped active military service, might at any
time be sent off and I left alone to get a living from the soil.
We decided, therefore, that risks which, for my husband's

sake, we had not wished to run, should now be taken: we must in some way "steal" or hide some of our property. Also a part of the grain, as soon as it was threshed.

A woman lived with us, very polite but watchful, who, we knew, reported our movements, so that we had in some way to outwit her. We had honorably kept faith with the peasants when they had told us we could touch nothing, and they themselves had refrained from taking anything from the house, waiting for a paper to state how our property was to be divided. In fact, nothing was ever touched by the peasants. All we lost was through Bolshevik liquidation.

Since Bolshevism had come in, every visit made us, under whatever pretense, ended in an open or secret requisitioning of whatever suited the visitors. One day, after such a business visit, when I went to the landing, driving our "visitor," it was at the same time to meet Oka, who was returning on that steamer. Our guest had appropriated Oka's last decent suit of civilian clothes, and was wearing them. It was as good as a play to watch the expression on Oka's face as the steamer drew up and he looked at the man standing by me and gradually recognized his own clothes. I introduced the two men and the incident was closed!

Though we needed many things, food, bread was our chief thought, and we decided that in some way, when the grain was threshed, we must hide a part and also try to barter or conceal what would save us in the black days that we knew were before us. We could not dispose of anything we had without serious danger, for in the inventory of the contents of the house, abridged and edited as it was, a cross marked every article given to us to use, and the documents were safe in the archives of the county Department of Agriculture in Ostashkov. Unexpected friends, however, always appeared in unexpected ways at critical moments. A man we had never known personally, who had charge of the archives, suggested the possibility of further "editing." He said he would choose a busy moment and risk letting us have the document for two or three days. With the help of V, the papers were copied, only all the crosses that would identify the articles in our possession being omitted. As we had no typewriter, the handwriting presented considerable risk, but we counted on the mentality of those we had to deal with, and V volunteered not only to copy the list but the several signatures! All this was done, and the papers returned to their place.

From this time on, we gradually smuggled bits of furniture, bedding, curtains and such articles as would be least noticed, out of the bungalow, either hiding them or, with V's help, bartering them for what we most needed. Then a heavy blow came to us in the removal of V. Several men of various kinds followed, but all of them in one way or another were hard on us, so that not only was there no hope for help from them but we had to carry on all further operations secretly under their watchful eyes. We had become expert, however, and from the attic by night carried boxes and bags down to the lake; from there Oka rowed them to the opposite side, where peasants waited for him in the darkness. So gradually we had things hidden in twelve different places. It was amazing to see how easy it was, in some ways, to dupe our over-lords, owing to their ignorance. We had a large eight-sectioned screen which in olden times divided the bedroom occupied by my husband's parents. The work was exquisitely fine and the colors unfaded. This screen we had succeeded in proving to be necessary to us, and though he could no longer see it, the knowledge that the screen was there had been a great satisfaction to my husband. He had urged me to try to save these pieces of embroidery, as well as those in two large fine screens of the same period. Incredible as it seems, we were able to get these beautiful and valuable embroideries out and replace them by bright colored magazine pictures without any attention being paid to the change! These were among the few articles that we managed to get out of Russia on our backs, and we had the great satisfaction of giving them to those who had made our escape possible—the Clement family and Clement Cochran.

When the time came for threshing our grain, we began to plot some way of concealing a part of it. In the fall of 1919 all the grain was carefully checked, and only as much left to the farmer as was necessary for food and seed. The remainder was taken from the peasants at a nominal price scarcely covering the cost of raising, and from us without any payment. Indeed, they even tried to make us pay for the privilege of threshing it in the barns of our own former estate.

For years we had done all our threshing by machinery, but since Bortniki had been turned into a state farm the leather belt of the threshing machine had been converted into soles for the workmen's boots. Threshing, therefore, both on the estate and on our own little farm had to be done in the old, primitive way of beating with flails. Oka and G, the girl who lived with us, did the threshing, and the grain, carefully measured with her as witness, was stored in one of our rooms, to be divided at the end of the threshing season. Pretending fear that members of one of the many domiciliary raiding parties to be expected might appropriate some of the grain if it were all exposed, and thus get us into trouble, we discussed with G the advisability of having at least a part of it somewhat out of sight. So we brought into G's own room one of the huge chests always to be found in the attic of the old estates. We were able to get many bushels of rye into this chest. Then we brought two large packing cases and, placing them on top of the chest, filled them with the books that had been piled on the floor when our bookcases had been taken. Our Russian library had gone early in the Revolution, but we had a valuable collection of books in various languages, some already out of print, dealing with the several countries in which we had lived. There were also Persian manuscripts, still more precious, which we had succeeded in saving so far. Hundreds of books were packed into these boxes, a labor that took all of us a long time. Then it was impressed upon G that if people came she could protect the grain in her care. The next step was for Oka and me to steal the same grain from G without her suspecting the theft. Our flour was giving out and it became necessary to send rye to the mill, ten or twelve miles distant, to be ground. Oka being at work, it was quite natural to send G. We asked a trusty peasant, R, to take his grain at the same time and help G in lifting the bags of grain. It was possible to go and return the same day, but this did not suit us, so we arranged with R to have his grain put through first and then persuade the miller, who was a friend of ours, to have something happen to the mill that would detain G overnight. So Oka and G packed the bags in the cart, and she, climbing on top, started off in high spirits. Soon after Oka came home in the evening, R appeared, reporting loudly in the presence of bystanders that something had broken down, and poor G did not get her rye ground. He could not wait for her, as his horse was needed at home, and so she was left to follow. He drove home and then rowed in the darkness from his village back to our landing. The three of us went to work, feverishly unpacking the books that made the boxes too heavy for us to lift. Then all the rye was put into bags, and the two men carried them down to the boat and rowed them up to R's village.

Fortunately, his house was situated on the very outskirts of the village, so that there was little danger of their being detected when they carried the bags there, to be hidden in R's haystacks. This done, they returned, replaced the large boxes, repacked them, being careful to have the top layers as they had been. It was after midnight when we finished, congratulating ourselves on the night's nefarious work.

G returned the next morning in very bad humor, complaining that R, "who you think is your friend, deserted me after putting through his own grain, and left me to manage alone as best I could with all those bags. Thanks to others, I loaded them, but he showed how much he cares for your interests."

Naturally, we agreed with her in regard to R's unfaithfulness. Apparently G suspected nothing.

CHAPTER TWENTY

Destitution and Disease

THE winter began with Oka still "militarized" in the Forestry Department, receiving less and less of the necessities of life that were promised as payment. Still, we had nothing to complain of compared with city dwellers, who had no fire-wood and were obliged to break up wooden buildings or use furniture. We had plenty of rye bread and vegetables, though no meat or eggs or groceries of any kind. At one time, horsemeat was occasionally to be obtained. One of the most serious of our deprivations was salt. The civil war cut off our communications with salt-producing parts of the country, and very soon it became our currency, as later did saccharine. Potatoes, which we had longed for, we now had, but a steady diet of boiled potatoes without salt becomes deadly. We were sometimes permitted to send to Alec rusks, potatoes and dried fruit, but no salt, peas or beans. Other things I occasionally was able to smuggle through, but salt never.

The schools suffered for want of books, paper, pens and pencils. We hunted up old copy-books stacked in the attic, kept by fond mothers of many past and gone Ponafidines. By turning them upside down, the children were able to write between the lines. We also found many old pen nibs, which the teachers carefully cleaned and hammered into shape. And yet reports of the wonderful schools and the "wiping out of illiteracy" were spread all over the world. The curriculum of the peasant schools was broadened (on paper); languages, physics, chemistry and other kindred subjects that none of the village teachers had studied were reported as being taught. Even my name figured at one time as a teacher of English and French in a village school!

An attempt was made to have evening schools for teachers, to coach them in the subjects they were to teach, but, so far as we knew, this was dropped almost as soon as begun, except as the schools existed on the program and in reports.

Crops were poor in our part of Russia in 1918, but plentiful in the south, where two years later the terrible famine swept away large numbers in spite of the heroic efforts of the American Relief Administration under Mr. Hoover. Like the sons of Jacob, who journeyed into Egypt to find bread, our peasants went south; but the war and the Revolution threw this burden largely on the women.

As is generally known, amid the destruction that came with the first period of Bolshevism, in the years of military Communism, the railroads suffered in the universal break-up. The Nicholas Railroad, running from Petrograd to Moscow, was badly paralyzed. Lack of management showed itself on every side. Locomotives broke down. Fuel was not prepared in sufficient quantities. There were times when a train stopped and able-bodied passengers were called on to go out and help haul wood, a barn or other convenient building being broken up if there seemed no other way of getting fuel. The number of trains decreased, and it became necessary to limit the number of passengers. Except for the army of peasants going for grain, private persons could not get tickets unless with a medical certificate. The Government officials, Red Army men, and now "baggers" so crowded the trains and railroad stations that the long journey to the southern part of Russia was a formidable undertaking. And yet the women bravely shouldered their bags, endured the terrible crowding, where coupés for four would be occupied by over a dozen, and even corridors and roofs were packed. No conveniences, buffets, inns. And yet they went, old and young. Not to bring back sacks checked in baggage cars but usually only what they could carry on their backs! Their own wants were forgotten, their own baggage reduced to a minimum. Every fiber of their being was strained to carry one pound more of the precious flour the family was waiting for. It was wonderful how much the women learned to carry; it was a labor to which they were unaccustomed.

The South, more fortunate than we at that period as to food, was suffering from typhoid and typhus epidemics; and now, along with the flour, our peasants brought home disease. Like fires, the epidemic broke out all around us. By this time our zemstvos were hoarding their very last medicine, using it only in extreme cases, and my usually large stock was dwindling away. Doctors also were scarce, the war having called for them. I found my hands full. Of all the villages I visited, the sickness could invariably be traced to a member of the family who had been south. Whole families were laid low, with no one to take care of them. Village *skhodkas* were called to discuss the question. In one village where I happened to be, they asked my advice, and I had a long struggle to get them to give up the wild plan they had drawn up. Their idea was to have the whole village take turns in nursing. I tried to make them understand that with the plague of vermin which the baggers brought back with them, the contagion would be carried to every house. I begged them to isolate the few families that had been seized and to get volunteers to devote themselves to the work, and not have any communication with others. In some cases we found old women who consented, or a family whose different members promised to quarantine themselves while nursing their neighbors. But it was a hopeless job; owing largely to the vermin the epidemic spread and spread. No one can realize what it was. Often in unbottoning a shirt and passing my hand inside to place the thermometer under the arm (the universal custom among Russian doctors), I would have to pick the loathsome creatures off my hand and wrist. An apology was not needed when in conversation you drew the attention of your friend to a creeping object on his body or clothes. Soldiers from the front, lack of soap, and, in big cities, of fuel to furnish hot water, made the battle a serious one. In one of his speeches, Trotsky once said, "We are facing three foes—war, famine, vermin, and I think the last is the most dangerous."

How we escaped I do not know. When Oka passed through two villages on his way to the Forestry Department, he would sometimes stop to take the temperature and pulse of some of my patients, sending back word to me to save my going if I were not needed. And yet neither he nor I took the disease. There was little I could do except keep up the heart's action, and fortunately I had a good supply of such remedies, but diet and nursing were not to be had.

A previous epidemic, of Spanish flu, had exhausted all our resources. When that unknown foe faced us I was in despair, and went to our doctors for help. They were themselves not only inexperienced, as were those in this country when that epidemic appeared, but in addition they were limited in hospital nurses and drugs. They told me that if I could get the peasants to take measures in the very beginning, something might be done. As in our cooking, when standard provisions gave out, combinations sometimes the most bizarre gave unexpectedly good results, so in the treatment of Spanish flu, the combination of lying on the Russian stove, pouring down raspberry tea, quinine and Dover's powders and castor oil, which were then to be had, seldom failed in the first stages. Fortunately, the peasants around us obeyed implicitly, and called me in at the first sign. Dried raspberry tea was always the panacea for anything that began with a chill. All druggists carried it, and we all had plenty. Tea having disappeared after the Revolution, wild raspberries and other fruits were dried to take their place, so that there was a tolerably good supply of dried raspberries, which were saved now for sickness. I remember days when I had over twenty patients at a time in the surrounding villages, all packed on top of the stoves. The women folk kept busy providing changes of dry linen as the tea took effect, and somehow the treatment worked. Our priest, who was very busy in those days, told me that at every funeral he made inquiries, and added, "I seldom have buried a patient of yours, and then I was told they called you in too late."

And again none of us took the disease. Medicines that were needed for my husband's sickness were sacred, but so long as we had any others in the house I could not steel my heart against cases I knew I could help, even if we had none for ourselves. The time came when all the needed drugs gave out, and then I turned charlatan. One could not refuse to do something, and no other help was to be had; so, knowing the power of faith, I always gave something, if only "surrogates," as we called the substitutes that passed for bread and coffee—and often the most unexpected results followed!

In none of the many domiciliary visits, when our property gradually disappeared, was our medicine-chest ever touched. "Leave the medicines; she gives them to the people," was the invariable verdict.

CHAPTER TWENTY-ONE

Bolshevism and the Church

WHILE from 1917 to 1920 Oka and I were in Bort-niki, we saw Alec occasionally. During the later part of this period, he was stationed at the headquarters of the staff of the Bolshevik army on the Polish front. After his father's death, when attempts were made to drive us out, he came and was able to postpone the evil day. When finally we were ejected, it was Alec again who was able to soften the conditions and prevent our expulsion from the county and even the State, as had been repeatedly threatened, for it would have been starvation if we had been sent away among strangers. His lot was worse than Oka's: he was alone, while Oka was at home, where together we faced what came; and in the second place, Oka's youth had prevented his being in the old army, and he did not bear the stigma of being "an old officer," a situation that for Alec carried not only hourly suspicion and insult but also hourly danger to his life. Besides he starved worse than any of us. We never lacked something to put into our stomachs; he did. We had (everything was comparative then) comfortable beds and quarters, and were surrounded by loyal friends we knew, even when they had to efface themselves. He, on the other hand, was for a long time stationed in a small town, quartered in a huge room formerly a store, without furniture or any conveniences. The officers, among whom were several of his own kind, made themselves beds for their hay-pallets from boards; the river near by was their only bathroom, even when cold weather set in. Once a week regularly were executions, and with strained nerves he would sit, unable to do anything, listening for the volley—then isolated shots, the finishing off of those not yet dead. There was a young woman who cleaned the offices, a Lett. During the first years of the reign of terror, the most unsavory work of the Cheka was carried out by Chinese mercenaries and Letts, who had the reputation of being the most cruel of all the races in the Empire. This woman certainly bore out the reputation that had been given her people. Every execution evening, she went out with her revolver, getting a stated sum for each of those she "finished off." Imagine having so sinister an individual working around you, and knowing that you yourself were a promising candidate for one of the firing parties and might be the victim of this woman's possible services!

Alec's position was a difficult one, as he was constantly watched. Attempts were made to draw him out, to have him commit himself to some expression against the Soviet Government. Every day he knew that one word of false accusation from any of the Cheka men about him would bring his arrest and death, as was happening all around him.

One of the many incidents he told us of illustrating the insidious work of the Cheka was this. A fellow officer, his wife and Alec often met a Communist whom they all considered a good fellow. Around the samovar, one day, while they were discussing various subjects, that of torture came up. The Communist stoutly denied the existence of anything of the kind in the Bolshevik régime. Alec and his friend were too prudent to follow the question or dispute his statements. The lady, however, was so sure of the friendship of the Communist that she pushed her argument, citing an instance of a friend of theirs. As soon as she began, Alec tried to stop her by touching her foot under the table, but she went on. "We are all friends here," she said, utterly regardless of consequences. The case in question was that of a mutual acquaintance whose scars both Alec and the lady's husband had seen and the woman now described. The Communist, good-naturedly contriving to discredit all such tales, stood by his former assertion. When he had left, both men bitterly reproached the woman for her words, urging that she should have known the danger of confiding such statements to any one in these days. Shortly after, the acquaintance, who had escaped from the clutches of the Cheka after suffering torture, was seen, conducted to the headquarters of the Cheka, and later, so they learned, "died" in prison. It was this atmosphere of fear, spying, treachery, that remains as the most poignant memory of those years, rather than that of physical discomforts, cold and hunger, that have made such deep scars in the brains and hearts of those who survived.

Of George, during all this time, we knew little. Once in the course of the winter of 1918 he wrote he was coming on leave, bringing Vera and the baby to stay with us; that he probably would be home almost as soon as the letter. With what delight I prepared for them the up-stairs rooms where all the Ponafidines had been brought up. We set up the little bed George and all our boys had slept in and, as best we could with what we had in the house, trimmed it up. Day after day we watched the long fir-tree marked road along the lake, but they never came. During one of the domiciliary visits, headed by the chief County Military Commissar himself, the little bed attracted attention. "I did not know you had a baby in your house—where is it?" I told him we had expected our grandchild.

"Ah, the child of that son of yours who we have reason to believe is in society little agreeable to us. It's a pity he is not here to-day," and with a gesture he tore the netting from the bed, running his sword through the mattress in evident regret that there was no one in it! That day

GEORGE PONAFIDINE

George's wife and child (the two Veras).

I became reconciled to George's not coming, and hoped the Commissar was correct in intimating that he had escaped the Bolsheviki. One day, I think it was the next summer, a woman stranger in Ostashkov gave a folded soiled bit of paper to the woman who kept the little inn where we always put up. The paper, without envelope, was addressed to Alec, and both the address and the letter itself were written in pencil. It was from George. He wrote, "I am writing in the fields and sending this by a sure hand. Come and join me if you wish a good time. I am going to visit Ivan Ivanovich of Persia and we will have horseback riding." Interpreted, this read that he was going to join Karniloff's cavalry, of whose movements we had heard rumors, and we had adopted the pseudonym of Ivan Ivanovich of Persia, as that great patriot had been our guest in Meshed. We were thankful to know that in some way George was free—but what of his family? The letter was read until committed to memory, and then destroyed. I urged Alec to take the risk that might come to us, and try to join George, but he would not do it, being sure it would bring vengeance on us. I felt it was all a bluff and that we would not be touched; anyway it was worth the risk; but later experience proved that Alec was right. Had he gone, we three would most assuredly have paid the penalty, and all of us have lost our lives. Once more a letter came from our boy, written in Chernigov, where he was, together with Vera and her mother and her sister's family. Why he was there we did not know, for the letter was very carefully written. We only had the comfort of knowing that they were all alive up to the date of the letter.

Many changes were taking place in every way, but deeper and more significant in cities than in the country. In spite of propaganda, the stolid peasants of middle and

old age were little moved down deep in their hearts. The
first Revolution had not touched their religious faith. The
Provisional Government had abolished the Holy Synod,
separating Church from State, and in August a Patriarch
was chosen by the Church to fill the position abolished
by Peter the Great, who did away with the Patriarchate in
his policy of holding all the reins of the State in his own
hands.

At the beginning, Bolshevism, though demanding atheism from the Communists, used no force in repressing
religion. It was ridiculed, icons were forbidden in Government premises, but as yet no real persecution took place.

One of the unfortunate situations in the past was the
restriction in preaching. The Russian form of service is to
me most beautiful, but preaching not being the essential part
of it, the clergy seldom touched on any social or political
problems of the day, and so negatived church influence. The
charges often heard now of the Russian Church having been
a weapon of the Tsars is, I think, an exaggeration. While
controlled, as I have said, it had no active influence, and the
majority of the priests with whom we came in contact in the
country were inclined to the left. That this is correct is
proved, I think, by the indifference with which the Bolsheviki
treated the Church during the first months, seeming to regard it as not a dangerous political power in their anti-
religious program.

Red Army men would come home, ridicule their elders
for going to church, sometimes arguing noisily outside the
church, but stirring up no real disorders. All church services were so mocked that perhaps while the boys were at
home the family refrained from outward support of the
church, but no sooner had they returned to the front than
church-going was resumed. This attitude continued during
the years following, when the "anti-religious front" became

active and bloody, though I am convinced that it had and has had little influence on any but the younger peasants. In political meetings, the psychology of the peasant is as clearly shown: speaker after speaker of absolutely opposite views may take the platform, and each is warmly applauded; and the sphinx-like peasant, we may be sure, is either true to his inner instincts, whatever they may be, or is only for the moment carried away by oratory. No audience is more easily swayed by a clever orator who knows how to handle them. Another factor in the religious life of Russia at this period was that on our side there seemed to be a truce, an apathy, that made religion a foe to be safely ignored by the Bolsheviki. What had happened was so unexpected, so appalling, as to leave the country, as a mass, in a dazed state. Every preconceived theory and manner of thought and of life were overturned. The immediate necessity of finding food and medicine and of evading danger of arrest was so imperative, we were urged on by problems and dangers so overwhelming, events followed one another with such rapidity, that no time was left for the inner life, and religion was, so to speak, unconsciously pigeonholed. Then came worse days, and the sufferings all about us of innocent people, of little children, of animals, so brutally treated when ownership failed them, made one feel that God had forsaken us—that perhaps there was no God, for how could a good God permit such deeds as were daily committed by the few on the millions of helpless, unarmed, terror-stricken people! Perhaps I am unjustly attributing to the many my own weakness and absence of strength and faith. I think, however, that I was not alone in this moment of spiritual emptiness and bewilderment. The propaganda said, "Don't go to church—there is no God." "All right," said the peasant—and he did not go while the propagandist was in sight; but afterward he went again.

As the reign of terror continued, and famine and disease followed, a jolt came. As people became accustomed to adapting themselves to the conditions forced upon them, a realization came that their only hope was in something higher, that they needed a Power greater than any human ally to help them. The automatic closing of many of the churches in cities, which naturally followed when pastors had to seek work to support themselves, and there were no means of heating or lighting the churches, had taken place without persecution. Now the despairing people turned to the Church. We were told now, in 1919-20, that the frigid and formerly empty churches of the cities were filled even late at night with people silently praying, prostrating themselves on the cold floors. Priests were hunted up and support for them and the church was promised so far as possible out of the parishioners' own far insufficient supply of food, fuel and lights. A new era began that the Bolsheviki did not foresee when they carelessly answered requests for reopening churches, "Go ahead, if you are fools enough to wish for a church, but don't expect help from us."

The Russian clergy, who in olden times had not been at the height of their obligations, now fully atoned for any slackness in pastoral duties. Fearlessly they preached Christ, and urged their parishioners to withstand all propaganda against their God. In those days it took more courage than any one knows to preach the sermons they did when the agents of the Cheka stood listening at the door. I am sure that the martyrs among the clergy, beginning at this time, ran into tens of thousands. Fearlessly they alternated between pulpit and prison. We had in the Ostashkov Cathedral a very influential, highly educated priest who was too well loved for the Soviet to dare at this period to kill him, but his life became monotonous in its regularity: a powerful sermon denouncing atheism, arrest at the close of the service, an almost triumphal march to the prison, for most of the congregation followed him with smoldering sympathy that the Bolsheviki did not dare to increase by taking too severe measures. His time in prison was occupied in composing a still stronger sermon, which was again followed by arrest. The Russian clergy begins the morning service fasting, eating only at the close, at noon. So this man, reaching the prison after the dinner-time there, went hungry all day. His people would take him food, however; I myself did so once. After coming to this country, we heard that he had been finally sent off, no one knows where.

The peasants were little affected by this movement, until the Bolsheviki, realizing that religion was something to be considered in their future program, began open persecution. The time came when the impossibility of killing religion by persecution was finally understood, and since then all anti-religious propaganda has been centered on the young: to bring up the present and the future generations in absolute denial of a God and a future life is one of the chief factors in the present program of an agricultural, political and conscience slavery.

We found that a great deal of the anti-religious talk was, as preached by instructors who came to the villages, skin deep, a glib repeating of party slogans that one felt were not uttered from conviction. Trotsky said, "I feel that our Communists are like a radish—a very thin slice of red that, if scraped off, will show white beneath."

Once when a party was conducting one of the many raids on our house, something was said about including icons in the list. The leader retorted, "We won't even write down such trash." I answered, "Every one has a right to his own convictions, but we have no right to force them upon others, nor to make light of what any one holds sacred." To my surprise, neither he nor his companions said a word. It was easy, at least in those first years, to answer these raw Communists, who could argue no further than the vocabulary given them permitted.

CHAPTER TWENTY-TWO

Children and "the New Freedom"

BEFORE we were turned out of the house, and while we still had several horses, we were frequently ordered to entertain and drive to their next destination the instructors sent from Moscow. When I could, I went to the village to hear these men talk. Once, two were sent, one to explain Communism, the other to talk on agriculture. The largest izba in the village was packed with men and women listening with what it soon became evident was a half-insolent, half-curious, but wholly sullen attention. The agriculturist spoke pityingly of the ignorance of all advanced agricultural methods in which the Tsarist Government had kept them. In a crude way he told them of things I had heard laboriously drilled into them in clearer form by zemstvo instructors. One could see in the faces of the peasants the amused looks, which they dared not let go further, at the oft repeated statements of the speaker: "Of course, you have never heard of this or that implement or method which I have described. Of course, in olden times you were not taught this or that."

When the Communist took the floor and preached the blessings of Communism, describing the absolute equality of mankind and the equality that each citizen had a right to, and would get under Communistic rule, one old woman forgot her prudence and gave way to her feelings. "Eh, young man," she said, "you don't know what you are talking about. Look about you. Are all men alike, equally stupid or good? Go into the forests. The same sun shines on all the trees, and the same rains water them, but some are tall and mighty, others small and puny. Don't talk about equality."

One of the first fruits of Bolshevism was complete anarchy in the villages. A "society for the poor" was formed. It worked, not to raise the poor, but to pull down the prosperous, well-to-do peasants—the *kulaks*, so much talked of to-day. In practise it meant the destruction of everything that stood for thrift and prosperity. The peasant who had planted an orchard, who had a better tended garden than his shiftless neighbor, had it destroyed. The one who had a few bee-hives saw them overturned and the bees frozen in the snow. No one dared leave a pair of oars or a loose board in the boats; the children would break them. Life was made miserable by the wild license of the children and the resentment shown against well-to-do farmers. "Any one who has been idle and a drunkard, and has ruined himself and his family is a good citizen. Those of us who by hard work have improved our lot, built a good house, have decent clothes, are outlaws. To be in favor with the Bolsheviki, you must be good for nothing." These were comments daily heard.

The children were taught that they were independent beings, to develop without any "bossing"; control by parents, teachers or moral authority a bourgeois prejudice to be ignored. And they did ignore it. One day I drove through the village where every child knew me, on my way to see a sick peasant. In former days, we always took hard candy with us to throw to the children who opened the gates. All the plowed land of the village being on one side and the fallow fields on the other, fences and gates protected the planted fields. Getting out and opening and closing gates was such a bother that it was the universal custom for those who had restless horses to throw candy or pennies to the children who opened the gates. As soon as bells announced the approach of a carriage, children rushed to the gate and a scramble that ended in waving legs

and arms in a pell-mell pile followed. After the Revolution, when candy and finally even copper coins disappeared
in the mysterious way that things had of vanishing in those
days, this custom had died out.

On the day I speak of, I saw a number of children, both
boys and girls, run to the gate and stand on either side of
the road, each having something in turned-up apron or
blouse. As I came up to them, each little hand brought
out a stone, and a volley, poorly aimed fortunately, was
hurled at my horse. Fearing for him, I shouted in as stern
and menacing a tone as I could, "Stop it! Don't you dare
to throw another stone!" It took effect, and the next stones
remained clutched in their fists. I then drew up my horse
and said to them, "Now, children, tell me what you did
that for? What has my poor horse done to you?"

"It is liberty, we can do what we wish."

"All right," I said, "it is liberty. You all pass us every
day, going to the woods for berries and mushrooms. To-
morrow my sons and I will stand by the road and throw
stones at you."

This was an unexpected development of the idea of
liberty, and for a few seconds it struck them dumb. Then
one voice piped up, "We can throw stones at you, but *you*
can't."

"Why can't we? We throw as straight as you can."

"You don't dare. You are bourgeois."

I talked with them for some time and then drove on
unmolested. There were adults watching in silence—people
in the streets, faces in the windows, immovable, silent. Later
we heard that a gathering had taken place and that some
had protested against permitting the children to throw
stones. Others claimed that the children were within
their rights: if I didn't like it, I could "keep out of the
village."

"But she was going at the call of one of our own people—to see a sick peasant."

The discussion was long and spirited, it was said. The conservative party demanded that the children be punished. Just how it ended we never knew, but it was the last time any of us were troubled in this way.

Throughout the winter of 1919-20 we were constantly being menaced in one way or another. One plan was to get all the remaining families of landowners together in the house of a former farm manager of ours, a man owning a small estate himself. Again, we were all to be sent off to a camp in Siberia. More and more we learned that sufficient unto the day is the evil thereof. At the beginning of the Revolution, the boys and I would sit in their rooms after their father was asleep, discussing the prospects. It seemed as if we could not be reconciled to this or that humiliation that loomed before us. We soon learned, however, that the trouble we so dreaded seldom materialized, and it was a wholly unexpected crisis that confronted us. And to meet it, we always found unexpected strength. So gradually we were taught to shut the future from us, as we had the past, and to try to face bravely whatever the new day brought. Everywhere the same greeting passed between acquaintances:

"Well, how is it?"

"Thank God, the night is past. God send strength for the day."

CHAPTER TWENTY-THREE

Driven from Bortniki

THE summer of 1920 we soon realized would probably be our last months in what was left of our old home. After various rumors and menaces, the blow fell. A "paper" received in Ostashkov from Moscow brought to us one of the groups of visitors we had most learned to dread—well dressed, with high boots and leather jackets, and carrying the ominous portfolios under their arms. Where did all the portfolios come from, we often wondered.

A copy of the paper delivered to the manager of the estate is the only document we succeeded in bringing out with us. Translated, it runs thus:

R. S. F. S. R.
N. K. Z.
From the Ostashkov Central Department of Soviet
   Farms.
10/14 1920   No. 8998
   City of Ostashkov—Raisovkhoz
To the Manager of the Soviet Farm of "Bortniki."
   In accordance with a telegram received from the State Agricultural Department, dated 25/viii/1920, No. 1700, the Ostashkov Central Department instructs you to take measures for the expulsion of the family Ponafidine from the estate under your care, within two weeks time.
   (Signed) President of the Committee of Sovkhoz
   (Signed) Executive Secretary
   This copy certified as being identical with the original.
   (Signed) Manager of the Sovkhoz Bortniki.

Determined not to give up without a struggle, we at once based our defense on the fact that we were, after all, a "Red Army Family," once Alec was taken by them. As such we could not be turned out, nor could our needed horse and cow and the crops raised by us be confiscated. Also we had been given the right to live as peasants.

Oka went to the Military Commissariat, stated our case, and asked that Alec be informed. The Commissar appeared deeply sympathetic, said no one could touch us, bade us sit quietly, fear nothing, hide nothing, for the Agricultural Commissariat could do nothing to us, as we were under military protection. "Even if you are arrested, make no resistance. It will in the end make your case stronger."

Somewhat reassured, though troubled by the lack of confidence in all official statements, we awaited Alec's arrival. He came with a strongly written paper given by his military chief, saying that the house and property of Comrade Ponafidine, serving on the staff of the Ninth Army, could not be touched. With this, the boys went to the Agricultural Commissar, who, after reading it, tossed the paper aside, saying, "That is all right for the proletariat, but you have no rights, being *pomeschiks*. Your place is really not in the Red Army at all. You should be made to work."

"Let me work, free me from the Red Army, and we will thankfully plow and live the life of peasants," Alec replied.

"No, you can have no privileges. You will work where we put you. We need your knowledge and education, and will use them, but you have no rights and your family must go."

Days dragged on. The Military Commissar was, to our faces, always polite, sympathetic, promising immediate results that never came; the Agricultural Commissar, our real boss, cynical, hostile, brutal. One day, driven to desperation, Alec said, "I won't leave it like this, I will carry our case to the State Commissar in Tver, and if he does not give us justice, I will go to Moscow and ask Trotsky if this

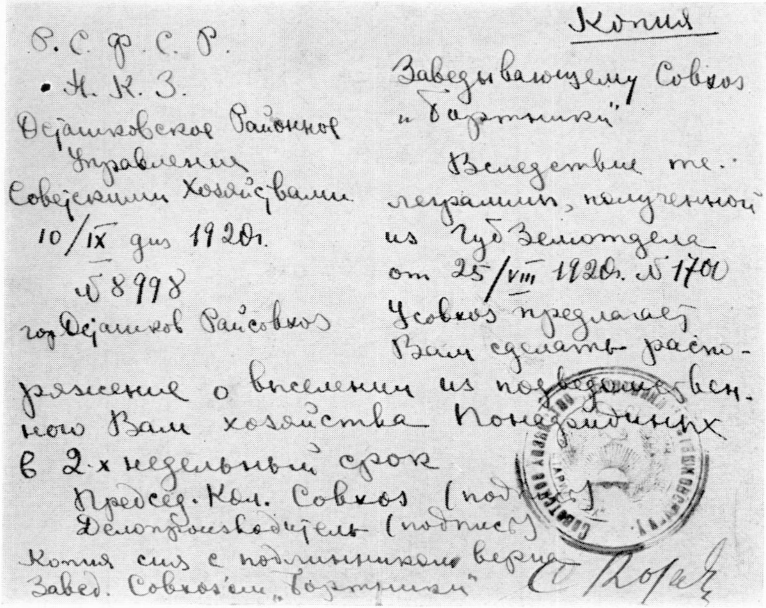

Копия

Р. С. Ф. С. Р.
Н. К. З.
Осташковское Районное
Управление
Советскими Хозяйствами
10/IX дня 1920 г.
№ 8998
гор. Осташков Райсовхоз

Заведывающему Совхоз
„Бортники"

Вследствие телеграммы, полученной из ГубЗемотдела от 25/VIII 1920 г. № 1700 Усовхоз предлагает Вам сделать распоряжение о выселении из подведомственного Вам хозяйства Понедельниных в 2-х недельный срок

Председ. Ком. Совхоз (подпись)
Делопроизводитель (подпись)

Копия сия с подлинником верна
Завед. Совхозом „Бортники"

Facsimile of eviction order.

The bungalow—the last home from which we were evicted.

is all the protection a Red Army man can have for his family."

The Commissar listened quietly and in an ominously sweet tone said, "Go, I have nothing against your doing so. Even if a Commission is sent and you are supported in your petition, remember, the Commission returns to Moscow but I remain here, and the carrying out of instructions is in my hands."

We knew too well what that meant! Several times Moscow had sent Commissions to Ostashkov to look into any complaints that might be made against the working of local Commissariats. One such came at a crisis we were experiencing, and many urged us to take advantage of this seemingly just move on the part of the Soviet; but we were distrustful, and refrained—fortunately, as events showed, for though the Commission was quite fair in its decisions, the iron fist of our "local power" came down so heavily on all our friends who had complained, that in the end they suffered more. In this case, too, Alec realized the rashness of carrying out a threat which, if fulfilled, would undoubtedly be the end of us.

The peasants came to our aid, and had to be held back from too active measures. They went to Ostashkov and insisted that we had the rights not only of a Red Army family but of peasants. They claimed that Oka worked as no peasant did. "By day he works for you in the Forestry Department, and by night, when we are asleep, he does his farming." Thanks to them, a year's supply of flour, based on the rations then given, was left for me, to which were added the vegetables that the peasants claimed were partly my work. They succeeded in saving us from hunger, but they could not ward off our expulsion. Oka was not counted in the flour supply, as he was supposed to receive all he needed from the Forestry Department. I asked for a bed to be left for Alec when he came home, but was told he "could buy his own, like all other good citizens," and I dared not say, "And how about all the beds and bedding that you have taken from him as a good citizen?" One of the hardest things in those days was to keep from "answering back." There was no danger of our breaking down, or even asking for what were our rights, except in unusual cases, as was the present. The Soviet brutality somehow did not cow, it angered me, and I felt above lowering myself by asking favors. For myself, I never did. It is a satisfaction, as I look back, to feel that none of them can boast of seeing us appear frightened or of shedding a tear for any humiliation brought upon us. Nor did we ever hide our principles. One of the many revelations that events brought to us was the knowledge of how little we understand ourselves. How impossible it is for any one to say confidently, "I would do so and so under given circumstances." We found that we often bore without flinching what we would have declared we could never endure, while on the other hand courage failed us when we least expected it.

The decision was made. We were to leave Bortniki with only a few necessary articles—our vegetables and one year's supply of rye flour for me. No cow, no horse, and as for money, of course we had none. Oka managed to get himself transferred to the Fisheries Department, for the fish were also nationalized and largely "militarized," sixty per cent. of those caught going to the army, thirty per cent. to institutions (hospitals, etc.), and ten per cent. to employees. A commission came to decide what was to be given us, and they worked in a most characteristic way. The inventory (the one that we had edited) was brought from the city, and we gathered around the table, going over it preparatory to checking up what we had in the bungalow. The Commissar studied the sheets with a frown, and then said,

"I thought everything given the Ponafidines from the house was marked, but I see nothing." A lively discussion ensued. Some of the city members "distinctly remembered" that crosses were to mark everything "loaned" us. Others knew nothing. The present manager of the *sovkhoz* was a recent appointee. He also remembered being told that a cross was to mark each article. Well, they were not there, that's all. Evidently the Comrades had not been equal to their sense of revolutionary duty, and in copying had carelessly omitted the crosses! The question now was how to verify the articles. One man spoke up with a logical suggestion that made my heart skip a beat. "After all, Comrades," he said, "the matter is very simple. We have a full inventory of everything possessed by the Ponafidines. So let's go to the big house and check up on everything there, and whatever is not there is, of course, here."

"Right, right, let's go."

A cold chill went over me, and I imagine my equally guilty sons were no happier, for we knew that "everything that was not there" was not here, either! One had to think fast in those days, and Alec calmly said, "No, that can not be done. You yourselves know how many requisitions have been made by you officially, and furniture and other property have been taken since the date of this paper. I see nothing here to indicate the articles taken. Perhaps you have a separate list?"

A pretense of inquiry and fumbling of papers took place. All knew of these "official requisitions." Some had taken part in them. The less said the better, and it was decided simply to drop what was past and make an inventory of what we had. A member of the Commission, a peasant from a neighboring county, was commanded to remain with us, keeping us constantly in sight until we left, seeing that we took only what was permitted. The question of our future destiny troubled no one at all. During the two weeks of grace given us, we were to look after that detail. We drank tea together, joked and talked, and the Commission as usual left in good humor, departing like the best of friends.

The woman who had been with us was discharged, and I was left alone most of the time with the Commissary, whom I will call X. Before leaving, Alec went over the list with him to separate what was to be ours; and here the fun began, for it was the last time any comrade would have a chance to get anything from us before we were reduced to a "proletariat" state. X seated himself, pencil and paper in hand, the boys and I around and opposite him. "The trouble is when once a thing is written, it is written," he began sagely. "Now before we write, let's think. Can not we write in a way that will be good for you and for me? Remember, though, that I have only pockets."

Just what he meant by that is a question, for when he finally left us, his pockets were represented by good sized boxes.

"You are in charge here. You know the size of your pockets, and can choose," ventured one of the boys, as an answer or comment seemed to be expected.

"All right, then we can begin."

We went carefully over the bungalow, not so packed with furniture now as in the first days, for with the help of V much had disappeared unnoticed. X made a list of "soft" (upholstered) furniture to be left, giving us only three stiff "Vienna" chairs. When it came to taking them, I told him I could not spend the rest of my life sitting on a cane-bottomed chair, and suggested that in return for some of the things we had not objected to seeing go into his pockets he leave me an upholstered chair.

"I would gladly, but the number is already written and witnessed—so many soft chairs."

This was an obstacle we all recognized; but his face suddenly brightened, and he said, "Look here, if we fasten those cushions to a chair, won't it be a 'soft chair'?"

In the end, by hunting up cushions of sorts, and fastening them to chairs and benches, we were able to save a number of pieces of comfortable furniture, upholstered with rare Persian rugs and embroidery that, owing to their subdued colors, had survived the various requisitionings, when the bright cretonne-covered furniture had gone. Several times astonishment had been expressed that "such a rich house had such dull furniture and such low chairs, with no place for one's legs."

Those last weeks were among the most trying of our experiences. I was virtually a prisoner; Alec had to return his post in Vitebsh, and Oka was gone most of the tim was a good-natured fellow, rough, uncouth, but not b We had become fast friends, for all he did to make my life a burden was quite unintentional—his ways were not our ways, that was all. He could see no reason why, if he happened to be talking with me in my room, he should not lie down on my bed with his heavy tarred boots on, or if he wanted to wash his hands, why he should not use my towel. But the horror came when he also found my tooth-brush and began to use it, a pleasing novelty, consigning me for the rest of our life in Russia to going without a brush. He, however, did not know that, for he obligingly left it in my room, "where we can both use it."

He always called me "old woman" in an affectionate rather than satirical way, and would constantly come into the kitchen with, "What can I do for you, old woman?" and would bring me water, chop wood and help in other ways when Oka was in town. He made me leave my bedroom door open, but I had a screen, the only privacy possible. He went to bed after I did, and was up as soon as he heard me moving. He followed me, if I took a step out of the house, went with me to milk the cow and care for the horse, both of which we were allowed to use as long as we were in Bortniki; but I knew I was watched every moment, though the man was very nice about it. He even offered me a position of cook in his house, and said he would treat me fairly and pay me something. The ban against hired help did not lie heavily on Communists.

Oka, in the meantime, had much to think of. We felt we must keep our cow, for we foresaw that hungry days were before us. Bribes were taken everywhere, but there was always danger for any one of us who proposed it. We ... w of cases where the comrades who had taken bribes ... heir own kind had found their consciences too tender ... here was the chance of getting a bourgeois into ...e. In roundabout ways, Oka found that he could ask the Agricultural Commissar to let us keep our cow, offering pay for "expense that might be entailed in drawing up papers," etc. Peasants bartered for us some of the things we had in hiding, doing it in a distant county, and finally Oka had half a million roubles, which was the sum needed for retaining the cow. Encouraged by this success, he thought of the possibility of also getting the piano back to "use" in giving lessons. Famine and revolution could not wean Russians from music, and he might be able to give lessons for food or the equivalent of it. The piano, however, came under the Department of Education, which we feared might represent a higher standard of morals as well as of intelligence, but diplomatic soundings proved that a Commissar of Education was as approachable as the Commissar of Agriculture had been, and we were given the "use" of the piano.

The object most dear to Oka's heart was his motorboat, which had already been confiscated. When it had been drawn up into a shed for the winter, the motor was taken to pieces as usual, and each part carefully oiled, wrapped in paper and packed away. Foreseeing its loss, Oka was determined that if he could not have it, neither should they, so he hid away a small but essential bit of the machinery, knowing that, as an English engine, no parts could now be replaced. The sequel was interesting and characteristic of the times. When spring came, the boat was needed for the Fisheries Department, to be used by Oka himself when inspecting the various places where fish were salted. One day the head of the Department sent for Oka, and alone in his office said to him, "I know perfectly well you have put your boat out of commission. See that it is put together and in good working order and nothing will be said." This man knew nothing, but he put himself in Oka's place, understood Oka's feelings and took measures accordingly, though he had never heard of books on psychology and "behavior." For the remainder of our stay, Oka ran his motor-boat for business purposes and, what was more, took visiting Moscow Communist Commissars, mostly much bejeweled Jews, on moonlight rides. In his capacity of chauffeur, he constantly feared being offered a tip. He used to say, "I don't mind anything, so long as they don't tip me. If they do, I'll drown myself." But they never did. No amount of soot or old clothes could deceive them, and the biggest of the visitors would give him their hands, call him Josif Petrovich, and use the plural in speaking to him—a very rare happening in those days of "equality and fraternity."

CHAPTER TWENTY-FOUR

A Narrow Escape from Death

THE new home which we succeeded in finding in Ostash-kov belonged to a merchant who kept fishing supplies. There was a large stone-paved courtyard surrounded by storehouses and the roomy two-story house fronting the lake. A high brick wall and gates gave to the place something of the appearance of a fortress. Our room, a large one, faced the back, with two small windows opening on the garden on one side, in front of which we eventually had our wood-pile—a convenient place to hide anything when retreat was ⸻ ff from the one door into the kitchen and from there ⸻ he yard. I went to the city to see our room, and took ⸻ urements with a view to stocking it as full as its di-⸻ ions and the good-nature of X would allow. There was no place for a cow, however. Oka came home one night to report that if we could find a door and window, there was a place in which we could keep "Maliutka." So one of the last crimes we committed in our old house was the theft of a window-sash and a door, a nocturnal adventure that gave us considerable satisfaction.

Here also we could have a pig and a lamb—the products of V's careful manipulation of our effects. These two animals had been the objects of much deliberation. Their tender age proved that they had been obtained by us since we had been reduced to the status of peasants. They did not represent the property of aristocrats and therefore we were allowed to keep them.

Maliutka's food was, however, a problem. We had a good supply of hay and clover that Oka had laid in from the land given us to use; but how were we to get it to the city? The navigation on the lake would be closed, and carting it and driving the cow around by land would take long and be expensive. This the peasants consented to do for seven pounds of salt a hayload.

No one was permitted to have any salt above the ration, and we had scarcely enough to make our own food palatable, nevertheless we told the peasants that if they would bring us the hay and cow, they would eventually get their pay in salt, just when we could not say. "We never lied to you, did we? Will you believe us?" They did. Again to anticipate, I must add that as soon as we had settled in Ostashkov, I went to some Jews who had no cows but I knew had other things, and offered them fresh milk every day in exchange for salt. They consented gladly. It took us from November, when we got our cow to town, till May to pay off the debt of salt, though we gave all the milk each day, with the exception of just enough for our "coffee."

A few days before we left, X was sent for, another man replacing him for the time. When he returned from Ostashkov, I saw immediately that something had happened, his face was so changed. I asked if Oka was safe. He said, "Yes," and that he expected to come on the steamer the next day if he finished some work in town. Then the storm broke. "Oh, why have you been so foolish! It is all up with you. G has reported to the Communistic Party that you have concealed a quantity of rye in the house of R. To-morrow a Commission from the Agricultural Department of the Communists and the Cheka will come, and if it is found that the charge is true, you and your son will be shot on the spot where the crime was committed, as an example of what happens if the people's property is touched. I can do nothing, and I like you. Why were you such fools as to risk it!"

Here with a vengeance was one of those bridges to cross that we had not expected. I thought hard and fast. The man spoke regretfully, sympathetically, but could I trust him? Was it not one of the cases of "provocation" so-called that were constantly taking the lives of our friends? No, he was not to be trusted. I must brazen it out in some way. I did not have to feign astonishment, for I was fairly breathless with surprise that, after all this time, we had been found out. How could it have been done? G never had the opportunity of getting all those books out to verify the contents of the chest. Oka and I had never left her alone in the bungalow long enough. To this day we do not know if it was simply a shrewd guess, a bluff, or that she had found a few grains of rye which I, in sweeping up, had over-looked. The harm was done, and it seemed to me we had never faced death more closely. I still tried not really to lie. I told X that I was astonished and angry at his news, but let the Commission come, they would find nothing of the kind. Resolving in my heart that in some way we would make my words come true, I answered X's steady look. He seemed partly relieved, it seemed to me. "Tell me truly, have you hidden the rye? They will come to-morrow, and if you have, you will certainly be shot. I won't stay to see it. I can't, for I like you, old woman, and I can not save you if the rye is found, but my eyes won't look at your being killed."

I thanked him for his friendship, and said, "Well, to-morrow will show you that we have nothing there." What could I do? I could not stir alone nor was there a way I could get word to R. Fortunately, his house was on the outskirts of his village, but it was a second one, a less friendly one being between us and where R lived. I decided I must make the attempt in the night to get to his house by going through the fields that skirted the first village. X was a good sleeper. I had never heard him move in the night. At two o'clock I listened. I could hear him if he moved, but all seemed quiet. Hastily throwing on my clothes, I was almost ready when suddenly at my window I heard X's voice! I was stricken speechless with sheer fright. "Emma Josifovna!" he called. "Old woman, wake up! There is a big fire. Come and look." In the darkness of the room he could not see that I was dressed. My long silence he took for sleep, and did not know that I was standing not far from him, tongue-tied with fright and dismay. Finally I stammered, "I'm coming—let me dress," and when I joined him, it was to find the sky bright, with a burning village lighting up the road I was to have taken, and every one on the place and in the villages running out. Sleeping with my one good ear down, I had heard nothing. I think the realization of the failure of my plans crushed me less than the feeling of awe that came over me. What if the fire had broken out just a little later, and he had found me gone! It was hard keeping up conversation about the fire that made everything as bright as daylight around the village where somehow I must get word. Gradually the light faded. People on the estate went back to bed and so did I, but not to sleep. It was too near morning, and too many people would be prowling around for fear of the fire breaking out again, to make it safe for me to go out.

When morning came, and I realized that at noon the steamer would come, the rye be found, and not only we but poor, loyal R and his family would be doomed, I was almost beside myself. Think as I would, I saw no means of warning R. Not a soul could be trusted.

Soon after breakfast, a troop of children passed who had been early in the woods gathering mushrooms. Among them was R's little boy, a tiny lad, not more than seven. His father always told him when passing to stop and bring him word if I was well. God sent him that day. I found from him that his father had gone to town and was expected back on the steamer that noon. I gave the boy a picture book to look at, and while X was lying smoking, stretched out on his bed in sight of my room but apparently not giving attention to the boy's chatter, I managed to write a note to Oka, merely saying, "Rye discovered. Search party on steamer. Take measures." This I tucked inside the child's blouse, telling him to meet the steamer and give it to Oka so that no one would see him do so. Would he do it? Would Oka be on the steamer, and R? Could I detain the Commission long enough? I tried to crowd all these questions that would force themselves upon me out of my brain. The morning wore on. I tried to act as usual, so that X would not know I was worried, but I took good care to have no water in the house nor kindling for the samovar. At last the steamer whistled! In fifteen or twenty minutes they would be here. X was pacing the room, evidently sincerely distressed and puzzled. Presently we saw coming down the road the typical group, armed and portfolioed, and with hard cynical faces. They were all gruff and antagonistic, repeating the accusation and telling me to come with them to the house of R. I tried to appear indignant and hurt only. I said I would go with them willingly, but could not let them leave without tea after the long cold ride, and they must have left so early as to be hungry. Early or late, every one was more or less hungry those days. They fell in willingly, taking off hats and stacking their rifles. I left them talking with X, while I went down to the lake for water. Then I had to try to split kindling wood. Those days had taught me to do most kinds of work, but I never did learn to manage an ax. So I was long in starting the samovar, in spite of X's repeated, "Hurry up, old woman."

Finally he came out and, pulling off his boot, the best bellows ever invented, slipped it over the top of the tube, and soon had my samovar singing.

We gathered around the table for our meal: tea (a "surrogate"), a little sugar that we always hoarded to sweeten our enemies' dispositions (it generally did), boiled potatoes and bread. Seeing how heartily they fell to, I feared it would not take long to finish, so I began telling them stories of the wonders of America. They were so interested that they slowed down, and I went on and on. When the many, to them amazing, facts connected with America became exhausted, I gave my imagination full play. I don't know what I told them. I only know that I was determined to hold them until I could see from my seat at table Oka's figure coming down the road. In all the lying we did during those years, I have one profound satisfaction, the knowledge that neither my sons nor I ever told a lie that injured any one or was intended to avenge ourselves. They were always lies to save ourselves or our friends, and so perhaps not all black.

After what seemed years, I saw Oka coming! And *he* was carrying a portfolio, too! He walked in with his usual calm, self-possessed manner, but I, who knew his uncanny ability in keeping himself neat, noticed signs of dust and of trickles of perspiration on his face that raised my hopes. The moment he appeared, one of the visitors exclaimed in a suspicious voice, "Who is this? The young fellow was on the steamer with us."

"That is her son," said X, pointing in my direction.

"Then where have you been? Why didn't you come straight home?"

"I work in the Forestry Department," said Oka, coolly laying his portfolio on the table, "and I stopped at our branch office for some papers I must work at to-night."

"Is he speaking the truth?" turning to X.

"Yes, he is working across the lake, but they have an office in the village on this side too."

If Oka had not had the wits to go for those papers, the first suspicions would have been followed up! Then I broke in with great indignation and told Oka what these men were here for and of the libel G had circulated against us— and that a search of R's house was to be made for the rye.

"Rye?" said Oka, looking the men square in the face. "We haven't a grain of rye at R's. You are quite welcome to search."

And search they did, in the house from attic to cellar, and in the barns, but not a grain was to be found. Puzzled and baffled, they gave up. X did not dare say a word, but I could see his relief, and my heart warmed to my uncouth keeper, and even my tooth-brush was forgotten.

The Commission returned by the afternoon boat to report. They had finally thawed, as was always the case if we were given time, and though I think they had suspicions, they went away rather relieved than otherwise, it seemed to me. It was only after they had all gone that Oka told me how he and R had taken the bags in loads of hay right through the village to the barn of R's father-in-law. Every one knew that in his new place R did not have his hay-barn finished, and that he intended keeping the clover in his father-in-law's barns. Every one in the village also knew that R was in the habit of helping us with his horse in our work, while Oka and Alec in turn did what they could for him. If any one noticed any coincidence connecting the search with such untimely haste just after R and Oka had returned from town, not a voice was raised in the crowd that watched the search. So again we were saved.

CHAPTER TWENTY-FIVE

Moving to the New Home

AT LAST all was ready for our leaving. What was to go with us in the way of clothing and small articles, had been piled on the floor of my room. X had a private heap in a dark corner of the attic for the time when boxes should have to be carried instead of pockets. My pile I found was decreasing rapidly: X had a way of turning things over sometimes.

We fought hard for the safety of our valuable books and manuscripts. These consisted now only of books in foreign languages and Persian and Arabic manuscripts. Though lost to us personally, they were too valuable to be destroyed. Oka went to the Department of Education and told them we did not ask to keep these treasures for ourselves; he merely asked that they be taken charge of until they could be sent to a library where they would be intact. No, like everything else they were to go to the Department of Agriculture. On the last day, when everything not given us was to go, we begged to be allowed to pack the books in boxes. No—and they were jumbled into dirty, muddy sacks that had been used in bringing in potatoes. The day was drizzly, and the books in the bags were thrown on the deck of the steamer and finally consigned to the cellar of the Department of Agriculture. Later, when a burglary brought an investigating committee to the cellar, one of the members told me that he saw our books on the floor. Some were picked up by them as they passed, and handfuls of pages torn out, to be used for rolling tobacco, as we had a paper famine. Illustrations caught the attention of others and were torn out. When settled in Ostashkov, we at last succeeded in interesting the Department of Education sufficiently to have them appoint a woman of education to make a catalogue and turn the books over to our local library. Madame K told us of the terrible state our library was in: the books were mutilated and whole volumes were missing. This small library was only one of many, sometimes vast, libraries that were destroyed from 1918 to 1920, some of them literally going up in smoke.

We parted very touchingly with X, whom we never saw again, and found ourselves with Daisy, our fox terrier, a cat, and a little mongrel who had adopted us, Tsigan, intended for a big dog but with apparently sawed-off legs. His marvelous sagacity as watch-dog had saved his life, and all on the estate had taken part in providing his board, but his affection and loyalty were confined to us. "Eat their bread, yes, but have nothing to do with Bolshevism," seemed to be his motto. Early in 1918 we had gone through the heartache of having all our many hunting and cattle dogs shot rather than see them starve. Daisy we could never part with in her old age, so long as we had a morsel to divide with her. She ate very little anyway, and the cat had a good time with mice that were beginning to overrun us.

The peasants brought a boat, such as we had for the funeral, and left it moored in a deep place some way from the shore. Oka, with the help of R and other peasants, carted down furniture, the piano, flour, personal belongings and fire-wood. When night came, all was put in except the precious vegetables. The last few days had been growing colder; the edges of the lake froze slightly. None of us can remember the date, but it must have been in November. Oka dared not leave the boat without a guard, so he built a fire on the shore, and when I went to bed I saw the light, and his form stretched against it—Tsigan by his side.

We were up early for a good start but found to our consternation that winter had set in. We could not risk exposing our precious vegetables in an open boat to such low temperature! A hasty council decided that the vegetables be left in R's care, to be brought to town gradually, well wrapped up. No time could be given to carting them that day to R's house, for every hour was precious. The lake might freeze, so that the boat would be winter-bound somewhere, and the owners were pressing for haste. The vegetables could not be left alone in the bungalow; they would be annexed—liquidated. Who was to stay by them? Oka put it up to me to choose. I told him he was more needed to unload the boat in Ostashkov: I could not do that but I could watch our vegetables. It was therefore settled that Oka should go to the city, and R return by the steamer next day, if it could navigate, and take all the vegetables over to his house. I with our dumb friends could then go on the return steamer to join Oka. Hastily a few things were thrown out to me. The boat pushed off, the rowers worked hard until a kindly breeze filled their sail. We watched them go; then Daisy, Tsigan and I went back home (home?) with my arms full of what I had asked should be left me. These two faithful friends trotted ahead, my "lanterns," as we called them, for when in the dark autumn nights I used to visit our cow and horse (the last thing before going to bed) and had to thread my way to the very farthest barn that had been left us, on snowless nights Daisy's white figure was my "lantern," since she knew my errand and seldom turned from the path, while if there were snow, Tsigan's black coat saved me—I could see him and follow. When we reached the bungalow, like Robinson Crusoe I took stock of my belongings. In one room were stacked the vegetables, so I had plenty to eat. I had a little cooking pot, but no knives or spoons, a blanket and a bottle, but neither kerosene nor matches, a little salt—and that was all. I went with my pot to the nearest village and asked for some burning coals so I could light my stove and boil some potatoes. We had forgotten bread. The day dragged on. I kept to the bungalow. We had our dinner of potatoes, and the darkness beginning to settle down, I thought of preparations for bed while I could still see. The only bit of furniture was the table upon which the silent form of my husband had lain those days and nights when Oka and I had watched and hoped in vain that Alec would come and see his father's face, so beautiful and calm. On this table I spread one blanket half under me, lifted up Daisy and the cat and, lying by them, covered us with the other half. It was bitterly cold, and the night was very long and very dark—this last night, passed in the same room where my first months in Russia had been spent almost thirty years before, when I had come a happy bride into the little home my husband had lovingly had his brother fit up for us.

Never was daylight more gratefully hailed than the next morning when I climbed, stiff, from my pillowless table and with the dogs ran down to the lake. There was a crust of ice some distance from the shore, but our steamer came at last, though late, and R drove over immediately with his cart, bringing a lot of hay and rugs to cover the vegetables. When they were all safe, I put the cat into the basket and went to the landing to wait for the steamer. The herd was feeding in a field near the road. I had always avoided getting near it, but now, even after so many months, as I answered the words of farewell spoken sympathetically by the herdsman, the cows lifted up their heads at the sound of my familiar voice, and one after another came to me until the whole herd was moving. It was the last straw. I hurried on, choking, determined that as I passed through the village no one should see a tear. Tears were so kept back all these years, I seemed to have a foolishly liberal supply near the surface now.

Oka met me at the steamer at Ostashkov and took me and the cat and the dogs to our new home. We made our one room which contained all we possessed really very home-like and cozy, and it became a center where nearly every evening more came in than we had chairs for, and music helped us all to forget.

That first night, as Oka lay in the combination American wardrobe bed, and I on the chest (of rye fame), that made a very comfortable divan by day with a rug we had saved, Oka suddenly asked, "Mother, how do you feel?"

"Why, very calm and comfortable," I replied, surprised myself, as I came to think of it.

"I am happier than I have been for years," he went on. "We are quite safe—proletarians in every sense. There is nothing more they can take from us. We can not sink lower and we shall be unmolested."

In one way, I look back on that year as the most care-free we had. The peasants brought us the remainder of our wood, and later on, the cow and hay. We had no social or other responsibility. We had no money, but no one else of our friends had any. One was not ashamed of old clothes, or shoes with holes in them, for every one else was in the same condition. Oka, transferred to the Fisheries Department, was at home, except for trips of a few days at a time when he was on inspection. The owners of the house were very agreeable to us, and among the others crowded in was Madame K, our old neighbor in the country. We each took turns in heating the big Russian stove in the kitchen. Communistic cooking demands great honesty and fairness, two qualities already nearly extinct, and it was a constant struggle to keep one's pots from being pushed out of range of the hot coals by some one else, or one's rye patties from disappearing. When in one's only kettle water was heated and counted on, one would often find it empty.

The owners of the house, Madame K, and I were a solid front against other tenants, transients, who came and went, and so we managed pretty well. When Oka was home, he would go, ax in hand, to the lake, where the large hole through the solid ice might be frozen over, and bring me water. When he was away, this was my hardest work, as I always expected to slip and "take a header" as I stooped over the deep holes.

In spite of our having been reduced to the one room, domiciliary visits were made a few times. One night, when I was hastily dressing behind my screen, I heard one of the comrades, who had come to search us, say to his companions, "Now notice this room. They are living packed in like sardines, but it is clean. Look under the bed—no dirt. That is because she is a lady. We are going to another place, where the woman wasn't a lady, and they live like pigs." This was an expression of facts that had been forced upon the people. At first, the conviction was universal that the sign manual of breeding, of bourgeois culture, was in outward possessions. Take away clothes, jewelry, money, and the aristocrats were the same as any one brought down to the lowered standard of equality. It came as a surprise that this was not so, that, even starving and in rags, there was a difference based on culture, education and breeding, and not obtained through jewels and clothes. We often heard the expression, "Yes, we see you can do our work, but we can not do yours." One day, as I was passing through a village where some people were gathered, animatedly talking in a group, one of them, an old man, hailed me and asked me to stop. It was at the worst time of the peasants' antagonism to us, and I was a little frightened; but I joined them, and the old man went on to say: "We were just talking of you. These foolish women were saying how lucky it was that our *barinya* (lady) had such a good disposition, for though they had seen you having your property taken from you, and humiliated by insults, you never cried nor said anything."

"If we had been treated as you have," said one of the women, "every one would have heard us!"

"Let them touch one of my cups or kettles and I'll teach them!" said another.

"Do you hear them?" queried the old man. "I have been trying to make them understand that it is not good disposition, but *this*"—and he tapped his forehead significantly with his finger.

The gradual realization that there was something to be had that could not be obtained by occupying fine houses and dressing in silks was penetrating the consciousness of city people as well as peasants.

CHAPTER TWENTY-SIX

The Page from the London Times

THE winter in Ostashkov was very different from those spent in Bortniki. We had friends near us, and we had a fair supply of kerosene. It was a relief, also, to be away from the old home, with all its recollections and now so much changed. Our Tsigan had been hailed as a watch-dog by the whole house, who helped with his board, but he found his duties perplexing and his loyal heart divided in responsibility for the cow, the house and each one of us. If Oka and I went anywhere in the evening, he would follow, and sit patiently on the door-step, but run home every little while to verify the safety of our room and the cow. Sometimes, when Oka and I were in different places, the situation was still more complicated for the faithful creature.

The next summer, when it became hot, finding that Maliutka was stifling in her narrow quarters, we put a basket of hay in the yard in front of her stable and let her loose when the front gate was closed for the night. The first time this was done, we were aroused by Tsigan's loud barking, and going out we found him trying to drive the cow back into her prison. We explained the case to him, petted him and the cow, and the wise little fellow, though disapproving, understood, and lying down beside her with a sigh, seemed to say, "Well, I am used to it—one thing more to look after," and from that time he slept close to the cow instead of in front of our door.

Added to other privations, Ostashkov was suffering from want of hay. During the winter before, rumors ran through the villages that statistics regarding horses and cattle were to be gathered. The peasants generally felt that this was a move for fleecing them, and it would be wise to hide as many of the animals as possible—and so they did. One man unfortunately had the brilliant idea of hiding his sheep in his cellar—and his house was the one in which the Commission happened to take lunch. The sheep, objecting to their new quarters, gave voice, with the result that they were confiscated and their owner fined.

The statistics gathered, the matter was forgotten—till spring, when a new Commission arrived to apportion meadowland to each family according to the number of cattle owned; all the rest was to go to the State. (This, when the peasants were fondly supposed abroad to own the land for the first time!) As the allotment was based on the statistics, of course the animals that had been hidden did not come in for any provisions for the winter. What was done was secretly to dispose of many needed cattle and horses, and when a sale was impossible, to slaughter them. This increased the steady decline of live stock that marked and is still marking the Soviet agricultural destruction of the country.

Our supply of hay ran low toward the end of the winter, and Maliutka joined her companions in misery by being turned loose in the streets in the daytime. Peasants are always prodigal in the use of hay thrown into their low sleighs to serve as warm seats and to feed the horses while in town. In the market-places, rows of blanketed peasants' horses stood eating hay from deep baskets or from the pile thrown on the ground. In the sleighs, probably covered with home-made rugs, was more. Here the hungry cows would gather. Horses would snap and drive them from their baskets, but the cows, who also were getting an education along new lines, would nose under the rugs and chew hastily, with one eye out for the irate owner, who would soon discover and descend upon them. No amount of beating off kept the cows away for long, so Maliutka and her friends would come home in the evening probably smarting and aching in numerous places but with hunger somewhat appeased; and after all, that was the chief thing in life. As the spring came on, rushes and reeds grew around some little islands in the lake, and grasses began to sprout. Before going to his work, Oka and I, armed with bags, would row to these islands, and on our knees pick the short grass and cut the rushes, thus helping out with our Maliutka's food. She had become as companionable as a dog, followed me whenever she saw me going out. Oka, seeing her standing calmly chewing the cud in front of a house, would know that I was there.

Living in the city, we were able to realize how much more difficult it had been for town-folk to live than for us who fortunately had been on the land where we could get food.

Soon after settling in Ostashkov, Oka, finding his piano in need of tuning, called in a tuner. We asked him what he would charge, not being at all sure we could afford the cost. The man seemed very much embarrassed; he said there was something he needed badly, but it was so much that he hesitated to mention it, knowing our circumstances. Finally, he blurted out, "You know I live with my sister. We have only one cup and saucer between us, and when I am hungry it is awfully hard to wait till she finishes her tea and I can have the cup. Can you give me a cup and saucer?"

Where had everything gone, that not even a cup and saucer could be had? The sudden disappearance of everything that we had been accustomed to consider indispensable was one of the many mysteries of the new order of things. Of course, much can be attributed to waste. Before leaving Bortniki, I had seen in refuse piles in the villages bits of our broken crockery, pieces of the costly, treasured dinner service that had come down from the far past. In one village I saw a beautiful high-backed hand-carved chair belonging to my sister-in-law, the work of past generations. The izba was crowded with such unusual furniture, and this chair of real as well as sentimental value had found a final resting-place close to the big Russian stove, replacing a wooden bench that usually stood there, convenient for setting pots on when drawn from the fire. The seat of the chair was already scorched and stained. The same waste was shown in collecting grain and vegetables, for taxes in kind.

One day a Commission came to the owner of the building in which we lived, to get storeroom for a quantity of rye. The only available place was a stable, the board floor deep in manure. There was plenty of time to clean it out, and to throw down straw, and in our horror of seeing food needlessly destroyed we all who had gathered around begged to have the place cleaned, even offering to help. In spite of all we could say, the grain was dumped on the damp foul floor, and of course the waste was great. Our eccentric friend, Madame K, had the courage the rest of us lacked to say, "It is clear why you do this. It will give you a chance to report the rotting of more than the bottom layers, and you can make thousands out of the deal." To our surprise, nothing happened to her! Another mystery of the Communistic psychology: one might be arrested, or, in 1918-20, even executed, for a careless word, and yet at times something like this would be passed in silence. We found we could say almost anything to their faces: it was the reported statements that were the most dangerous.

Potatoes also were taken in lieu of taxes. Peasants were ordered to deliver them on the steamer landing nearest their villages. The potatoes, brought in bags, were emptied and piled without cover, and it was a rainy, drizzly season, often with slight frosts at night. The one steamer a day could seldom clear all the piles left on the landing,

and often after days of exposure the potatoes were taken
and shipped or stored without drying. In Moscow, one
day in the autumn of 1920, a long string of carts passed me
in the street, from which a little stream of liquid that kept
dropping attracted my attention. It proved to be a large
consignment of completely rotten potatoes that had been
frozen and, now thawed out, were being brought into starving Moscow, only to be thrown away.

It is difficult for any one to realize the isolation of our
lives. In the fall of 1917, with the rise of Bolshevism, all
communication with the outside world was cut off. No newspapers from abroad were permitted, and only by a miracle
occasionally a letter evaded the watchful eyes of those determined to keep us in ignorance of affairs beyond the borders of Russia. Scarcity of paper made it impossible to pub-
lish enough newspapers for private circulation, so they
would be posted on walls to be read; but we now know how
false was all the foreign news given us. We were led to
believe that Communism was spreading all over the world,
and this made our case more hopeless and stopped our
dreams of getting out of Russia.

The first inkling we had of the true state of affairs came
when a Jewish acquaintance, returning from Petrograd,
brought us secretly a bit of the *London Times* that had been
used to wrap something in. Our friend had seen it on the
floor of an office, and with considerable risk had managed
to transfer it unseen to his pocket, and now brought it to us
for translation. As always in such crises, we locked the door
and saw that the window nearest the wood-pile could be
quickly opened in case of surprise. Then we all gathered to
read this, our first touch from "over there." It proved to
be part of an advertising page of the *London Times*, and at
first we were bitterly disappointed, as we had hoped for
news; but from this crumpled bit of advertising we were

able to build up the then existing economic and social status of England and, from inference, the world.

We had been told, for instance, that Communism had extended to England and Europe in general: that all houses were nationalized, that no private ownership existed, and no hired help. Here, with growing amazement, we read in the help columns long lists of cooks, scullery maids, parlor maids, waitresses, butlers. Most fantastic of all, here were hunting boxes for rent! Did that mean that somewhere in the world were people living their own free individual lives, with time, inclination, permission to indulge in sport? In Petrograd, we knew there were no dogs or cats—all had been eaten or had starved. Here we read of dogs of various breeds for sale, among them fancy lap-dogs at fancy prices!

That bit of paper was a revelation. It opened our eyes, and we thanked God that all the world was not as we were. But that very fact made our present conditions more unexplainable. How could the outer world be living a normal life and yet be callous to our situation? As no one could admit this supposition, we were constantly being buoyed up by rumors of foreign intervention. Even if Europe and America, the Allies whose success was so largely due to Russia's self-sacrificing advance in the first years of the war, should forget this debt, there was the menace to them, as we began dimly to recognize, of Bolshevik doctrines. Was it possible that this was not felt? Would not steps be taken for self-preservation, if for no other reasons?

CHAPTER TWENTY-SEVEN

The Journey to Moscow

FROM 1917 all direct communications were so cut off that these years, Rip Van Winkle-like, have been dropped out of our lives so far as knowledge of international affairs goes. It can be imagined, therefore, what it meant to us when two letters came in 1920, one from the United States Consul in Esthonia, in which he said that he had sent similar letters during a long period, attempting to locate us; that our friends were "actively" (how that word went to my heart!) trying to help us. The other letter was from Mrs. S. M. Clement, and enclosed one from my nephew, Clement H. Cochran. Mrs. Clement repeated what she said she had written us throughout the past years—in this one letter condensing events of years. Her own daughter had died, and also my eldest sister; my two other sisters had lost their husbands; our dear friend, Mrs. Roper, who had been almost like one of our family, had gone, too. And yet, while keenly realizing Mrs. Clement's sorrow, I found my feelings more of gratefulness that at least that many of those I loved were released from this horrible world. Death had lost all its sting for us, and even personal pain was quite annulled by joy in the thought of their escape, for still we found ourselves thinking of life everywhere as ours was.

As we read these letters over and over—urging us to come to America, offering financial help to get out—it was again made clear to us how the Bolsheviki had distorted facts. If the Revolution had spread throughout the world, would our friends be in a condition to help us materially? Would they consider our case unique and look for betterment if we left Russia, unless their own country was in a normal state? We showed these letters to a few trusted friends and translated the sentences; but they themselves *handled* the bits of paper that had come from an outside world and proved to us that there were people living in happy lands where one went to bed at night sure of being undisturbed, and of waking a free person and with food enough for the day.

These letters set us thinking. First, how could we get word to our friends without discovery that would ruin us? Secondly, how could we begin the work of planning the simultaneous escape of all three? To get out singly would bring ruin to the others. All but George; wherever he might be, we felt sure he was far from any harm our movements might bring him. We had no communication from him, and only a carefully worded, unsigned letter from Vera, speaking of herself and George in the third person. She had written: "I met our mutual friend Emma Cochran and she told me of the young couple she had been interested in— Vera and George. Vera is alone in Theodosia. She and George were together out of Russia, but he would not stay there while his child and parents were in Russia, so came back. They could not find the child nor get in touch with his family. They were together until a *dreadful thing happened*. Since then Vera has lost George."

This letter exercised much of our newly developed ability to read between the lines, but there was much quite incomprehensible to us, for the Soviet papers we now know so distorted facts concerning the white movement that we had altogether wrong conceptions. We knew where the child and her greataunt and grandmother were, and by sending simply the address on a postcard and mailing many of them one at last did reach her, and Vera eventually found her family near Odessa. Her mother had already died at last of insufficient food, and the others were in a terrible condition. Of George, she knew nothing until we, from America, wrote her in 1923 all that we knew of his falling in battle in 1920. Though this is anticipating, I will say that as far as we have been able to put together the events of their life, Vera was separated from her child about three years in all, and lost sight of George probably in 1919. She was never able to give us the details coherently. We were all in the same condition, for those years were like a long, continuous nightmare, with so few conscious awakenings to facts that it is impossible to give accurate chronological accounts of what took place.

To return to our problems: the question now was how to continue with our correspondence. We dared not post a letter in Ostashkov. We learned that Esthonia had received recognition as a separate state, and that there was a diplomatic mission in Moscow. We felt sure that through these channels letters could be safely sent, and in all probability I should find something there for myself. Oka felt that I ought to make the effort to get to Moscow.

Ever since my husband left us we had been revolving plans for escape, but had found no possibility of doing so, if the plans were to include us all. Oka had thought of getting transferred to Lake Pskov, which on one side borders Esthonia, where in his tours of inspection of the winter fisheries it might be possible for him on a dark stormy night to lose his way, and land on the Esthonian shore. But we could think of no way to include Alec in the party. And now these letters, and the existence of an Esthonian mission to Russia, seemed at least like straws floating our way and to be taken advantage of. Those letters reaching us so miraculously seemed to give us the right to believe that God would help us, if we did our share. But—how to get to Moscow?

The chaotic management of the railroad, added to the strain the war had laid on transportation, had reduced the number of trains running on our line. Instead of several a day, only two or three a week were going, and they were of course crowded. As a political move, too, traveling was discouraged, and tickets could be bought only under certain conditions, namely, with an official document proving that the holder was going on government business, or with a certificate stating need for medical treatment that could not be had locally. Naturally, I would have to come in the latter category. Twice a week a Commission met to deliberate on requests for travel. It was made up of a physician and representatives of the Communistic Party, Red Army, peasants and workers. Oka contrived to keep track of the appointments, and when a Commission that was of promising members was to meet, I went to them with a written statement from my doctor, asking for permission to go to Moscow for treatment of a serious eye-trouble. I found the rooms full of waiting men and women, largely peasants and petty merchants, going, of course, to do some "illegal" bartering for their pressing needs. The wife of a Jewish tailor (probably wishing to bring some merchandise for her husband) was just ahead of me with her medical certificate. With doors closed, I could hear nothing, but she came out very soon, crying, and whispered to me in passing, "They refused me."

So I went in with very little confidence to face a long table with a tiny lamp on it, and some eight or ten men around it. At one end before a pile of papers sat a physician whom I knew. I handed my paper to the doctor, who, looking up, said casually, "I know her. She is in bad shape and should go to an oculist." A peasant said, "That is our *barinya*. She is all right." Still another, "I painted their house. I know her—let her go."

And so I received a pink paper authorizing me to go to Moscow for medical treatment, and to report at a certain place—good for so many days. The next step was to get a ticket. Of course, Oka was told that all tickets had been sold for two weeks ahead; of course, also, we knew what that meant. The man who sold the tickets was like every one else, totally unable to support his family on his pay, and was looking for outside sources of income. So Oka obtained some meat, through barter, and took it to the man—and the ticket was at once forthcoming, without any explanation of the sudden change.

Then came the planning for the details of the journey. Moscow was on rations given those who had cards. I could hope to buy nothing; food must be carried, bread, raw potatoes, a little salt. The distance was not over two hundred miles but, with the frequent "sickness" of locomotives and other incidental delays, my absence might drag on to a week or even more, so that a good supply would have to be packed on my back, as that was the only way by which my hands would be free to push and pull myself into a train, and to hold on with, once I was inside. So I started all alone on a more adventurous, uncertain, even dangerous journey than I had ever undertaken, for Oka could not go. The train left at eleven o'clock, a cold winter night. Oka and a friend went with me to the station, crowded with a noisy struggling mass of people, all with bags on their backs. When the train pulled in, the rush and confusion were indescribable. The train seemed full before our torrent struck it, and by the time the boys got me through the crowd, the cars were overflowing on to the platform and I was unable to get inside. People with bags on their backs were swinging themselves up on the roofs, clinging to buffers, and I sat down on the steps with my feet crowded between people on the lowest step, thanking God that I was not like those seated *there*, with feet dangling in space. It was bitterly cold, but I was well packed between my neighbors.

Toward morning the guard made some people shift, and offered me a place in the crowded, filthy toilet room that was already occupied by passengers and a squealing pig in a bag. But though warmer, I exchanged places with one more frozen than I, and got back to fresh air.

In Bologoi, the junction where our branch joins the main road, we found a great crowd waiting, the aggregation of several days, but sufficient cars were hitched on to handle the throng, though we were horribly packed. I was fortunate enough to find space for sitting on the floor of the corridor, opposite the door of one of the coupés. In most instances the coupés, intended to accommodate four, were packed with a dozen or even more, but in this case two men, representatives of the newly recognized Esthonian Republic, were traveling in former comfort. Stiff and cold and hungry, for my bread had not thawed out enough to cut, I sat on the floor, eagerly craning my neck whenever the door opened, to see the unusual life going on inside. I felt like the poor man watching the rich man's table. Never have I seen any luxury or splendor that so impressed me and that seemed so unattainable, so unreal, as did what I witnessed here. Two well-dressed men in really pressed and brushed suits, polished shoes and white starched linen! Had I in some other life seen such beings? From a valise one of the men took out a neat toilet case, then a white towel (evidently where this person came from soap was used in laundries!); and as he elbowed his way through the packed corridor toward the toilet room my eyes followed him with a wondering feeling that he had come from another planet. Then I saw these fortunate creatures cut pieces of cheese, which they laid on well buttered slices of white bread! I doubt whether the world can ever again furnish me with a greater exhibition of luxury!

We arrived in Moscow after midnight. The city was

not lighted. There was not a single hotel, inn, tavern of any kind to which private citizens might go. I could not in the darkness find my way to the very distant part of the city where my relatives lived, so I joined my fellow baggers in hunting for a spot to rest in. Every available square inch seemed occupied. Even ledges of windows, high up and narrow, had men curled precariously on them. Stepping over and on and among the hundreds of sleeping forms, I found a little open space among a mass of khaki-covered figures. Here I slipped off my bag and, using it as a pillow, lay down, huddled up in the small space, and slept soundly all night. In the morning I woke stiff and cramped and very cold and damp. The snow that was frozen on our felt boots had melted from the heat of so many human bodies (though the place was not heated) and the floor had become quite wet.

As soon as daylight came, I went to my relatives. It was a long walk, made harder by the heavy bag on my back. The only trams running were for workers, who had cards indicating the distance they lived from their work. Even at hours when the cars were nearly empty, no one else could ride, and all other means of locomotion were nationalized, even bicycles, which were used by all the members of the Cheka.

My first duty was to report my presence in Moscow. My documents were carefully examined, and I was told to report daily. I had carefully committed to memory all the addresses I should need, for fear of bringing trouble on the friends whose houses might be kept under the baneful eye of the Cheka during my stay. This was one of the means used to make it impossible for people to get together who might plot a counter-revolution.

There was no mail for me, but I was able in the premises of the Legation to write a letter to Buffalo, such as I should not dare to send from home. It was difficult to believe that there, in the heart of Red Moscow, I was absolutely safe and could write what I wished.

The specialist I went to was one we knew, and he diagnosed my case as a very obscure eye trouble which, while not needing immediate surgical care, must be watched; and he recommended my coming to him every few months. This was done to make it easier if another trip to Moscow was called for later on.

Armed with this certificate, written on a blank of the hospital where the surgeon was working, I went back to headquarters to get permission to stand in line for a return ticket the next day. Presenting the doctor's certificate, I was told gruffly that the doctor's signature must be endorsed by the nearest local Communistic club! Unfortunately, I could see the doctor only in the afternoons, and the distance was too great for me to walk there before the close of his office hours. It meant an extra day—and my bread was coming to an end. The next day I went to the doctor's; he was surprised at the demand, and said he could get the signature only in the forenoon, but the next day being a holiday of the Communists, I should have to wait until the day after! Finally, the certificate having been duly adorned with Communistic seals and signatures, with a sigh of relief I walked, many miles, to the headquarters. The certificate was carefully examined, turned over, reread, evidently in the hope of finding some flaw. Suddenly the man held it out to me. "This is no good. The doctor does not say he saw you," he said.

"But how could he diagnose my case if he had not seen me?" I asked, aghast at this novel method of sabotage.

"That makes no difference. He doesn't say he saw you," was the stubborn reply.

"But look, it begins, 'Citizen Ponafidine is suffering

from——' Doesn't that mean that he examined me? And further on, it tells me to come again."

"He may merely have heard of it. Go back and tell him to write it over beginning: 'On such a date, I, so and so, saw so and so.' Then it will be in revolutionary order."

We had learned to obey, so I left, facing another two days' delay at least, many miles of walking in the slippery streets and an increasingly empty stomach. In the end, the man at the window was grudgingly satisfied, and I had permission to get a ticket. My friends lived far from the station, and it took me over two hours, so to get well up in the cue I had to leave at five in the morning. It was dark and there were no street-lamps. Had it not been for the white snow (it was January), the walk would have been impossible.

Reaching the square by seven o'clock, I found a crowd of some thirty persons already in line, and we could not hope to have the doors open before ten, I was told. At last we were permitted to march in single file into the waiting-room in such a way that by winding around and around we could nearly all be packed solidly in, each keeping his own place. When the ticket window was opened, all Red Army men were told to go first, then all on Government business, then all Communists, so that before pink tickets such as mine came into turn, the announcement was made, "No more tickets issued on the Nicholas Road. Come again to-morrow." This was repeated day by day, I forget now just how many times. I don't see why all of us did not catch fatal colds, standing for hours in zero, sometimes sub-zero, weather, after being heated by long walks, as many were. One day in particular was terrible. A strong wind made the cold worse, and as we all stood close together outside in single file, I could feel how the young Red Army man in front of me shivered. It seemed as if every muscle in his body was quivering separately, and I finally said to him, "But how you shiver!"

He turned a blue face but, laughing good-humoredly, said, "Don't you think I can feel *you* shiver?"

"But your lips—your face is livid," I went on.

"Well, you are no better. See here. Let's take turns watching each other's bags to keep our places, and run to get warm. You put your bag here behind me and I'll see to it, and you go around the block. Walk fast, slap your arms, and when you get back I'll leave my bag with you and go."

A moment of mistrust entered my mind when I thought of the big bag, filled with all my relatives could spare, that I was taking home to barter for flour to send them. But the face of the young soldier was so frank and simple, and we were so clearly in the same trouble, that I felt ashamed of my suspicions, and thankfully got the heavy bag off and started to warm myself by walking. We repeated this several times. Once the soldier came back with beaming face and told me to go to the "workers' rest house" around the corner, a former hotel, where I could sit down on the stairs and keep warm. "There is no heating but there are so many people it is warmer, and anyway you will be out of this cursed wind."

I found the place—and a sentinel at the door. When I asked if I might go in for a few minutes and get warm, "Why not?" he said. "There are lots of women there, waiting to begin work shoveling snow when it gets lighter."

So I went into the large vestibule, the whole width of which was a flight of stone stairs, on which were seated women and also some men. The air seemed decidedly warmer, and I found a seat among the women, thankful to rest myself. It was evident that I was being noticed, though really dressed more shabbily than some, and I had not been there more than a few minutes before a woman, well dressed but evidently a common person full of her own importance, came down the stairs, spoke to one and another in an arrogant way, little in keeping with the spirit a matron of a workers' home should show in a country run by "workers, soldiers and peasants." When she reached me, standing on a step above me, she said, "What are you doing here?"

"I am resting a few minutes and trying to get warm."

"You have no business here. You are a bourgeois. Get out!"

"I asked the soldier at the door if I might come. I did not do so without permission."

"He is a fool. Get out I tell you!" And she gave me a kick in the back that raised an approving laugh among the women around me.

When I returned, my friend asked why I came so soon, and he was fearlessly outspoken in his condemnation of the way things were going on. "Equality—there is no more equality now than there used to be. The difference is that there was education and brains at the top before."

We got into conversation, and he told me he was on leave, returning from the fighting line in the Crimea. We had read that the Whites had been "liquidated." Baron Wrangle had escaped, but most of his staff had been taken and all his ammunition and supplies left behind when a part of the army got out. At home we had discussed this report but could not understand how the Whites had not been able to hold the narrow neck of land connecting the Crimea with the continent. And why had Baron Wrangle not destroyed what he could not take with him? Here was a chance to learn something from an eye-witness, but I would have to be careful to conceal my interest and sympathies. So I began, "You boys evidently gave those Whites a pretty hot time."

"Well, it is a question who got the worst of it. I was

never in such hot fighting, and when at last we did break through, it was to find the Crimea deserted of the army. They had evidently got together a lot of ships and gone to Constantinople."

"Anyway, you took the staff prisoners, and all the guns and ammunition," I said.

"Not a bit of it. Scarcely any prisoners—and every gun was ruined and no ammunition found. The place was clean. They fought us to the last while loading the steamers, and it was mostly over dead bodies that we entered the Crimea. It was awful."

And was there nothing to tell me that one of those dead bodies was that of George, my first born! . . . And so we stood, day after day, until in the end we were told that, owing to the crippling of the railroad, no pink tickets would be given out until Easter! It was now the middle of January. I had no food. I could not send a telegram. Letters took weeks, and Oka would think I was dead. I started back with a heavy heart and eyes down, thinking, "Isn't there a soul in Moscow to help me?" when a cheery voice said, "Why, Emma Josifovna, what are you doing here!" I saw before me a wealthy Ostashkov Jew whom I knew only to bow to.

I told him all my troubles. "Come with me," he said. "It is a pity if I, who owe all my present prosperity to the help your husband once gave me, trusting me when no one else would, can not now repay a part of that debt. My brother-in-law is high up in the transportation department. He can get you a ticket."

This good angel took me to a well-furnished house where a table was set for breakfast, such a table as I had not seen for so long that it seemed like a fairy picture. The hostess presently came out in an elaborate negligee, and a maid (shades of Communistic equality!) brought in coffee, white rolls and butter, and a platter of cutlets. They were so fragrant! She sat down to the table alone. Her husband, who had evidently had his breakfast, was talking with me, saying it was perfectly impossible to get a ticket. He had been trying in vain for days to get a pass for his sister, and gave me little encouragement, sending my risen hopes down to zero. My newly found friend came to the rescue, saying, "Your sister can wait, but we must get Madame Ponafidine through, and in the meantime have her sit down and eat. No one ever left their house hungry in the days when they had food, and now she must not go away hungry." I shall never forget that breakfast! And two days later a ticket and "platz-carte" entitling me to a seat were obtained, and I traveled in luxury until we reached our junction at Bologoi, where we were packed into a baggage car.

It was bitterly cold, but as long as we were tightly packed we were comfortable. Ours was a branch line, however, and presently the soldiers began to drop off, until finally only a few men and myself were left. Some one discovered, with a shout of joy, a tiny sheet-iron stove, a *bourjuika* so-called, and by it some bits of wood. The soldiers with knives and bayonets tried in vain to cut off pieces small enough for the stove. Approaching a station, we saw some peasants sawing wood near by, and one of the men, bringing me his big overcoat, said, "Lie down and I'll cover you. Keep still and I'll get wood." As soon as the train slowed up, he rushed to the peasants and said, "Cut us some small bits of wood. There is a baby just born in that car, and if we can't have some wood small enough for a *bourjuika*, the child will freeze."

The kindly peasants at once set to work and soon had plenty of short wood, which they helped carry to the car. They dropped it by the stove with a pitying glance in my direction, and as the train moved, the soldiers made a fire, with many a joke as to the possibility of living well even in our hard times, "if you know how to do it."

Our joy was somewhat damped, however, when we found that there was no chimney and that the grateful flame warming our fingers was at the same time filling the car with bitter smoke. We tried putting the stove in the middle of the car and opening the sliding doors on each side, but the *bourjuika* gave out so little heat that we had to get close to it, while the draft from the doors, bringing in the below-zero air, was unbearable.

I think I was never more nearly frozen than when in the middle of the night I reached home. Oka made a good fire in the Russian stove, and I climbed upon the shelf, where our friend the doctor kept me for two days, telling Oka to heat the stove twice a day. This heroic treatment probably saved me from the serious illness that several of my companions of that night suffered.

CHAPTER TWENTY-EIGHT

An Amazing Offer

FROM this time on, in one way and another, an irregular correspondence was maintained through which we learned something of the tireless work our friends were carrying on to effect our escape. My nephew, Mr. Clement Cochran, the eldest son of my brother, whom I had not seen since as a boy of sixteen he had visited us in Russia, was apparently delegated by our friends to do the correspondence, knocking at every door in America and Europe that might lead to some way of helping us and finding George.

Of the outside world we knew nothing, and we seemed to have settled down to a steadily monotonous life, our chief ambition to get somehow enough to eat and wear, and our greatest hope to keep out of sight and avoid suspicion. One day Alec, who happened to be at home for a short time, came to me with the startling message that our County Military Commissar wished to see me. We could not imagine why I should be called, and only the unusually decent reputation of this Commissar somewhat relieved our fears. Alec and I went together to the military headquarters. We found much bustle and going and coming of Red Army men, and the Commissar very politely invited us to go into his reception-room until he finished some important conference.

We found the reception-room wonderfully familiar: a salon set of furniture upholstered in rich French material, pale yellow with embossed designs, slim Louis XV chairs, and hangings at doors and windows of the same rich but perishable material. The sofas and chairs were already stained and frayed, having been used by soldiers in rough military clothes. The furniture we at once recognized as the cherished property of one of the richest families in

Ostashkov—and more inappropriate office furniture for a military department could scarcely be imagined. This kind of waste explains much when one is asked where everything in Russia disappeared.

The Commissar soon joined us. He was exceedingly friendly, and made the following amazing proposal. He said that he had been endeavoring in vain to establish a "military farm," where enough pasture land and winter fodder for the reserve cavalry horses in Ostashkov could be had, and also the grain, vegetables and dairy products that the soldiers needed. "But all my efforts have been in vain," he continued. "I can not get a manager who does anything but think of his own pocket and of doing as little work as possible. Inefficiency or dishonesty, or both, have made every government farm we start a failure." Then came the most startling statement. "I realize that you former *pome-schiks* are the only ones on whom we can depend to do really efficient productive farming. Your own estate Bort-niki was the best managed in our State. I know that you as an American had much to do with it, and I know that if you undertake a thing you will carry it through honestly. My proposition is this: Choose any of the five following estates (he named them, including Bortniki) as the most suitable for your needs. You will have full charge, and either one of your sons you select as an assistant will be freed from his present service. I will not now determine your salary but you shall have everything you want, and you will have full authority."

I was speechless. My first thought was an overwhelming consciousness of exultation that we, the despised class, held up as enemies of the people, were by this man at least admitted to have been of use in the economic life of the country, and people to be trusted for efficiency and honesty. I can scarcely describe the glow of gratitude that filled me.

As soon as I found my tongue, without waiting to talk it over with Alec I absolutely and emphatically declined. I tried to express my appreciation of his having acknowledged what the large landowners had done for agriculture, and thanked him for his good opinion of us in particular, but I told him that we had, after years of persecution, escaped from the noose that hung around the neck of every *pomeschik*, that we had been reduced to the rank of the proletariat, which relieved us somewhat from daily fear of arrest, and I would not willingly put my head into the noose again. If I accepted his offer, I would carry out my responsibilities, insisting on obedience that would insure the work of the farm being done properly and in season, and the cattle and horses being cared for by reliable men. "All this," I argued, "would now be obtained with great difficulty, for, as you know, the comrades' idea of liberty is to work when and how they wish. Every order my son and I should give them that they did not like would be reported at headquarters as a desire on our part to establish 'serfdom.' We should be 'tyrants,' 'blood-suckers,' again."

"No, no, you would have absolute authority, and I would uphold you in it. Military discipline would be established."

"That would not save us. We should be the direct intermediates. Orders would come through us and we should be the sufferers. I am sure you would stand back of us—but suppose you got a promotion and were removed. Can I count on any other man who may take your place as having your broad views? Won't your possible successor be met with full accounts of this resurrected bourgeois family which has returned to the *pomeschiks'* favorite tactics of oppressing the poor peasants? Would not these accusations bring my sons and me 'to the wall' that we have so far escaped? No, I thank you warmly for your confidence, but I am afraid to accept the offer."

We had a long talk and finally the Commissar gave us two weeks to consider the proposal, hoping, as he said, that we would see our advantage in accepting it. The one sinister note in his arguments, one that brought to me a feeling of dread, was his remark, "Think it over, and I believe you will voluntarily consent. Of course, as you are a woman I would bring no force to bear upon you. With your sons it is different." We parted with a cordial hand-shake—but what did he mean?

To-day I can ask, was it the shadow of the coming "voluntary" consent of thousands of peasants now, in 1931, being so cruelly forced to "voluntary" collectivization?

As we walked home we discussed the plan. There was much to attract us to it. At least one of the brothers would be safe from military service, and probably the other could be drawn in too. It was a work into which we could conscientiously throw all our energies, showing what an honestly administered government farm could produce and proving that the grain-producing sources were the large landowners. On the other hand was the certainty of opposition to any controlling head and policy. None of these workers could be counted on to do more than the strictly allotted eight hours of work, and to do it as he pleased. Farming, when sudden rain came in harvest-time, a strayed cow to be recovered, sick animals to be cared for in the night—things like these could not be done by voting. Who was to do the extra work, and how? We could never make the work a success, however carefully we handled the workers, without arousing all the people against "bossing." After much debate we all three decided to stand firm in refusing.

Shortly after, the two weeks were up, but we decided to wait. Finally the Commissar sent to know why we had not come to give the answer. The boys felt it safer for me to keep away, and Alec went alone. The Commissar was as

cordial as ever and listened to Alec's statement of the reason
for our refusal. When he had finished, the Commissar said
with a laugh, "Well, you are more nearly right than you
know. I am leaving, and the one who is to succeed me certainly will not see things as I do."

Later we learned that this Commissar had not been pro-
moted, as I had diplomatically put it, but was dismissed not
only from his post but from the party, as not being sufficiently "true to the revolutionary party spirit."

About this time an acquaintance brought a large portfolio crammed full of papers, asking us to hide them for him,
as there were documents compromising many, which if found
would lead to certain death. Oka was still in the Fisheries
Department and his motor-boat was kept in a little inner
harbor surrounded by the store-houses of the Department
and guarded by Red Sentinels day and night. No outsiders
were permitted to enter. So Oka managed to conceal, in
this safest of hiding-places, the dangerous package, placing
it inside the motor, where it was securely locked. A few days
later Oka left for Petrograd on official business, and Alec,
who happened to be still on leave, went from time to time
to see to the motor-boat or to take it out when needed.

One night during Oka's absence a drive was made on
Ostashkov and over fifty arrests made. One young man was
taken from our house. There was no warning knock at
the gate, but swarming over the wall they came to our door.
We were awake, thanks to Tsigan's barking, and ready.
These night visitations were so nerve-racking that some
families we knew never retired until after two o'clock, when
they had a pretty good chance of sleeping the remainder of
the night unmolested.

The day after the arrests, the wife of one of those taken
came to us privately, begging to have us burn in her presence
the package her husband had given Oka to hide. So far the

arrests had been made on suspicion, but these documents would furnish names and facts involving them all, and there would be no hope of saving their lives.

I told her we should not dare to burn so much in our room, where, if interrupted, we could not hope to conceal our work. Besides, her coming to us would certainly bring more suspicion on our house. I insisted on her going away and not coming again, promising that Alec and I would decide on a safe way of getting rid of the dangerous package. The terrified woman was loath to give up seeing with her own eyes the destruction of papers that were virtually the death-sentence of her husband and all his friends, but I persuaded her to trust us. Alec and I had a long talk as to how the package could be destroyed, and finally went to a friend who had so often saved us by his advice and influence. He agreed that our room was not safe, and suggested our doing the burning in his house, where there were many rooms and stoves, and where we could keep watch from the windows for any one's approach. Alec took a large basket of implements, cleaning rags, and the like, and went to the harbor, grumbling to the sentinel in passing that his brother had left him the dirty work of cleaning the motor. The entire morning he spent taking the machinery to pieces, oiling, cleaning and polishing the brass in plain sight of many. When he had finished and started home, under the implements in the basket was the large package that if discovered meant death to some fifty people and would involve us in the same fate for having attempted to conceal the documents.

Passing the sentinel and walking through the streets with the compromising basket was one of Alec's worst experiences, for he had every reason to expect that he might be challenged. Opening the package, we took out several millions of paper roubles, which we hid, and then went to work to destroy the papers, the great importance of which a hasty perusal proved and made us the more eager with trembling fingers to start them burning. The family was divided, some stationed at windows to give alarm, others in the various rooms feeding the fires as fast as they dared. Every one breathed freely when the last bit of paper was burned beyond danger of being read and the envelope containing the money was eventually got to the woman with the assurance that all was well. The arrested men were kept for some days in freight cars on the tracks outside the city. They were fed on scant rations of salt herrings and bread and water. No bedding, not even straw, was provided. On the second day Alec went to the cars taking some food and clothing. A switchman, seeing him, asked if he was going to the prisoners, and advised him not to. "Every one who has come to see them has been arrested," he said, "and you will be too."

As the victims were Jews, Alec felt he was in no danger, so he went on to where a Chekist was guarding the platform of one of the cars, and asked him if he might give what he had brought to——(naming the man). "What is he to you?" was the answer. "These can not be related to you, they are Jews."

"No, not related, but this young fellow is sick. He has no relatives here, and happening to lodge in the same house with us, he has interested us. That is all."

The Chekist proved to be a decent fellow and called our friend to the platform. After that, Alec went every day—a walk of several miles—and occasionally, when he could not go, I went. The order of procedure was always the same. I stood on the ground, our friend on the platform, the guard between us, and whatever I gave had to pass through the guard's hand. We spoke as through an interpreter, not being permitted to speak directly. "Tell him to give me anything he wants washed," I would say. "Tell

her to get me some cigarettes if possible," he would sometimes add—and we would wave good-by.

A few days later the prisoners were sent to Moscow and
thrown into prison, where they were kept many years. Here
again occurred one of the many coincidences that so often
came to us in such unexpected ways.

Among the town-folk who went into the country to get
food, a Moscow dentist came to Ostashkov, and we took him
in. There were no hotels or inns of any kind, and people
would get a note of introduction or, more often, because less
dangerous, an oral message from a mutual friend, asking us
to give shelter—a floor to lie on, that was all. So we often
had one or several men, virtually strangers, with whom we
shared our one room and our hot water in the morning for
them to make their tea. Then they would go into the
villages as we directed them, carrying clothing, bits of
jewelry, pots and pans—any of the things the peasants could
not buy and for which they would gladly exchange food.

The next time I went to Moscow I took advantage of this
dentist's invitation and slept at his house, on the floor in a
tiny vacant room, and sat at table with him and his wife,
sharing their hot water and eating my own bread and potatoes. At this time I managed to get in touch with our
friend in prison. Friends were permitted to take food to
the prisoners once a week, but not to see them. I carried a
few things in a knapsack and asked the guard to bring
it back so that I could use it again. Under the lining I slipped
a note, and when the bag came back I found a few words
penciled on my paper, saying he was coughing badly and
doubted whether he would live long if he remained in the
damp basement where he then was. And here the coincidence came in. My dentist's father was the prison doctor!
Thanks to him, our friend was placed in the infirmary, where
he had comparatively luxurious quarters and where it was

easier to send him food; and there he was kept all the rest of his imprisonment. Even after our escape from Russia, while the American Relief Administration was saving so many millions of lives, we sent through this organization packages that we know reached him in prison.

CHAPTER TWENTY-NINE

My Search for the A. R. A.

In July, 1921, we heard that an American relief expedition had been organized on a large scale under the direction of Mr. Hoover, and was even then in Moscow. Nothing so wildly exciting had come to us, cut off as we had been from all regular and reliable news from the outer world. My boys felt that our friends in the United States would surely take advantage of this opportunity for direct contact, and they advised my going to Moscow to see the A. R. A. people. Again the red tape of getting permission to go for treatment for my eyes. At length, however, I arrived in Moscow, and was told by my friends that the letters A. R. A. and the American flag had been seen on cars and trucks, but no one could tell me how to locate the Administration.

It seems incredible now that a city like Moscow could be in so chaotic a state as to make it impossible to locate so big an organization. But so it was. There were no telephone books that I could get, no address department, which was so useful in old times, no stores, groceries, bakeries from which one could learn something of the neighbors. No possible way seemed safe for me to get the desired information.

Finally I decided to go to the Foreign Office, where I had already had, in a previous visit, a very disagreeable interview with Comrade Weinstein. To him I went, saying that as an American I was anxious to know where I could find the Hoover people.

"I remember you," were his first words, disagreeably spoken. "You came to me with a cooked-up request to resume American citizenship and yet have grown-up sons here. What do you want now?" He went on to say that he, too, had heard of the proposed Hoover Commission, but that they had not yet arrived in Russia.

"Then could you give me the address of the Friends whose work I learn has been going on here for some time?"

"They were here, but we have sent them out of Russia," was the curt reply.

"Well, there is an English Commercial Mission somewhere in Moscow, isn't there? They may know some of my friends."

"They too are gone," he said, rising, and added in an exasperated tone, "You may take a broom and sweep Moscow and you won't find an American or an Englishman here." At the same time, he kicked shut a drawer in his desk that my eyes had been glued upon, for I saw a pile of English newspapers. The words "Minister to the Republic of Georgia" had fixed my attention. What had happened? How was Georgia a republic? The drawer safely closed against my imprudently inquisitive eyes, the comrade turned and gave me a twisted smile that I felt meant "No, you don't!"

I went out convinced that every one of those whom the most responsible Under-Secretary of the Foreign Department had said were sent away were still in Moscow. I also knew that all foreigners would have to come to this office many times, and so I decided to take up my abode there, so to speak.

In the outer room a simple woman, wife of the janitor of the Tsarist Foreign Office, sat by the window at the information desk. I told her I should have to wait for an answer to my petition—could I sit there? "Why not? Sit down." We got into conversation. She told me much of her life but soon turned her attention to a Red Army man who came in and, sitting on the window-ledge, visited with her. "Look," the woman exclaimed, pointing out of the window to an elderly woman who was crossing the street with a saw

over her shoulder and whose ragged dress ironically indicated her former prosperity; "isn't that a good sight, a *bourjuika* obliged to go and saw out some of the building wood
to make a fire? That is the kind that used to come into the
kitchen and make a scene if the soup was over-salted, or tell
the laundry woman whose back was aching that she did not
make the linen white. Now let her ache!"

The Red Army man's eyes, as did mine, followed the
woman crossing the street, then turning to the speaker, he
said, "Eh, comrade, do you think it is better now, and that
all are equal? There are just as many on top now—the only
difference is that those people were learned and knew how
to make themselves rich and the country comfortable. Now
there is no salt to over-salt any one's soup, and our women's
backs ache from trying to wash clothes without soap. That's
our equality."

I could scarcely believe my ears at such open criticism.
I do not know how long I sat there, carefully scanning
each of the many persons who kept coming and going,
hoping to see a foreigner; and at last I was rewarded.
A tall, slim, clean shaven man, with English written all
over him, entered.

Hurriedly I intercepted him and explained my trouble.
"We certainly are all here," he said. "I belong to the
English Commercial Mission. The Hoover people have
been in a hotel but have just moved to new, and I hear very
fine, quarters that have been assigned them by this office,
but I do not know the address. If you would go to the
Friends, they would surely know, for they are American."
And he gave me their address.

Fervently thanking him, I made my way to a former
hotel, where the Quakers' offices were. Going up to the
man at the information desk, I asked (and here ensued another characteristic conversation), "Will you please give me

the number of the rooms occupied by the American Quaker Relief Organization?"

"Whom do you wish to see?"

"Any one of the Organization."

"What name?"

"I do not know any individuals. My business is with any one of the Americans."

"Listen to her!" he appealed to space, throwing out both hands. "She comes to me to see some one and she can't tell me whom she wants to see!"

"But I tell you," I patiently and meekly urged, "I want to see any one officially connected with the Organization.

"How am I to know all the offices here—it is a big place," he parried.

I ventured: "Have you a list of tenants?"

"Of course."

"Well, if you would be so good as to read them, I could recognize an American name."

"The lists are secret," he fired at me.

When I had nearly given up hope, he called to a man near the door, "Here, take this citizen to the American Relief rooms," and after being made to deposit all my documents, passport, etc., I was escorted up-stairs (elevators had long since succumbed to Communistic principles) and ushered into what was evidently a whole floor of offices and storerooms with boxes and packages reaching almost to the ceiling. I found only one of the Friends in charge, a sweet-faced Irish girl. A stenographer, sitting at the far end of the room writing, was evidently a Russian Jewess. I stated my case and my difficulty, but found the Friend as vague as had been the Englishman in regard to the address of the A. R. A. She told me they had moved from the Savoy Hotel, and added that such a large organization could not have moved without their destination being known at the hotel.

We got into conversation and I asked the woman, who had already been in Russia for some time, if she felt that in their work the Americans had been able to see below the surface and to sense what was really going on in Russia. "As to conditions in general," she replied, "no, but as to child welfare, I think we are able to judge. In this department I think that much is being done and many of the methods used here could with advantage be adopted in other countries."

Knowing from experience the difference between Bolshevism in theory and in practise, I gasped out, "Well, you have evidently been shown and told just what the Bolsheviki wish you to believe." The girl at the far desk suddenly raised her head and gave me a deadly look that convinced me she understood my imprudent exclamation, and I realized too late my foolishness. In a few moments she left the room for just long enough for me to whisper, "That girl understands English!"

"Oh, no, she has been with us some time but does not understand spoken English. She only does our Russian work and can read to copy English," she calmly replied.

"Indeed, she does," I said, and, as the girl was returning, I added with my lips only, "She is a spy." And the dear unsuspicious Quaker woman answered me amiably, "Oh, no, she can read and copy English, but she has never been able to learn to understand spoken English nor to speak it."

The girl modestly took her seat and I decided that my business was to get hold of my documents and disappear (if it were not already too late) before she got word down to the office. Hurriedly taking leave, I rushed down-stairs and asked for my documents, trembling lest they be refused me. But they were handed over, and pocketing them, I put as quickly as possible a good distance between me and that sinister girl whose eyes I can still remember.

To the Savoy Hotel I went, only to find the people in

charge there as uncommunicative as the others had been. What could be the object in trying to conceal the whereabouts of people I should sooner or later find? I talked to the hotel folk for a long time. "Yes, the Americans have been here, but no one knows to what address they have moved." Of course I knew this was a lie. At last, however, I was told that there was a man living in the hotel who would know. He was out just then but would be back in half an hour, and he gave a name that decided me *not* to be there in half an hour! So, thanking the man, I said I would do an errand while waiting, and immediately put as many blocks as I could between me and the hotel. I wondered what steps to take next and walked on aimlessly, until I nearly ran into Oka's chief, a man very influential and seemingly very friendly toward us, but one of the most unprincipled persons I ever met. He was a gentleman, a man who had occupied high civic positions in olden times, a most delightful person in society but one not to be trusted. When I told him of my day's work and failure, he promised to get all the information I needed. Just then we saw a car pass us with a small British Union Jack on it, and my companion ran to the corner to see where the turning car was headed. He waved to me to come on. There, just around the corner, the car had stopped before a building over the door of which were the words, "British Commercial Agency."

Here was another one of the institutions which Comrade Weinstein had assured me had left Russia! I went in and found, among a number of others, the very Englishman I had met in the Foreign Office. He was greatly amused at my story. "Just like them," he said, "to lie when there is no real need to do so, and make a mystery of what they know will be uncovered."

Here in the office I was given at last the address of a well-known house, or twin houses, built in lavish semi-Oriental

style by two wealthy Armenian brothers. It was some distance, and I had been walking all day—the relatives with
whom I lodged estimated, when I told them where I had been
during the day, that I had gone over ten miles, and on bread
and potatoes. Here at last I found the headquarters of the
A. R. A. Everything was in confusion there, furniture being
moved in and office equipment being set up. I saw some
young Americans carrying chairs, and my heart beat fast as
I looked at them—as beings from another world. While
waiting for my name to be taken to some one in authority,
I watched these boys. They were bothered with the doors,
which, having no latches or locks, would not open and shut
easily. "Queer people, these Russians! Such a magnificent
house, such floors and decorations—and what a hodge-podge
of furniture! And no locks on the doors!" It evidently
did not occur to them that they were in the house of people
who had been driven out; that everything removable, even
the door-knobs, had been taken away; that the ill-assorted
furniture now there was loot from other places. But I
said nothing, for there were Russians going and coming.

Finally I was received by the director of the Moscow
branch, Mr. Carroll, and Mr. V. A. Turner, who had letters
for me. Both these men were so cordial, so understanding,
that for the first time in years I felt safe and among my own
kind. I shall never forget their kindly reception and the
fight I had to keep from breaking down and sobbing. Mr.
Turner gave me a letter from my nephew, Clement Cochran,
the first one I had had that was written clearly and without
fear of censorship. I was told that, according to the agreement between the United States and the Soviets, the relief
work was to be carried on under certain conditions, among
them the release of all American citizens, my name being included on the supposition that I would automatically renew
my American citizenship after the death of my husband.

Many arguments were used to persuade me to take advantage of this permission and to leave Russia. All my friends in America considered it the thing to be done, and so did Mr. Carroll and Mr. Turner, who urged me to apply for a passport and go at once. But the permission would not include my sons—and that ended the question. To leave them and go where I should be safe and always have food, while never knowing day by day if they were alive, was not even to be considered. We had suffered so much together that none of us could think of separation. Whatever happened should come to us together. I do not think that those kind American men, brought up in an atmosphere so different from that of present Russia, could understand my point of view. Then and in the months that followed, the arguments always were, "You can do no good by staying. Your sons will be happier to know you are safe. Your being with them in hard times makes it worse for them." All these words failed to touch me. Nothing could induce me to leave Russia by myself. All I had was my sons, and my only happiness could be in sharing whatever fate was theirs.

The Hoover Commission was very loyal in keeping to their agreement not to interfere with any internal politics, and I soon realized that I could not advise with them as to all of us getting out of the country in an illegal way. So I could only enjoy the unspeakable comfort of talking with trusted friends and of sending messages to those in America. I was given money, too,—English pounds, sent by my friends, and a package of food to eat on my way back. In the package was a can of chicken à la king, which I took home and which furnished an almost forgotten flavor for our potatoes for several days. A can of *café au lait* also was made to last for several days by using just a little each morning to flavor our rye coffee. There were besides some chocolate and a package of candles, perhaps the greatest luxury of all.

My experience in hunting up the A. R. A. made the Englishman laugh, but he did not realize the tragedy back of it—the deceit practised on the people. My friends in Moscow knew of the Quaker Mission as practically a Soviet institution, for the Quakers trustingly worked through the Soviet, who found it easy therefore to spread the impression that the relief work was prompted by political sympathy, that it was in fact the American Bolsheviki who had sent over help to their comrades in Russia. When the Hoover Commission arrived, every means was used to keep them from coming into contact with anti-Bolsheviki. This was proved in the childish attempt of officials even to keep me from finding them. The rumor was spread everywhere that the provisions brought by the A. R. A. were also sent by the American proletariat in token of political sympathy. To recognize any more idealistic motive was not in their Soviet program. That this was and is still one of the regularly practised measures for leading the Russian public astray was astonishingly illustrated in the report of Mr. Hoover's election. The Soviet press, in speaking of it, said, "The name of the newly elected President is familiar to our peasants, as Mr. Hoover, one of the greatest capitalists of the great capitalistic country of the United States, was engaged at an unusual salary because of his great executive ability to deliver and distribute the food and medicine bought by the Soviet in America at a high price during the Russian famine."

It was hard for me while in Russia to convince those with whom I talked that the A. R. A. had come as a humane institution to save the starving; that the money had been given by individuals, churches, institutions, regardless of political or denominational views; that the money voted by Congress was also sent from motives of sympathy for suffering and by no means as a political gesture.

I turned my face homeward, cheered by the letters and the knowledge that there were friends in Moscow to whom we could perhaps appeal in case of trouble. The money I had received I sewed into my fur cap, and I remember my dismay when, slipping on the icy pavement, I lay for a few moments unable to move, while my cap and its precious contents rolled away from me on the sidewalk.

This time I was lucky enough to get a ticket and, what was more, a seat in the train. The cars were almost dark in the daytime, for the glass in the windows had been broken and replaced with boards. Only an occasional small pane had been put in, for glass, too, had disappeared. At night, the train was not lighted, so I took out one of my candles,— and became the most important person in the car! Cigarettes would be passed up, handed from one to another, for the "comrade of the candle" to light. Now and then, some one trying to locate his belongings would ask the "comrade of the candle" to lend it for a few minutes. The car was crammed, the corridor so full that people could pass only by crawling over the shoulders of those seated on the floor. At last we settled down to sleep as best we could, packed four and even six on a seat. As I blew out my precious candle and went to sleep sitting bolt upright, my feet crushed between the people on the floor sitting between the seats, I was suddenly wakened by loud cries of "Catch him, catch him, he has stolen my meat!" Then, in a babel of sounds, a shout went up, "Here he is! We have him. Comrade of the candle, light up!" And presently my candle disclosed a confused struggling mass, in which was a man hugging tight the stolen bag of meat. A court martial was immediately held around the candle. A man made a statement that was upheld by his seat-mates, that he had put the bag of meat under his head in his upper berth, which he was sharing with several others. He woke by feeling the bag being drawn from under his head. It was meat he had bartered for his overcoat. Food was more precious in those days than diamonds, and the man who at such a time stole food could not hope for mercy. Once the guilty fellow had acknowledged his theft, the method of punishment was discussed most callously. About this time, I wished that Mr. Turner had not put candles into my package. The judges decided to administer fifty blows on the naked back, given with the buckle end of a military belt. The man was stripped and the blows began, the buckle doing havoc on the poor back, while the howls of the thief rose louder and louder. There were a number of women, and we stood it as long as we could, for we felt that stealing food was too serious a crime to be overlooked, but still it was hard to see so brutal a punishment. We all set up a protest, but as no attention was paid to us, I blew out the candle. The confused curses and howls that followed showed that some of the blows were going wild. Gradually things quieted down, and each traveler clung tighter than ever to bags and packages.

CHAPTER THIRTY

First Move toward Freedom

THE report I brought back to Oka convinced us that our only hope of leaving was to escape illegally. The A. R. A. could not be involved in it, and for their sake we had better keep away from them.

We realized that in some way we must all get together in Petrograd or some other large city, from which our escape would attract least attention. In Ostashkov every child knew us. We should be missed, perhaps caught, and in any case bring trouble to our friends. We could not see far ahead, but we had a very real sense of the miracle of that first letter reaching us, and we felt that the Hand that had guided it to us would lead us on if we did our share. Our first duty was to get together—all three of us.

Oka took his chief into his confidence sufficiently to ask him to help get Alec back from the Polish front to be with us. An official trip to Moscow was invented, and Oka started to see one of the Commissars high up in the military service, who when in Ostashkov had been exceedingly friendly to us. A sincere Communist by conviction, he was about the only one we ever met who had any human kindness in his nature. He had told Oka that if ever he needed a friend to come to him. So Oka went, taking with him a sack of grain to cement the friendship. He told the Commissar frankly that he had come to Moscow to ask for a transfer of Alec to Ostashkov, putting the request on the ground of my loneliness and desire to have both sons near me in those times. The Commissar at once consented. He told Oka to go home and send a written application from his chief. This was easily procured—an application for transferring Comrade Ponafidine, "an expert in forming fishers' co-

266

operatives, to Ostashkov." So Alec was transferred, though his ideas of fishers' cooperatives were decidedly hazy. He was given a few days' vacation before entering upon his duties, as he came home sick and running a high temperature.

During those days one of the sudden changes to which Bolshevik policy was accustoming us took place. The Fisheries Department in Ostashkov was wound up and was to go out of existence. That would mean the return of both my sons to active military service. Fortunately, we knew it would require some weeks to liquidate so large an organization. Something could yet be done.

None of the results of Bolshevism has reacted more disastrously on the character and morals of the country than the daily deceit and lying that became necessary for existence. Not a step of a normal life could be taken normally. To get food and clothes, deceit had to be practised. To evade expulsion from your own house or to travel on legitimate business—in a word, to obtain any of the privileges that we consider the rights of decent citizens—one had to bribe and lie. We looked upon all this as a temporary condition that we must face as one does the unethical, and even illegal, demands forced upon individuals in time of war. We felt that we had as much right to do our best to outwit and deceive the Bolsheviki as we would any other band of robbers.

To carry out the simple plan of moving to another city, therefore, we had to employ all the ingenuity developed during the four years of living as hunted animals. All our resources of hidden property had to be drawn on for carefully placed bribes. Oka went to his chief and told him that all that remained to save him and Alec from military service was to get a transfer to the Fisheries Department of Petrograd, which had not yet been cut down; or, if this plan failed, at least he must get to Petrograd to take other measures for finding employment. So Oka went to Petrograd officially, as transferred to the Fisheries Department there, since some reason for traveling had to be given before tickets could be obtained. He was well supplied with money that we had been collecting by selling some of the hidden property.

Thanks to friends and underground measures, Oka succeeded in getting Alec into the military engineering work as a specialist in bridge building, and himself as chief of one of the sections of astro-physics. Truly, one could turn one's hand to anything in Soviet Russia! Here was Alec, a university graduate in law, whose military training had been in the Air Department, supposed to be building bridges; and Oka, who was also a lawyer by education and had been doing work in forests and among fish, considered competent to be employed in a department the very name of which carried little meaning to him! When this was arranged, a lodging was found in a very inconspicuous street far from any of our former connections, and some fire-wood laid in. This done, Oka went to the Fisheries Department to get his documents signed, permitting him to buy a ticket for his return to Ostashkov. Here a new blow awaited him: he found that the Petrograd branch of the Department was non-existent; it had been liquidated, and there was therefore no way to get a permit. So here he was, stranded, though not for the first time. Once before, in 1918, he had been absolutely unable to get out of Petrograd. It was only through a Jew that he eventually succeeded in returning home. Without the help of the Jews little could be done in those days, for they held all the strings in their hands, and for friendship in some cases, as we often found, or money or its equivalent, in others, they could and did do much.

So again Oka went to them, and this time received a much bestamped and sealed little passport book which contained his photograph and described his mission as "A revision of the Red Cross work in Ostashkov." Thanks to this document, he reached home safely.

We then began to prepare for openly leaving Ostashkov. Our cow and piano did not belong to us, since there was no private property; they had been given us to "use." But again the difference between Bolshevism in theory and in practise, and the slogan, "All things are possible if you know how to go about it," saved us. We sold our cow and piano to Jews, the one for four and a half million roubles, the other for five million. I had never dreamed of being a millionaire, much less a multi-millionaire, and though well knowing the worth—or worthlessness—of the rouble, I was rather awe-stricken. A million of anything, be it matches or bacteria, is an impressive concept!

The payment for the cow was made in two nights. The first time, a bag was brought containing, the purchaser said, two millions. "I haven't counted the money," he added, "but I am sure the different packages are correct as marked and tied in thousands. If you care to go to the bother of verifying, do so, and let me know if there is a shortage. I am ready to make it up." Even after years of Communistic training had accustomed us to the disappearance of gold and silver and to dizzy falls in paper money, I could not reconcile myself to such carelessness in handling millions. The boys good-naturedly yielded to what I now realize was a foolish insistence on my part, and we gathered around the table, with doors and windows locked, and the bag open on the floor, ready in case of alarm. The money was in notes of one hundred, one thousand, though some were of smaller denominations. That counting has given me a little more adequate conception of what a million units are! We found in the first payment a shortage of a few hundred roubles, but the second instalment had a surplus that brought the total to a fairly close balance.

All that was left of our hidden property and what we did not take with us was turned into food—dried fish, cereals and flour. This we placed in the care of a friend, to be taken to Petrograd as needed, if our escape was not soon effected. In case "anything happened to us" and we did not return, we asked the friend to notify Vera, who would find some way of getting it.

Our dear faithful Tsigan was taken by the cousin who had been with us at the time of my husband's death and who often had come to us in Ostashkov. Tsigan, very conservative in his affections, had struck up an unusual friendship with this cousin, and we knew he would have a good home with her. She has written us how completely he has constituted himself her body-guard, and day and night keeps close to her. The cat had died, and Daisy, the fox terrier, old and crabbed with strangers, went with us and made a great sensation when the crowds struggling to get into the train saw a dog! In her old age, even a meager diet went to fat, and I feared that her plumpness would add to our complications, so that I tried to keep her out of sight. A man who knew us slightly was just behind us, and he probably heard, as we did, the increasingly ugly remarks around us. Suddenly he said in a loud voice, "Americans love dogs. This is an American woman come over to see what help can be given us where there is lack of food, and she has brought her pet dog along with her."

At once the chorus changed. "Let her pass. Give way, this is an American woman." And thanks to Daisy, she and I had a comparatively comfortable seat in a coupé all night, while my sons sat on their bags somewhere in the corridors. Even though there were familiar faces around, no one betrayed me by disputing the story that even made it possible for me to get, through the guard, a drink of water.

It was about two in the morning that a refined-looking,

white-haired gentleman opened the door of the back stairs of his apartment and ushered us into our new and last home in Russia. His was a fine, almost richly furnished apartment, with piano, good library, all as yet "unrequisitioned," for in cities less of that was done than on the scattered country estates. Oka had succeeded in getting us a small room in which the two boys were to sleep, and a corner of the large living-room, where, behind a bookcase moved across, was put up a small camp-bed for me. So, though all might share the living-room by day, this corner was ours. Our landlord, a bachelor in delicate health, let us have this free of rent in return for the housework and cooking I did. There were others in the various rooms, and the kitchen was common property.

Tired and cold, we unpacked enough to make ourselves comfortable for the remainder of the night, and discussed the best plan for hiding, for the moment, the very bulky package on which our future depended, for it contained, with other things, the precious dollars and pounds that little by little Mrs. Clement had got over to us, and a few valuable documents. These, for the night, were put under my bed and we were soon asleep. Suddenly I was awake. Some one was moving. I rose and very softly opened my door, and looking through the large dining-room with its polished hardwood floor shining in the half light, and through still another room, I could see the hall leading from the kitchen, which was lighted. I heard men's voices and heavy footsteps, and then my blood froze as I saw, one after another, several blue-jackets pass toward the room of our host. A domiciliary visit conducted by sailors, the most dreaded class at that time! There was no hope of a familiar or friendly face to save us here, and our documents were very incriminating. I closed the door, praying that Daisy would not give way to the fox terrier shrill bark, and hurried to the

boys. I touched each one, and whispered, "Sailors are
searching the house." In an instant they were both in full
possession of their wits, and turned to find a hiding-place
for the money and documents. They asked if our neighbors
in the opposite room were awake. I told them I thought not.
"Then we must warn them—they may have things to hide."
And one of the boys, stealing out and knocking softly,
warned our fellow lodgers, while the other and I were undoing the package. We felt very much as I imagine rats do
in a trap—and with about as much hope. The letters we hid
between the leaves of various books in the library, hoping
that if search were made, some at least might be overlooked.
The Soviet money we decided not to attempt to conceal, as
it was too bulky and less incriminating than anything else
we had, and it would perhaps avert further search. Then
we turned off the light and lay down to seem to be asleep
when they came. For a long time we could occasionally hear
voices and heavy-booted footsteps, but none came toward
our rooms. To us it seemed hours that we lay, trembling
at every sound. At last we heard the outer door slam
heavily. Peeking out, we found all quiet, though the lights
in the kitchen were still burning; then we heard our landlord
moving about. One of the boys crept toward the kitchen
and, assuring himself that no sailors were there, went to our
host. Gradually other doors were stealthily opened and all
the occupants of the apartment gathered to hear how, as
by a miracle, we had been saved.

This was the explanation. At this time all houses were
nationalized. There was no private ownership and therefore no one responsible for repairs. "House Committees"
were then formed, recognized by the Soviet and made of
great use by them. The House Committee would lay nominal
rent on the large apartment-houses, such as we were in, and
from this fund make repairs that were absolutely necessary.

The Soviet held the Committee responsible for each inhabit-
ant, and even for any casual lodger for a night, all of whom
had to be reported. This simplified the policing of the city.
Our landlord was chairman of our House Committee, and
these blue-jackets had come to him to get information concerning a "counter-revolutionist" they were after, who had
been traced to this house and to the apartment of a doctor
living several floors above us. To that apartment our host
had been obliged to take them, and there this man, a brother-
in-law of the doctor, was found spending the night. The
place was searched, the man sought arrested, and with him
the doctor for having failed to report the visitor. The chairman, our host, would also surely have been arrested but for
the doctor's taking all the blame upon himself. Our landlord was therefore made only to act as witness, and then allowed to return to his broken night's sleep. When we left
Petrograd, weeks later, the doctor was still in prison, and his
wife unable to get in touch with him or to learn of his fate.

CHAPTER THIRTY-ONE

The Struggle for a Passport

OUR new life began. We found a comparatively safe place for our compromising packages. Alec went daily to his regiment of engineers, where his bridge building was confined to clerical work; but he had to report regularly and work under the menace of very compromising documents. We felt, therefore, that he was all the time living over a volcano. Oka for the time being was safer; his documents showed that he had a temporary release from military service on account of his health. His work in the astrophysics department was limited to the examination of libraries for the selecting of such literature, and only a knowledge of languages was here required, and no regular hours of service were set. This was a tremendous advantage, making it possible for him to get about and do much that Alec's confined life under constant suspicion rendered it impossible for him to do. But we knew that at any moment his "age" might be called into military service, to be sent off somewhere to the front. Haste was therefore imperative. But in what way was it to be made? We had done all we could—had settled in a large city—could be easily lost— but how to find the next step? What measures could we take? All communication with the outside world had again ceased. We thought of trying to get at least one of the boys or myself a job in the Petrograd branch of the A. R. A., but met with no encouragement there. To-day we are glad I failed, for after the A. R. A. left Russia most of those who had worked for that organization and been suspected of giving information displeasing to the Soviet were imprisoned, while others were exiled, never yet to be heard of.

Days passed. Our millions were disappearing. Between

them, the two boys were getting nominally thirty-four thousand roubles a month, but often lack of cash left them without pay, small as theirs was. It will be remembered, however, that at that time meat cost forty thousand roubles a pound, butter forty-eight thousand, sugar one hundred and forty thousand. Shoes I had bought just before leaving Ostashkov were one and one-half million roubles. We were not so well off, therefore, as one might think, and for that reason, if no other, we must set out before our means were exhausted. But how? Every door seemed closed. It was not only that the Russian frontiers were guarded with almost inconceivable closeness, but even if we slipped through the Red line we should be caught and sent back, as were most persons, especially the men. It seemed useless to attempt anything without first making close contact with the other side, where, as we had learned from Mr. Cochran, arrangements for our safety had been made. But how to get in touch? Our family council finally decided that it would be wise for me to go to Moscow and get permission to leave Russia. That permission the A. R. A. could obtain for me, and once legally out of the country, I could from the other side prepare the way for the boys' safe reception if they succeeded in getting out secretly. I fought this plan for a long time, dreading above all the separation, for fear it might be permanent, but finally I yielded to the boys' insistence, mentally reserving for myself the decision as to whether I would ever make use of the passport when once obtained.

Though the train was crowded, I traveled in comparative comfort, and found that since Lenine's N. E. P. had gone into effect, with many temporary changes for the better following, life in Moscow was more tolerable. There were street lights, few and dim, and some open stores, though everything was impossibly high in price.

I was disappointed to find that none of those I knew in

the city, except Professor Archibald C. Coolidge of Harvard, who was in charge, was acquainted with our case. He, however, was very ready to help me get my passport at once. Evidently he had not been able to understand Bolshevik ways and mentality, and was confident my business could be settled quickly and simply. He was therefore more surprised and disappointed than I was when day by day found us thwarted at every step. Professor Coolidge wrote a letter to the Department of Foreign Affairs that dealt with passports, stating that I was one of the Americans that came under the agreement regarding permission to leave Russia, and he was sure that with as little delay as possible a passport would be made out. With this I went to the same office where I had had unpleasant experiences before and where I anticipated nothing good.

Unfortunately I have no diary to fall back on in describing the unique methods of Bolshevik bureaucracy but, though I know much is omitted, I will give the details as nearly in order as I can remember them.

My first interview, though anything but cordial, still raised no obstacles. I was sent to various departments where blanks were to be made out, and after three or four days everything seemed to be arranged. The last day I went supposedly to receive the passport, only to be told that the documents made out would have to be verified and, as it took time, I could return for them in about two or three weeks. In vain I pleaded the complications attending a second trip from Petrograd. Comrade Weinstein's temper and personal regard for me had evidently not improved, and I was roughly informed that if Americans wished to have dealings with the Soviet they must bow to Soviet laws and not think they were in America.

My return surprised Professor Coolidge, but there seemed a shadow of reason in the delay and, though he made a protest, it was so friendly as to produce no impression. I went back to Petrograd. Sometime later, I can not remember how many weeks, I received a summons from Moscow, so imperative and threatening that any one would think I had been evading the law and hiding. I started for Moscow, where there followed days of the most exasperating and insulting red-tape negotiations I had yet experienced. It took a good two days to get a certificate that was satisfactory as to Communistic guarantee. Two well-known Communists had to certify as to my being eligible to leave the country. Next I had to get the signatures of two members of our family in Moscow, stating that they would be personally responsible for my "absolute loyalty in word and deed to the Soviet Government while abroad." In case of my failing in this respect, the undersigned undertook to bring me back to Russia or personally to bear my punishment! I told Professor Coolidge that under such circumstances I would drop all further thought of obtaining a passport—and in my heart I was glad of so legitimate an excuse to give my sons for no longer considering my leaving the country.

Professor Coolidge, however, would not hear of it, using every argument to induce me to leave while the A. R. A. was in Russia and had the power to help me. Finding me very stubborn, he called in several of the members of the staff who had been in Russia the longest and who felt that conditions were likely to become worse rather than better. As I sat looking at the ring of men in front of me, whose strongest argument was that I could do no good by staying and would only perish myself, with my sons, I felt so goaded that I finally burst out, "I just wish that the wives of some of you gentlemen were here. A mother would understand what you can not." I knew that Professor Coolidge was a bachelor and I hoped for little from him in appreciating my point of view, but one very sage remark of his came to me with a pang when my strength gave out in the darkness and blizzard on the frozen frontier of Finland. He said, "You must consider also the possibility of your hampering your sons in a crisis." This was the only worth-while argument brought out, and it made me decide at once to go on with the attempt to get a passport, but not to use it until the moment arrived when my presence might "be a hamper" to the boys. Even this fond hope was cut off when after long wearisome days I found the passport really in my hands and read that it was valid only for a certain period. The uncanny cleverness of the Bolsheviki in checkmating us at every turn was here again evident. With a sinking heart I told my friends of the required signed guarantee of my being loyal to the Soviet Government even when in America. Instead of magnifying the danger to themselves, the risk they ran of my saying something imprudent that the ever-present Soviet spies and *provocateurs* would get hold of and report, my people thought only of our being able to escape, and readily gave their signatures. Again days were occupied in standing in line before a little window to deliver the guarantee, then standing for hours in line before another window for an answer. At last the paper was handed out to me with a written notice that the signatures of my friends must be witnessed by two Communists living in their district! Why could they not have told me this the first day?

Finally, however, when every possible excuse had been used, the signatures of every one remotely interested in me obtained, all obstacles overcome, Professor Coolidge was notified that at a given hour I could go to get the passport. I hated to dampen his very sincere pleasure by expressing any skepticism, but I could not share his confidence. At the assigned hour I appeared in the large room where, taking my place in a long line, I worked my way up to the information table, at which I received a slip admitting me to the window where passports were given out. When my turn brought me to the window, where I had seen passports being delivered, and I presented the slip, together with the notice addressed to Professor Coolidge stating that my passport was ready and adding the name of the official who was to deliver it, I was told that Comrade X was absent, sick, and no passports could be given. I tried to remonstrate, for I had been seeing passports handed out, but was rudely told to move on and not delay others. I stepped aside, therefore, where I could still see passports being delivered. Evidently Comrade X's indisposition attacked him only when my passport was called for. Some one said that in the afternoon I might succeed better, so I waited. It must be remembered, there were no means of transportation for us private individuals. The relatives with whom I was staying lived almost on the outskirts of the large city, the A. R. A. was miles away. There were no hotels, restaurants, no place where I could go to wait or obtain food, nor were there any rest-rooms of any kind—in those days the front hall and stairs of private houses were the public toilet rooms! The residents invariably used the back entrances in going in and out.

I had a piece of bread with me, and all I could do to avoid being noticed as a loafer was to go out from time to time and walk about aimlessly in the snowy streets and then come back and sit in the waiting-room.

In the middle of the afternoon, feeling I had given ample time for the indisposition to pass, I again renewed the long process of reaching the window. The Comrade there recognized me and, before I could open my mouth, blurted out, "No passports given out to-day—pass on."

I plodded my way home, fully conscious that the usual process of obstruction was in full sway. Thinking it over, I decided to go the next morning to Professor Coolidge first. He listened to me seriously but still was inclined to call it a misunderstanding, and was quite optimistic as to my success that morning. One of the most valuable interpreters was present, a tall fine-looking man who had his own reasons for understanding Soviet intricacies. He said, "She is right— it is no misunderstanding. I am going to the Foreign Office myself and will take your note, Professor, but my opinion is—it won't be the last you will write on the same subject."

Something was said about my going on the A. R. A. car with this gentleman but, owing to complications as to time and routes, the proposition was dropped without their in the least suspecting the throbbing in my feet. It was the last straw, that showed how utterly impossible it was for these kindly gentlemen to take in the actual conditions under which we lived. They knew in their brains that taxis, trains, or any other means of transport about the city were things of the past; they knew the distance between the premises of the A. R. A. and the Foreign Office, and they had my ad- dress, in a well-known part of Moscow; but accustomed to normal living, they evidently were unable to grasp the vital connection between these facts and every-day life. Had I called their attention to the number of miles I walked every day, and given them my daily menu, they would have had a shock, and no minor complications would have prevented their offering me that longed-for lift in one of their many cars. But they fulfilled their task of feeding children with a devotion and an efficiency unsurpassed, while holding them- selves quite apart from the life around them.

The A. R. A. loyally and very literally carried out all in- structions forbidding them to enter into any contact with internal conditions or to mix in the politics of the country. In all my connection with the organization, in Moscow and Petrograd, with the exception of my first visit, when there were some who were personally prepared to find out all about me, no questions were asked me nor interest manifested in our experiences, and I never volunteered any. Neither did I now tell them what the scores of miles I covered during those weeks meant to me in my weakened condition.

And so I went for my passport. The interpreter, who was leaving as I entered, told me that all was settled, Professor Coolidge's note had been read and he had been assured that the passport would be delivered to me. It was evident, however, that, even so, the interpreter had little faith.

On reaching the familiar window, I was informed that a passport would not be given me, that I was refused permission to leave Russia! I was prepared for another attack of sickness somewhere, but not for this. Back I went to the A. R. A., and for the first time I saw Professor Coolidge lose his calm and his temper. His indignation called forth a very curt letter to Comrade Weinstein, threatening that if the passport in question was not immediately forthcoming, he would take the matter up with Litvinoff himself; that this instance was an infringement on one of the conditions on which the Americans had undertaken the work. He added that the next morning, at the hour originally fixed, I would be at the Foreign Office and that the passport must be given me. The interpreter still had his doubts, and said that he would drop in about noon to see if I really had it, concluding with his favorite expression, "No one can get anything out of these people unless he pounds the table with both fists and can swear at them in at least four languages." As a gentleman of refinement, Professor Coolidge could scarcely be expected to swear even in one language, and matters looked dark. I had little confidence that so inoffensive a letter as Professor Coolidge's would be considered.

The next morning I again made my way to the Foreign

Office. This time I was told that the passport would be given me, but it was not ready. In reply to the question as to when it would be ready, a vague "I don't know" was all the satisfaction I could get. So I sat down to wait for my friend, the interpreter, to "drop in about noon." In the meantime I watched the queues that came up to the girls at the information desk, receiving passes to one or another department, or refusals to certain requests. I was pleased to see the passes handed out, and the number of rooms indicated for audience: my indisposed Comrade was receiving, Comrade Weinstein was in his office, likewise several others with whom I had dealings.

"About noon" the man I was expecting arrived and beckoned me into the hall. I quickly told him in a low voice that the passport was "not ready." Swearing under his breath in one of the four languages, he told me to go back and sit down and wait. I could see his huge figure looming over the heads of the crowd. Finding the queue too long, he raised his hand and voice, requesting one of the girls to give him at once, on urgent business, a pass to Comrade Weinstein.

"Comrade Weinstein will not be in the office," said the girl, who knew the big man and evidently had received instructions.

"Then give me a pass to——," naming one after another, and receiving in each case the unflinching reply, "Not yet come," "Sick," "Not receiving." And I knew that every one of the men mentioned was in the next rooms! The big man evidently knew it too, for taking a good breath, he roared out, "Give me this instant a pass to the passport department" (my sick man). The girl recognized defeat when she saw it and without a word gave a slip that, being presented to the man standing with his back to the door, caused it to be opened at once with a polite "please," and the big man, as I found he was called, was ushered in. After a considerable time he came out and told me that the passport was said to have been delayed by some clerical mistake that was being rectified, and that it would be ready at two o'clock. "I don't believe a word of it, but I will be back here at two and see what has happened to you."

So again I killed time, nibbling at my piece of dry bread, and at two again went to the window, where the brief reply was, "It will be ready to-morrow." Soon my good friend came in and I reported. "Sit here and don't go away, however long I may be,"—and without waiting for a pass he brushed the doorman aside and disappeared into the forbidden precincts. I waited long—but some one coming out said, "The big man is in there yelling and kicking up an awful row."

Darkness came, lights were turned on. Then the crowds disappeared. Windows were closed—books and ledgers locked up. "Comrade, you must go. Don't you see the office is closing?" said one, approaching me.

"I can not help it, the big man told me to wait, and I am waiting."

"Oh, that is all right then." And he went away, evidently impressed by my importance.

Another, apparently a watchman, came up and more gruffly growled the equivalent of "Move on."

"I can not. I am waiting for the big man who is in there."

"Oh, all right."

A woman with a broom came by. "What are you doing here at this time? Go."

"I can not. I am waiting for the big man in there."

"Oh, all right. I heard him. He is making a big noise."

I hoped his voice would hold out, and my spirits rose

as I counted the hours—six o'clock—seven o'clock—a quarter to nine. Then a door opened. The big man stepped out and, mopping his red face with his handkerchief, gave a loud "pouf" of relief. Coming up to me, he unbuttoned his coat and drew forth the passport. Literally, the result of "pounding the table and swearing in four languages" for seven hours! He afterward told me how, when informed that the passport was in the hands of a clerk copying it because of some error, he forced his way into the next room and found on inquiry that it was not there. He had gone into every room, in spite of remonstrances, received all manners of explanations and excuses, and finally ended in the highest room of all—that of Comrade Weinstein, the last authority, who began to explain that the passport was not ready, that it was in the hands of a comrade who was not there that day. But the big man's ire was up and, with the instinct of a hunting dog or merely as a bluff, he brought his hand down on a pile of papers to which he had caught the Commissar's eyes wandering, and thundered, "Here is the passport. Give it to me or to-morrow we report and the Commission leaves Russia!"

The never-failing Bolshevik, cowing before a master, drew out from near the bottom of the pile—my passport! "But it is still lacking the signature of the Cheka. Come for it to-morrow."

"There are no more to-morrows for us. You have plenty of men here. Send some one with this to the Cheka and get the signatures—in the meantime I will smoke here."

"But the Cheka is closed at this hour."

"Have it opened," came the reply between puffs, "and I will wait with you in this room."

Nothing remained but to capitulate, and the two men chatted amiably while the passport made the last stage of its journeyings and returned with the Cheka signatures. I was sorry that so historical a document was taken from us later in Finland to be destroyed, as were all the Soviet documents we possessed, except the one regarding our expulsion from Bortniki, which was evidently overlooked. The next day I called at the A. R. A. to express my thanks for all the trouble they had taken. I felt mean and dishonest, however, in what I was concealing from them—the determination to use the passport only as a last resort, if the attempt to get out illegally failed. This I simply could not speak of, as it would involve the administration that stood for the greatest relief work ever undertaken, a work that saved the lives of millions of starving Russians and brought back hope to thousands whose pangs of hunger were doubled by the feeling of being forsaken, and who were losing faith in God and man. This kind of work was above politics, and I could not let my little affairs compromise them by bringing a charge of meddling with the laws of the Soviet Government. Leaving Russia, as we were planning to do, was contrary to the implicit decrees, and furthermore my sons would be deserters from the army. In no way must the A. R. A. be involved. So I took the passport and with shame in my heart heard the kind Professor Coolidge say, "Please let us know how you succeed. We have given help to many, but we never hear from them to know the practical results of our passports."

I may add that later, when in Boston, I went to see the Professor, who, I learned, had expressed surprise at my "having chosen to get out in so dangerous and sensational a way when a passport would have opened all doors for me." I felt I owed him an explanation and a humble apology. He was exceedingly cordial and friendly, offering me any assistance he could ever give me in my writing or lectures. I explained my conduct, as it was impossible to do in Russia, but I still felt that he could not get my point of view. I think and sincerely hope that he harbored no ill feeling, but I am sure he failed to see things as I did.

But to return to Russia. With my passport in my hands I went to Petrograd, fully realizing that it was only fear of losing the good-will of the Hoover Administration and the food and medicines they furnished that had induced the Commissar to put up with the "big man's" bullying, and that insured my own safety after all that had happened. The passport was securely put away with our other important documents, the date of the expiration (three months, if I remember correctly) noted, and we resumed our life, each day hoping for a lead that would give us a definite opening for escape.

CHAPTER THIRTY-TWO

The Dawn of Hope

WE HAD a friend of bygone times who was living very well for those days. She dwelt in a small room, every spare inch piled with wood and all sorts of things—as great a medley as a pawnshop. Exposed to all weathers, she would be out on her "business." No one put intimate questions in those days, but an unforgettable dinner she gave us one day proved that she was doing well, whatever the business was.

One afternoon at the end of a long call, she asked casually if I knew of any one who wished to leave the country illegally—she knew of a way to do it. I replied that some one had spoken to me of such a matter but I could not remember just then who it was. "Well, think it over, and if it is any one I can vouch for, let me know." Was this the beginning? Should we seize this offer?

The boys and I discussed the question until late into the night. Should we trust this woman and ask her to help us? We could not doubt her loyalty, but if the plan fell through she might some day imprudently speak of our having had an intention of leaving the country, and this would be enough to bring the boys under conviction for attempted desertion of the army. The woman was a young German nursery governess in my sister-in-law's house when I first went to Russia. As the children grew up, she became housekeeper, companion, loyal friend and mainstay of the family. When war broke out between Russia and Germany, she could not bear to be on the side of the enemies of her beloved employers and took out Russian citizenship papers to be able to remain with them. She shared all their privations and dangers, toiled for them, starved with them, and her loyalty and love extended to my children, who had been so much at their aunt's house during our absences. And now, the family dead or scattered, she was stranded, unable to return to Germany, in broken health, struggling for a living. Our having a shadow of doubt as to the advisability of being frank with one so tried as she is a striking instance of the effect of Bolshevism on one's character—mistrust, suspicion of even one's nearest, and the inclination to choose a winding rather than a straight path in every action.

The result of our long talk was, "Nothing risked, nothing gained." I was commissioned to go to M and ask for details, but not as yet disclose that the information was for us.

Of course it was all very transparent: I knew that M knew that it was for ourselves, and soon I talked business frankly. She said she was in touch with an organization working on a purely business basis that undertook to get people over the frontier. It was a hazardous proceeding on both sides. There was always the possibility of a *provocateur* applying, who, being a Red, would betray them. The organization therefore had to be very certain of their clients. M, having a large circle of acquaintances among the intelligentsia and aristocrats, could be trusted not to introduce doubtful people. "For three years I have been doing this, getting a commission on each person I introduce," she went on. "How else could I have existed all this time?"

She could tell me very little, as she herself knew very little, since she had dealings with only one man. Who he was or who were his companions and how they worked, were beyond her knowledge. She only knew that they had succeeded in hundreds of cases and that they seldom failed.

It was decided that one of the boys and I meet her late that night, when she would take us to this man, with whom in the meantime she would have made an appointment. The apartment to which Alec and I were brought was evidently of people of breeding, culture and former wealth. This gentleman, such in every sense of the word, said he would undertake our case on condition of absolute secrecy. The aiding of military men to get out of the country would double the seriousness of the crime if discovered. Not a soul in our own family or circle of friends was to be taken into our confidence. "The more who know a secret, the more difficult it is to guard against leakage." He laid much stress also on the calmness, courage and physical endurance that might be required. Were we ready to undertake it at any risk? If not, the matter could now be dropped with no harm to either party. But if we began negotiations and learned of the workings of their organization and then backed out, we would be a menace to them. There could be no turning back.

We assured him of our agreement with all his conditions. We were as anxious for secrecy as he was, not only for our own sakes but because we wished to avoid involving in any way the friends we were leaving behind us. As to dangers, we could think of nothing worse than what lay before us if we remained: certain separation soon, constant fear of arrest, hunger and privation. Life was too hard to be valued, all we cared for was to keep together and share whatever came.

The next vital question was the price. He named a sum to be paid in English or American money, which, thanks to the persistent efforts of the Clements and Clement Cochran, was safely hidden in that precious package of ours.

All the preliminaries thus arranged, we were told that I was to go with the other son (evidently for the purpose of implicating us all) the next morning to the old Polish bank on the corner of the Nevsky and Kazan Streets and there wait on the steps for his companion. "A very tall man in fur coat with collar turned up showing black eyes and beard will go up the steps. You go down and in passing speak to him—the right man will answer you." It was a bitterly cold day in December when Oka and I stood on these steps, shivering from nervousness, I suppose, as much as from cold. We stood apart and did not speak to each other. Eagerly, but we hoped with seeming indifference, we scanned each person who mounted the steps, and at last were rewarded. A figure perfectly answering the description was coming. Oka sauntered down, saying, "Hello," and holding out his hand as to an old acquaintance. "Why, how do you do! It is long since I have seen you," was the answering greeting. Then followed a string of questions as to members of the family, so that I had a chance of joining them. "It is too cold to stand here and talk. Let's walk down the street," said our new acquaintance, and we started down the main street but soon turned off into small, almost empty byways. Even the principal streets had little traffic in those days, and we soon found ourselves where talking was safe.

"If you are going to get faint-hearted and will give up, better do it now while it is not too late. After this you must go ahead."

On our assurance that nerve would hold out, he led us to one of the big empty buildings that were so common. I can still see before me the great empty corridor—and a new man. Our old guide disappeared. All the new man had to tell us was what we were to take with us. He particularly cautioned us against suitcases as likely to raise suspicions. We should go as the great army of "baggers" were traveling, with bags on our backs. We might carry all the valuables we possessed, only bearing in mind the possibility of much walking and the danger of being overloaded. Then he gave us still another address.

The negotiations of the following days were carried on

by Oka, and we at last had full instructions. We were to leave at three o'clock on a date to be decided only by the weather. A storm, if possible a blizzard, would be our best chance. We should then meet in a certain railroad station, where we were to arrive separately. There were to be five of us, ourselves and two guides. We were to have punched return tickets to a station short of Oranienbaum, on the gulf opposite Finland. As certain formalities that we had to avoid were still connected with buying tickets, we could not go out to the train with the crowd, but a man in the luggage-checking counter had been bribed to let us out on the platform. Then we were to get into different cars. The guides were to be ahead. Oka was to keep in touch with them but not near enough to be noticed as being of the same party. I was to follow between him and Alec, all of us keeping at a distance from one another. We were not to speak nor to strike a light during the night, and if anything suspicious happened to one of us to scatter and not return to our lodgings for several days.

So much for instructions from them; but we still had much to think of. How were we to leave without bringing suspicion and arrest upon our friends—on the chairman of the House Committee, our landlord, and friends who had been in the habit of visiting us—especially on our near relatives living near Petrograd? How could we leave them without a word of farewell? Would they understand that it was purely for their sakes, to avoid connecting them in any way with our doings, and not from lack of confidence in them? What were we to do with our faithful companion of fourteen years, little Daisy, who at every sign of packing would take her seat in a suitcase or on a bag? Long and careful deliberations resulted in a labyrinth of intrigue.

We began to drop hints among our friends as to Oka's going on business to Moscow. We intimated that Alec might have to go to Tver to get some of his belongings, and that I might profit by the occasion to go back to Ostashkov and bring some more flour and other provisions left there. We talked openly of Oka's trying to get three tickets in one day, with seats near together, and often Oka would report failure. Then we arranged with our landlord to care for Daisy until our relative came to town, who would take her home and keep her till we returned. We would have ended Daisy's life if we could have done so painlessly, but there were no drugs nor had we any firearms. To take her with us was out of the question, for with all their good qualities fox terriers can never be counted on to refrain from barking at the wrong moment. We have since learned that our relatives, whom she knew, took her; but, though affectionate and crying if left alone, Daisy refused food and pined away. She died two weeks after we deserted her.

Oka went daily to an address where a man was to tell him when the day arrived. One day he came home more downcast than we had ever known him to be. The price for their services had been raised to six hundred and fifty dollars, a sum greater than our hidden treasure, one that we could not soon raise. What complicated the situation was that we knew this organization was to close and the various leaders themselves slip over the frontier. They had, with few failures, got, according to their statement, over three thousand out of Russia, among other internationally known people, the mother of General Wrangle and the late Professor Maximov of Chicago and his family. They realized that sooner or later they would be caught, and therefore had set the date for going out of business and scattering.

But how were we to get the six hundred and fifty dollars in time—only a little more than a week? We were again quite out of touch with the "outside." We knew there was money for us in the consulates if only we could get it. I think that that day was perhaps the blackest we had experienced. Our hopes had been almost realized, and now it looked as if they would be dashed. As for me, I took the blow lying down. My courage completely failed and, still worse, an apathy came over me. I can remember how we three remained silent, I lying flat on the bed. Occasionally one of the boys would suggest a plan, only to be discarded. Suddenly I thought of a friend who might lend us the money if I could get to him in a distant city. I sat up again, and we turned over that plan. A letter was sent, but as no reply came and time was short, it was decided that I should go personally. A ticket was procured and I went, almost getting stranded, I may add, in my attempt to return. The result was a loan of six hundred and fifty dollars from this never-to-be-forgotten friend, who gave it to us with little assurance of its being speedily returned and at considerable inconvenience to himself. In passing, I would say that we did get the money back to him, though it was months afterward, but he will never know with what gratitude it was returned.

Christmas was on Sunday. Monday morning Oka took the money to the man who stood at the end of "the chain." Naturally we had no receipt, no guarantee of any kind, and the days that followed, full of anticipation, doubt and dread, seemed long. The organization was complicated in that it had to think first of all of its own safety; the members of the company did not know who the leader was. It seemed that only groups of three knew one another and, even so, the names they bore were probably assumed. Therefore the arrest of one could not implicate all.

The weakest link in our chain was the necessity of leaving at three in the afternoon, an hour that Alec could not possibly get leave to come home without raising disagreeable questions and involving complications. This obstacle was removed in a marvelously providential manner. While I was away, Alec had done the cooking, and in shredding cabbage had cut the forefinger of his right hand. It was nothing to which he would now give a second thought, but in those days we were all so run down from improper and insufficient nourishment that we had no resistance. On my return home I found Alec's hand and arm badly swollen. For two nights he had walked the floor. The regimental doctor having no medicines or dressings, we called in a well-known surgeon, who came late at night with his nurse. He sat and smoked for some time to "get his nerve back and his hand steady," his condition being the result of a harrowing operation he had just performed, in which the chloroform used had been adulterated and was worthless. Alec's case was of course very painful, and there was nothing to help, not even proper dressings. The next day, the surgeon gave him a signed slip to take to his regiment, certifying that Comrade Ponafidine should be freed from all duties for at least two weeks!

This was just one more of the small details of our escape that never cease to fill me with a sense of awe and deep humility whenever I live over that time.

CHAPTER THIRTY-THREE

Escape

ONE day about noon Oka came in from his morning visit to our "last man." A look at his white drawn face showed that the crisis had come. In a quiet voice he announced that we were to leave at three, and he laid down a package he had brought, unrolling a big loaf of white bread and some sausages, tea and sugar. "I had some Soviet money with me that we can't use now, so I bought this for the road," he said. We had not dared to be packed and ready, for a domiciliary visit might be made, but we had planned just what could be carried. We had to provide for possible exposure in the open, so each of us had a rug and a change of warm clothing. A knife, cup and spoon which we carried are all we now have of our home table service. We added all we dared of the embroideries I spoke of, and a good silk dress that had been buried in a peasant's cellar. I fondly hoped it would be of use but alas, it went to pieces in a few weeks after being made over—another illustration of what had been forced upon us, that human beings can endure what no machinery or manufactured things can. We made sandwiches, feeding our poor little Daisy the first ones, and when all was ready, the boys wrote two notes. One was to our landlord, who fortunately was out of the house. This said that, unexpectedly obtaining the three tickets, we had rushed to the train, and hoped that the informality would not get him into trouble. The second, to be dropped in a few days into the letter-box of our apartment by M, purported to have been written in Moscow and sent by hand, as was frequently done, and was also addressed to our landlord, informing him that having found better jobs in Moscow, the boys had decided to stay there, and as soon as we found a lodging they would send our permanent address; later we would come for what we had left in Petrograd. These two letters we hoped would remove all suspicion from our landlord and friends and carry the search for us, if it were made, to Moscow.

We slipped out of the house one at a time, our worst risk being that of meeting some of our fellow lodgers. By devious routes we all finally met in the crowded waiting-room. We knew well that among the throngs hurrying in and out were many Cheka people on the lookout for just such as we. Stories of arrests which had come to us made it difficult to carry out our rôles of ordinary travelers, interested only in getting seats in the train. Our two guides were lounging idly against the counter where baggage was checked, rolling cigarettes, laughing and chatting. I saw Oka a little way from them, and Alec was back of me. Carelessly the eyes of our guides met each of us in turn, and then they drifted behind the counter, joking with a man who held open the door to the train, and disappeared. Oka followed casually. I pushed on to pass through at a decent interval, when to my horror I saw the man preparing to close the door after Oka. That awful second seemed years. Were we to be separated? What would happen if the door closed between us? I dared not make a sign to the man nor look back to Alec for advice. But Oka had felt the man's movements and managed to put up his hand as if to scratch his head, and wiggled his five fingers. Like all of us, the man had his wits sharpened to signs and hints and evidently understood that something was amiss. He had been told it was an escaping party of three, and he had let three pass, but as there appeared to be five, he lazily let the door open again and I stepped through, trying hard to walk slowly and indifferently. Once on the platform, I distinguished Oka in the dim light. He stood with one foot on the step, but disappeared in the car as soon as he saw me. I went to the second car, and as I climbed up I had a chance to see that Alec, thank God, was close behind. With a long breath of relief I hunted for a seat in the rapidly filling car and felt that we were safely lost in the crowd.

Our instructions were to get off at a "half station" just short of Oranienbaum; the train would stop only a minute. On stepping down, we found ourselves facing one of the black blizzards of Russia, where wind and thick falling snow make it impossible to find one's way even by daylight. The platform was dimly lighted by brakemen's lanterns, and I saw obscurely ahead of me the figure of Oka. He looked over his shoulder to see if we were following, but the two guides were stalking ahead, glancing to neither right nor left. I followed, bowing my head to the blast, feeling Alec somewhere behind me. We were taken some little distance down the track to a shed that served as a waiting-room, enclosed on three sides and with a bench running against the back wall. Here, in silence, by gestures we were told to sit down. The bags were put under the benches and we were left alone. In the darkness we could see only small specks of lights— hear the train going on and footsteps crunching the snow near the tracks, which were patrolled, but we were surrounded by deep soft snow, so that our guides had disappeared noiselessly. We waited in strained silence. Where had they gone? Had they taken our money and deserted us? What if some belated passenger, a Red Army man, one of the frontier guard, should come in? After what seemed like hours, not two but, one after another, seven figures loomed in the darkness close to us, and only a reassuring whisper told us that they were friends. Our bags were seized. I felt a man holding each elbow and, after a few seconds of listening, I was run up a steep bank and into a ditch on the other side, where, rolling and falling, we all assembled. Again listening—no sound—no pursuit—we

were then run across what was probably an open field into
some woods, where three horses stood.   Each was harnessed
to a low long boatlike Finnish sledge, loaded high with what
we later learned were rugs that were being smuggled out of
Russia.   The loads were covered with something white, and
roped down.   On top of these precarious mountains we all
scrambled, still in the same uncanny silence.   The horses were
put to a fast trot and we were soon passing through the dark
streets of a town, what town we never knew.   Suddenly we
saw before us the figures of two men standing at a corner.   Instantly our drivers turned off into a by-street, putting the
horses to a gallop, and we were soon out of the streets and
into the open.   Then began the wildest ride of my life.   We
were going up a hill, evidently through grounds laid out in
flower beds with shrubs and plants protected by a high covering of some kind, for we bounded and jumped over obstacles that every moment threatened to upset us.   We clung
to one another and to the ropes that fastened the load as
well as we could, until we stopped under the walls of a large
building—a palace, large manor house or institution, apparently, dark and evidently unoccupied.   Our guides and
four Finnish smugglers put their heads together, whispering
softly; the fifth disappeared.   We saw something pass from
hand to hand—the smugglers getting their pay, probably—
and then our guides, the last link with Russia, with the past,
vanished in the darkness and storm, without a word or gesture of farewell, and we found ourselves alone with the
smugglers.

In these men we had little faith.   Smugglers had been
known to betray or rob or do away with those they had been
hired to get out of the country.   We had stipulated that we
three should be in one sleigh, but they now, with quiet firm-
ness, separated us, putting one of us on each of the sleighs.
Yet we waited, buffeted on this high point by the storm and

stung by the cold that was beginning to penetrate to our skins. Dimly out of the darkness the fifth man materialized, and after a short whispered consultation that we could not hear or understand, as they spoke Finnish, our five men distributed themselves on the three sleighs, and the same crazy speed took us down, lurching and bumping over unseen obstacles, lying flat as we dashed under what at times seemed arbors of creeping vines, until finally we were again going at full gallop through dark deserted streets. Suddenly a lamp appeared in a window of a corner house, and we turned down that street. What had seemed to us only a coincidence was several times repeated—evidently friends signaling the smugglers to safe routes. These men were getting people out as a side branch of their regular occupation. They were smugglers pure and simple, very likely from pre-war times, and had their own routes and friends and signals. We were only accidental, extra articles, well paid for probably, that they transported. Soon the town was left behind and we were on the frozen Gulf of Finland. At one point a lone sentinel challenged us, "Halt or I fire—once! Halt or I fire—twice!" but our very horses, answering to the danger, tore by, and the man did not fire.

We continued at an incredibly fast pace, with no tracks that we could see to mark the road. For hours the horses, pulling heavy sleds in snow knee-deep and often through huge drifts, never faltered or needed the lash. When, later, we dared whisper, and my driver and I became sociable, he told me they had three sets of grain-fed horses to use in turn, for their success and often their lives depended upon the speed and endurance of the animals. The drifts seemed to be over frozen lumps, and more than once our sleighs overturned, scattering us. Sometimes, when the snow had blown off, leaving clear-swept stretches, the men would jump off and run alongside to keep warm. Once I tried to do the same but could not keep up and was a hindrance, so without a word I was ignominiously picked up and deposited on top of the sleigh.

There was nothing to break the force of the wind on the open Gulf, and it seemed to pierce to one's very marrow. It was hard in the icy blast to realize that there was any clothing between the wind and one's naked body. Once, in one of the lurches, I was shot off without my driver's noticing it. Only we two were on that sleigh, and it was nothing but the timely good sense of those on the sleigh behind, who thought it best to investigate what they had dimly seen rolling past them in the dark, that saved me. I had scrambled to my feet but could never have overtaken the horses, nor, had I dared to call, would they have heard my voice against the storm, as all sat huddled, with collars raised above their ears. I was again seated and told to keep my hands in the driver's belt—but it was so cold that I couldn't keep a hold.

What added to the danger and was most wearing on our nerves was the searchlights that we soon found playing on the Gulf. The fortress of Kronstadt was an almost impassable barrier, making St. Petersburg one of the best protected harbors in the world. Cannon by day and searchlights by night could be made to cover every inch of the entrance. Now that we had to run the gauntlet in getting out, we felt there was little chance of evading the lights. Possibly the occupants of Kronstadt at that time were less skilful than those of old, or our smugglers were remarkably skilful in deftly corkscrewing their way through the sweeping approaching and disappearing streams of white light. Over and over it seemed to me as if it was within an inch of us, and we would instinctively shrink; then it would recede, only to give place to another snakelike white line moving toward us. Sometimes it seemed to me I must cry out, "Hit us and be done with it," but never while we were moving did the Bolsheviki catch us with the light.

Once we had a great fright. We distinctly saw a body of men approaching us. I could distinguish figures, rifles, bayonets. In my fear I broke the order for silence and whispered to the driver, "Look, the Reds are upon us." He chuckled and said, "Your eyes are big with fright. Those are the masts and funnels of a steamer that is sunk on a bar here." My sons also were deceived by the sight, though they suffered longer, as my driver was the only one of the five men who could speak any Russian. The silence broken, my driver whispered to me that a German steamer had made its way out that morning. We had anxiously watched for it ever since we had learned of our route. The Baltic ports are frozen in winter, of course, making navigation impossible during many months. This steamer, caught by untimely freezing of the Gulf, was intending to get out with the help of an ice-breaker. The "last man" had told Oka that there was danger if the steamer should succeed, for huge blocks of broken ice in a passage the width of an ocean-going ship would then have to be negotiated. And now we were told that that very morning the steamer had been taken out!

To be sure, the temperature was very low, and in the hours that had passed considerable freezing no doubt had taken place, but still the passage would be hazardous. "How will you manage?" I whispered.

"Oh, our horses are well trained. They will be unharnessed and made to lie down here," and he patted the load on which we were seated. "They will be securely roped and with strong iron hooks we will gather and push together the stray blocks of ice and make it solid. Then it will be easy to slide the sleighs over."

"That may be good for the sleighs and horses," I said, "but how about us?"

"Oh, you can do it! The ice will bear you and you can jump where it doesn't."

As I look back to that night, the deep Gulf and the danger of drowning are curiously absent from my mind. Our fear of the Reds was so much greater than anything else that the thought of being killed through any other agency or in any other way seemed to have little place in our minds. The cold was growing more and more intense, the storm worse if possible, but the brave horses never slowed up until the men began to pull them back into a walk. Finally two of the Finns, with long poles in their hands, went ahead, sounding the snow. "Here it is. Stop!" And all three sleighs drew together. We climbed down, stiff from cold. We could see the white snow-covered ice—a solid footing—then large black spots indicating the blocks of broken ice that had been washed clear of snow. Other dark spots that the poles of our explorers showed were crevices—open slightly congealed spaces between the thick pieces of ice.

In silence the men began quickly to unharness the first horse—mine. Some were still prodding and pushing the blocks of ice. Then, when least prepared for it—when we had forgotten that danger—a broad white light came creeping slowly toward us. The agony of that moment will always remain with me. As the bright searchlight struck us mercilessly, the chief sensation was of nakedness—nothing, ourselves, our thoughts, could be hidden. Descriptions of the last awful Judgment Day came to me as something like this. The light touched us—and passed! Thank God, it had missed us! But no—it stopped, and then slowly, very slowly, retraced its route until it picked us up, and stopped! I do not see why all our hearts did not stop too. The immediate effect was a loosening of tongues, and after the uncanny silence that babel of rough Finnish voices came as another shock.

"They see us! We can't risk the time to unharness the horses," explained the driver hurriedly, as his frozen fingers buckled on the harness. Then drawing out a long coil of rope, he prepared what was a familiar precaution taken by us on our lake when the ice was not safe. One end of the rope was securely fastened to the ends of the long shafts, the rest of the rope, perhaps thirty or forty feet, coiled on the driver's lap.

"Now get up and don't fall off as you have been doing so many times," he ordered.

I told him I wouldn't if he would give me something to hang on to. He gave me a bit of rope, which I wound around my hands. As the driver gathered up his reins and spoke encouragingly, the horse started, stepping on a block of ice three or four feet thick. As it began to sink, he plunged on to the next, our men pushing the blocks toward him when needed. Sometimes the detached piece we were on was not very large and both sleigh and horse would be deep in the swishing water, so that it seemed as if the gallant animal would fail to plunge on to the next piece. Shouting encouragement, the drivers managed to get two horses upon safe ice, but we heard a splash and shouts that proclaimed the falling of a horse between two pieces. All on the sleigh leaped off, raising the shafts and helping the horse to scramble out, while others with their long hooks pushed floating ice under him, till at last he was out and we were all safe on firm ice with the chasm between us and the Reds.

"Even if they come this far, they won't risk their lives as we do. They couldn't get over anyway, for Russian horses are no good there. They haven't seen oats for four years," chuckled the driver.

We drove fast to heat up the wet horses and soon my driver announced, "We are now out of Russian waters," and the cheerful talk that went on showed how real was the relief of our companions. As for us, it seemed that nothing now could frighten us. I asked the driver what our destination was to be, for details had not been given us further than that we were to be taken to one of the many quarantine stations established along the other side of the Russian border. This we had insisted on, because the official documents insuring our safe passage were in the quarantine stations. Otherwise, we risked being turned back. The man replied that they had not decided in what village it would be safe to pass the night, but the next day they would take us to the quarantine near Terioki, Finland.

I think the bitter cold sent me into a doze, for the next thing I remembered was a violent altercation going on. We had stopped, and my bags had been thrown into the snow. The driver, who had hitherto been very affable, shook me roughly by the arm and said, "We won't take you any farther. It is dangerous for us. You can find your own way."

The boys came running up to remonstrate with him. "But we can't walk. We don't know the way. Mother can not fight through such deep snow." (Was this the time prophesied by the A. R. A. people when I was to "handicap" and perhaps lead to my sons' death?)

"There is no time to talk. We won't take you any farther. You go so"—pointing vaguely into the darkness— "and there are woods and you will find people."

In vain we pleaded that we had no compass. It was dark and we might lose our way. They had the one answer and, gathering up the reins, they were soon lost to sight in another direction from the one they gave us, so that we did not even have the help of their tracks. We stood in the silence—around us the frozen Gulf, in the far distance back of us the faint moving gleam of searchlights. Somewhere in front of us, roughly north and south, ran the boundary-line. Should we strike the woods on the Russian or the Finnish side? How far we were from the shore we did not know, nor just where the Finnish boundary-line ran. A mistake of a few rods might mean death if we walked back into Russia, and in the storm it was next to impossible to keep our bearings. This is what probably was in all our minds, but we avoided the subject and started out as near as we could judge in the direction of the shore. The snow was sometimes fluffy and knee-deep, sometimes there were tightly packed drifts into which we would get and then flounder in deeper snow on the other side. My knees were so nearly frozen that they seemed at times useless and I feared I should go flat. The boys would pull me up, adjust my frozen bag on my back, but after a few steps down I would go. Sometimes, when the storm lifted, we saw a black wall—how far off we could not estimate—rising above the white: that must be the woods and land.

Seeing that it was impossible for me to go fast, Oka said that if we moved so slowly and daylight caught us near the open sea, we should be discovered and taken, even if we were in Finnish waters, and he suggested leaving his bags and going on as rapidly as possible, in hopes of finding a village where he could get a horse. So off he went. Alec and I each took a bag and, after following Oka's footsteps for some time, left the bags and went back for others. We had divided the food and money and rugs, so that in case we were separated each of us would have something to depend on. In this way, going back and forth, we advanced steadily but slowly until Alec, having carefully examined the snow, turned to me and said in a deadly calm voice, "Mother, if we go back once more, we shall never find Oka's footsteps. They are so filled in I don't know if I can keep them in sight even now."

What we had most dreaded had happened. We should be separated. I urged Alec to drop the bags and go as fast

as he could to find his brother's foot-tracks. It took much
urging, for he argued that we all might then be separated
and unable to find one another. But at last he gathered up
the bags and made a comfortable seat for me, saying, "You
sit here and rest and I'll try to overtake Oka soon and bring
him back, and then we'll stick together." Soon he was swallowed up in that darkness and I found myself alone. The
comfortable seat could not comfort me now; I jumped up and
began carrying the bags forward and then going back for
others as we had done before, keeping close watch of the
footsteps. I found action much easier than waiting idly,
besides I was going forward, even if slowly; but after making several trips I lost trace of Alec's footsteps, and then I
felt indeed that the end had come. I dropped the bags and
started to run in the direction of what I thought were foot-
tracks, only to fall, over and over again, in the deep snow.
Footprints were quite lost to sight, but I felt with my hands
for any irregularity that might indicate them. It seemed
ages that I had been alone, when a light in the far distance
appeared. Why I was so sure that it was Oka's message I
do not know, but all fear left me and I calmly retraced my
steps and gathered the bags and sat down.

Oka on reaching the shore had walked right into a
clearing and soon found a tiny log cabin. He had no idea
where he was—in Russia or in Finland. This might be an
outpost of the Red sentinels, for in the darkness he could
see nothing to help him identify the nationality of the
cabin. It was long before he could make up his mind to
knock. But the storm showed no signs of abating, and we
could not spend the night in the open. He nerved himself
to pound on the door and was rewarded by a guttural voice
calling out in Finnish, "Who is there?" A man opened the
door. "You are a Russian," he said.

  "Yes."

Just after escape.

EMMA C. PONAFIDINE

After a year in America.

"Well, come in."

Then Oka asked if a light could be put in a window over-looking the Gulf—that was the light I had seen—and then begged that something hot be prepared to drink while he went back to find us.

"It is the middle of the night and the children are asleep," the man grumbled.

"No matter, you must make some coffee and we will pay you well." And Oka again faced the storm and darkness, looking for us. Alec, too, had seen the light and was heading for it, so they soon met and then went back to find me. When we entered the cabin, a cuckoo clock on the wall pointed to five. The room was warm and neat. It was full of the delicious aroma of coffee, and on the table a whole saucer of sugar! That struck me as forcibly as anything that came to us that night—so much sugar, and placed before strangers! The young wife knew no Russian, but she had a warm heart and bustled around to get off our wet frozen clothes, sighing over Alec's bandaged hand, placing hot coffee on the table. While we were greedily eating, she bundled her two children on a big box and prepared a place for us to lie down and rest, giving up her own bed, while the good man went to a village some distance away where a horse could be hired. We ate and then threw ourselves down and slept. A pounding on the door woke us in a panic, but it was the master of the house with the owner of a horse. He asked a merciless price for driving us four hours to the quarantine, but so long as we had any money we were in no position to bargain. When we started it was just beginning to grow light. We could see what a tiny clearing it was that Oka's feet had been led to, and when our host told us it was not more than a verst and a half (less than a mile) east of us to the nearest line of Red sentinels, we realized how wonderfully God had cared for us throughout that dreadful night.

Our way lay for some time in a dense forest of magnificent trees like ours in Bortniki. Then we came to open ground and, looking across the wide expanse of the frozen Gulf we had crossed in the darkness, we saw the pink light of the rising sun bringing out in hazy relief the vague mass of shapes and smoke that was Petrograd. We drove in silence, looking as long as we could see it, at the ill-fated city, lying so near and yet forsaken and helpless in the clutch of the evil powers that held it. That picture against the ever-brightening rays of the mounting sun, for the storm had given way to a glorious sunrise, will always be with me.

EPILOGUE

SAFE at last in Finland! Our sensations? None. Yet
how many evenings had we spent making out the menus we
would order if ever we should again be where such things
existed. How often had we discussed the feelings that
civilized surroundings and nights unbroken by fears of sudden knockings would bring! And now all that we were
deeply conscious of was a sense of clinging to the representatives of an American business corporation as the only
tangible links between us and ultimate security, and a persistent fear that we might yet be separated. Not for a
moment could we bear to be out of the sight of one another.

There was no poring over steamship plans for a convenient cabin. All we cared for—and that we did demand—
was communicating cabins, and, in hotels, communicating
rooms. It was months before this feeling passed, as well
as the fear of speaking freely on the street.

My nephew had asked the agents of his firm in Scandinavia to look after us, and they did so in more than a
perfunctory way. The personal kindness of Mr. A, in
Helsingfors, and Mr. and Mrs. W, in Oslo, touched something deep in us that years of harshness and fear had not
killed. But we could express nothing, and I am sure we
seemed unappreciative. We were stunned, bewildered—
like beings from another planet. I still remember the flowers,
however, that Mrs. W sent to my room.

In Norway, while waiting for the steamer, we sent letters
to all the Russian newspapers published in Europe, asking for
news of George to be sent to Mrs. Clement's address. We
also wrote in English carefully worded postcards to those we
had left behind in the darkness, saying that my sons and I,
profiting by vacations, were traveling in Scandinavia, and

regretted we could not visit them, but asked that they continue to write us at the old address, again giving that of Mrs. Clement. Years later, when, in Europe, I met one of these friends, who for business purposes had a temporary pass across the border, his first words were, "Tell me—how did you ever get away without any of us suspecting it!" He described the excitement and conjectures that had followed our disappearance, ending with, "Now I can tell them all!" for the poor fellow had to return.

It was long before we dared write back in Russian, and it was a great day for us when the first word came from our friends in the old home. We could read between the lines the intense surprise, curiosity and envy that underlay the studiously simple acknowledgment of our cards, with regrets expressed that we had not found it possible to visit them.

When we reached New York we were met by relatives and friends. There were our benefactors, the Cochrans and the Clements, and there were Mrs. Lauderbough whose brother, Mr. Turner, had established the first direct communication with us, and my cousin, Chancellor Elmer Ellsworth Brown and his wife.

In looking back to that day, I again realize how apathetic, how deadened we were, how little impression anything made on us. It seemed as if I could never again be moved deeply by either joy or sorrow, however great. The wonders of New York—the electric display on Broadway—appeal to me now every time I am in that great city more than they did that first night when, at the risk of losing our train, Mr. Norman Clement stopped our taxi and made us get out in the middle of the blazing thoroughfare to look up and down the brilliant path of lights. I think that the friends who had so long worked to find us, and who finally rescued us from that living death, must have thought us singularly unresponsive. But I know that a deeper realization of the goodness of God to us, and the loving loyalty of our friends, grows within me as the years pass. No one has greater cause to know what friendship means, or to realize more keenly that no burden in life comes to one without the strength to bear it being added.

Three years later, Vera and her young daughter succeeded in joining us in America, but in 1926 we lost the mother, her death leaving to us the little Vera as a precious legacy,—all we have of our George.

The notices we had sent the papers brought a flood of answers giving information regarding George and also many friends and relatives, some of whom we had long counted as dead. The staff of General Koutepov forwarded the official report of George's death—that he was "missing" at the battle of Perikop, October 20, 1920. Later there came what I prize as one of my most precious possessions— the following statement of General S.

"Capt. Ponafidine was in the volunteer army during the Civil War, in the unit of the Imperial Ismaelovsky Regiment. Throughout the entire period he was in the Cavalry Scouts, first as an assistant to the Commander and then he himself in command. He took part personally in all the most dangerous expeditions and more than once, owing to the skill with which he carried out the reconnoitering, saved the battalion from falling into danger.

"During the expedition up from the Crimea to Poland, although one of the youngest officers, Capt. Ponafidine was always on the right flank or in the rear protecting the battalion from the enemy's attacks.

"On our return to the Crimea, Capt. Ponafidine was appointed to the third company (the Ismaelovsky Regiment) and was to have taken part in action but was prevented by illness. For two weeks he lay in the Reserve Hospital and then before he had fully recovered or regained his strength he returned to his post in spite of the remonstrance of his senior officers and took part in all the fighting during the evacuation of the Crimea.

"During the 'Perikop' battles, Capt. Ponafidine amazed every one by his untiring energy. He was everywhere, all the time on his feet, going into every detail, and personally supervising each step of the operations.

"During the battle of the village of Kurman Kermenchi (October 29, 1920) when the retreating company was entirely surrounded by the enemy's cavalry, Capt. Ponafidine was in command, his senior officer having taken command of the battalion. During the battle with colossal losses and extraordinarily dangerous conditions he was always at the head of his company.

"At the last moment he was seen personally firing the machine-gun in the face of the advancing cavalry, having taken the place of the last artillery man, who was killed. Several times the Reds had attempted to surround and take him, but he, standing at bay, successfully kept them off— until the field of battle fell into the enemy's hands."

THE END